MAN-EATERS

MAN-EATERS

by JIM CORBETT

THE ADVENTURE LIBRARY

The text of this edition of *Man-eaters* has been computer typeset in Adobe Garamond, designed by Robert Slimbach after original typefaces created by Claude Garamond of Antwerp, Belgium, in the 16th century.

Typography and binding design for The Adventure Library by Elton S. Robinson
Typesetting and production management by Martin Cook Associates, Ltd.
Printing by Data Reproductions Corporation, Rochester Hills
Binding by John H. Dekker & Sons, Inc., Grand Rapids

First Adventure Library edition 1997.

The Adventure Library
79 Nash Road
North Salem, NY 10560

Library of Congress Catalog Card Number: 97-72336
ISBN: 1-885283-11-3

Printed in the United States of America

CONTENTS

FOREWORD

BY GEOFFREY C. WARD

Heroes are out of fashion these days. We assume the worst of everyone who comes to prominence—and, sad to say, seem rarely to go too far wrong when we do so. But Jim Corbett was the real thing. He was just as courageous, as tireless, as fair-minded, as skilled in jungle-craft—and *almost* as genuinely modest about it all—as his remarkable writings make him seem. Even his initial motive for writing the first of his six books was worthy: the proceeds from *Man-eaters of Kumaon* (from which two chapters are included in this volume), were intended for the support of British and Indian soldiers blinded during the Second World War.

There was nothing unconventional about Corbett's private life, nothing unusual about his professional career. He was born in the Indian hill station of Naini Tal in 1875, and raised in the heart of the tiger jungle that in those days rolled without a break for hundreds of miles along the foothills of the Himalayas. He learned as a small boy to track and shoot game to fill his family's larder; his father had died young, leaving a widow with twelve children to feed on a sparse pension, so every shot was made to count. "Good shooting," an old friend remembered, "was to him an obligation rather than an accomplishment."

Corbett was a "domiciled Englishman"—born in India rather

than England—and therefore looked down upon by India's British rulers, whose own inflexible caste system insured that their "country-bottled" cousins rose no higher than they should. Corbett seems never even to have tried. At 17, he joined the Indian railway and stayed with it for more than 20 years, making sure there was enough coal on hand to fuel the trains running through his district and overseeing the transfer of goods from one side of the Ganges to another by ferry at a remote crossing called Mokameh Ghat. Then, he returned to his hometown, moved in with his unmarried sister, Maggie, and went into the hardware business, selling home sites on the side to officials of the Raj, many of them too exalted ever to ask him to dine. He never married.

During the winters, he and Maggie moved down the mountain to a small bungalow at Kaladhungi, on the edge of a cluster of thatch huts whose inhabitants tilled his lands. He disliked cities, preferred the company of his Indian tenants—"[s]imple, honest, brave, loyal, hard-working souls," he called them—to that of most of his fellow countrymen, and was never comfortable where he thought he might not be wanted. Even late in life, when his fame as a hunter finally won him membership in the Naini Tal Yacht Club, he rarely visited its clubhouse because, a friend remembered, he was unaccustomed to "elevated society."

Other Britons may have felt themselves superior to him in the drawing room, but at home, in the jungle, he had few equals; his accuracy with rifle and shotgun was matched only by his uncanny ability to read the forest floor for signs of animals. And when for five years, a man-eating tigress managed to elude a whole host of eager executioners in the nearby hills—accounting for well over 400 lives—it was only natural that the deputy commissioner in Naini Tal finally turned to him to track it down. His dogged pursuit of the maddeningly resourceful animal he called the Champawat man-eater was the first of at least a dozen similar hunts he undertook between 1907 and 1941. No one knows how many lives his efforts saved, but his quarry's combined total of human kills is said to have exceeded 1500 men, women and children.

Most books about hunting tigers and leopards—let alone accounts of hunting man-eaters—are filled with melodrama: intrepid hunters pursuing animals so savage, so merciless, they deserve nothing better than the bullet they get on the last page. Nothing annoyed Corbett more: "The author who first used the words 'as cruel as a tiger' and 'as bloodthirsty as a tiger' when attempting to emphasize the evil character of the villain of his piece," he wrote, "not only showed lamentable ignorance of the animal he defamed, but coined phrases which have come into universal circulation, and which are mainly responsible for the wrong opinion of tigers held by all except the small proportion of the public who have the opportunity of forming their own opinions." The tiger was in fact "a large-hearted gentleman," he continued, "with boundless courage." Man-eating was an aberration, not natural behavior: tigers adopted an alien human diet only because they were precluded from pursuing their normal prey either by old age or by wounds—often inflicted by hunters less accurate than he.

Corbett was a reluctant executioner, always hoping some other solution might be found, and, once his quarry lay dead, seems only to have been embarrassed by the crowds of grateful villagers who gathered to garland him with flowers. He insisted that all offers of rewards be withdrawn before he would begin because he considered them unsporting, and his accounts of his own adventures are rendered all the more compelling because they always include evidence of his own fears and frustrations, his bad decisions and faulty reasoning. We admire him all the more because he presents himself, not as a Great White Hunter, but as an ordinary human being performing as well as he can under the stress of truly extraordinary circumstances.

Some time during the 1930s, Corbett largely abandoned hunting big game in favor of filming it with a movie camera. And he grew increasingly concerned that the wildlife he had known as a boy was disappearing. He helped form two of India's first conservation organizations, edited a short-lived natural history magazine (dedicated to the proposition that "a bird in the bush is worth two in the hand"), and lobbied to have part of his beloved Kumaon Hills declared India's first national park. (He succeeded, and after independence, it would be named for him.)

He continued to organize tiger hunts for the rich and well-born, however—it must have been a source of satisfaction to him that they were dependent on his skills to bag their trophies, though he would never have been crude enough to say so. During a Christmas hunt he staged in 1946 for the viceroy, Lord Linlithgow, he took the opportunity to speak of his fears for the future: "His talk on tigers and jungle life was of extraordinary interest," Linlithgow noted, "and I wish I could have had more of it. He has rather pessimistic views on the future of tigers; . . . and [believes] that in many parts of India tigers will become almost extinct in the next 10 or 15 years; his chief reason is that Indian politicians are no sportsmen and tigers have no votes, while the right to a gun license will come with a vote."

Despite the best efforts of Indian conservationists and the Indian government, Corbett's melancholy predictions about the fate of the tiger and the rest of India's wildlife are sadly being borne out today. The jungles he loved have dwindled steadily, displaced by the relentless growth of human population, and a new kind of man-eating tiger has emerged since Corbett's time: intimidated young animals—as well as battered old ones—driven from the heart of national parks by stronger, younger rivals and forced to skulk around the periphery, where natural prey is scarce and domestic livestock and the men and women and children who herd them all too common. There is nowhere else for them to go. Unless new ways are found to safeguard what little remains of India's forests, the world Jim Corbett knew will soon survive only in his books.

New York, 1997

AUTHOR'S NOTE

As many of the stories in this book are about man-eating tigers, it is perhaps desirable to explain why these animals develop man-eating tendencies.

A man-eating tiger is a tiger that has been compelled, through stress of circumstances beyond its control, to adopt a diet alien to it. The stress of circumstances is, in nine cases out of ten, wounds, and in the tenth case old age. The wound that has caused a particular tiger to take to man-eating might be the result of a carelessly fired shot and failure to follow up and recover the wounded animal, or be the result of the tiger having lost its temper when killing a porcupine. Human beings are not the natural prey of tigers, and it is only when tigers have been incapacitated through wounds or old age that, in order to live, they are compelled to take to a diet of human flesh.

A tiger when killing its natural prey, which it does either by stalking or lying in wait for it, depends for the success of its attack on its speed and, to a lesser extent, on the condition of its teeth and claws. When, therefore, a tiger is suffering from one or more painful wounds, or when its teeth are missing or defective and its claws worn down, and it is unable to catch the animals it has been accustomed to eating, it is driven by necessity to killing human beings. The change-over from animal to human flesh is, I believe, in most cases accidental. As an illustration of what I mean by 'accidental' I quote the case of the Muktesar man-eating tigress. This tigress, a comparatively young animal, in an encounter with a porcupine lost an eye and got some fifty quills, varying in length from one to nine inches, embedded in the arm and under the pad of her right fore-leg. Several of these quills after striking a bone had doubled back in the form of a U, the point and the broken-off end being quite close together. Suppurating sores formed where she endeavoured to extract the quills with her teeth, and while she was lying up in a thick patch of grass, starving and licking her wounds, a woman selected this particular patch of grass to cut as fodder for her cattle. At first the tigress took no notice, but when the woman had cut the grass right up to where she was lying the tigress struck once, the blow crushing in the woman's skull. Death was instantaneous, for, when found the following day, she was grasping her sickle with one hand and holding a tuft of grass, which she was about to cut when struck, with the other. Leaving the woman lying where she had fallen, the tigress limped off for a distance of over a mile and took refuge in a little hollow under a fallen tree. Two days later a man came to chip fire-wood off this fallen tree, and the tigress who was lying on the far side killed him. The man fell across the tree and, as he had removed his coat and shirt and the tigress had clawed his back when killing him, it is possible that the smell of the blood trickling down his body as he hung across the bole of the tree first gave her the idea that he was something that she could satisfy her hunger with. However that may be, before leaving him she ate a small portion from his back. A day later she killed her third victim deliberately, and without having received any provocation. Thereafter she became an established man-eater and had killed twenty-four people before she was finally accounted for.

A tiger on a fresh kill, or a wounded tiger, or a tigress with small cubs will occasionally kill human beings who disturb them; but these tigers cannot, by any stretch of imagination, be called man-eaters, though they are often so called. Personally I would give a tiger the benefit of the doubt once, and once again, before classing it as a man-eater, and whenever possible I would subject the alleged victim to a post-mortem before letting the kill go down on the records as the kill of a tiger or a leopard, as the case might be. This subject of post-mortems of human beings alleged to have been killed by either tigers or leopards or, in the plains, by wolves or hyenas, is of great importance, for, though I refrain from giving instances, I know of cases where deaths have wrongly been ascribed to carnivora.

It is a popular fallacy that *all* man-eaters are old and mangy, the mange being attributed to the excess of salt in human flesh. I am not competent to give any opinion on the relative quantity of salt in human or animal flesh; but I can, and I do, assert that a diet of human flesh, so far from having an injurious effect on the coat of man-eaters, has quite the opposite effect, for all the man-eaters I have seen have had remarkably fine coats.

Another popular belief in connexion with man-eaters is that the cubs of these animals automatically become man-eaters. This is quite a reasonable supposition; but it is not borne out by actual facts, and the reason why the cubs of a man-eater do not themselves become man-eaters is that human beings are not the natural prey of tigers, or of leopards.

A cub will eat whatever its mother provides, and I have even known of tiger cubs assisting their mothers to kill human beings; but I do not know of a single instance of a cub, after it had left the protection of its parent, or after that parent had been killed, taking to killing human beings.

In the case of human beings killed by carnivora, the doubt is often expressed as to whether the animal responsible for the kill is a tiger or leopard. As a general rule—to which I have seen no exceptions—tigers are responsible for all kills that take place in daylight, and leopards are responsible for all kills that take place in the dark. Both animals are semi-nocturnal forest-dwellers, have much the same habits, employ similar methods of killing, and both are capable of carrying their human victims for long distances. It would be natural, therefore, to expect them to hunt at the same hours; and that they do not do so is due to the difference in courage of the two animals. When a tiger becomes a man-eater it loses all fear of human beings and, as human beings move about more freely in the day than they do at night, it is able to secure its victims during daylight hours and there is no necessity for it to visit their habitations at night. A leopard on the other hand, even after it has killed scores of human beings, never loses its fear of man; and, as it is unwilling to face up to human beings in daylight, it secures its victims when they are moving about at night, or by breaking into their houses at night. Owing to these characteristics of the two animals, namely, that one loses its fear of human beings and kills in the daylight, while the other retains its fear and kills in the dark, man-eating tigers are easier to shoot than man-eating leopards.

The frequency with which a man-eating tiger kills depends on: (*a*) the supply of natural food in the area in which it is operating; (*b*) the nature of the disability which has caused it to become a man-eater; and (*c*) whether it is a male or a female with cubs.

Those of us who lack the opportunity of forming our own opinion on any particular subject are apt to accept the opinions of others, and in no case is this more apparent than in the case of tigers—here I do not refer to man-eaters in particular, but to tigers in general. The author who first used the words 'as cruel as a tiger' and 'as bloodthirsty as a tiger,' when attempting to emphasize the evil character of the villain of his piece, not only showed a lamentable ignorance of the animal he defamed, but coined phrases which have come into universal circulation, and which are mainly responsible for the wrong opinion of tigers held by all except that very small proportion of the public who have the opportunity of forming their own opinions.

When I see the expression 'as cruel as a tiger' and 'as bloodthirsty as a tiger' in print, I think of a small boy armed with an old muzzle-loading gun—the right barrel of which was split for six inches of its length, and the stock and barrels of which were kept from falling apart by lashings of brass wire—wandering through the jungles of the terai and *bhabar* in the days when there were ten tigers to every one that now survives; sleeping anywhere he happened to be when night came on, with a small fire to give him company and warmth, wakened at intervals by the calling of tigers, sometimes in the distance, at other times near at hand; throwing another stick on the fire and turning over and continuing his interrupted sleep without one thought of unease; knowing from his own short experience and from what others, who like himself had spent their days in the jungles, had told him, that a tiger, unless molested, would do him no harm; or during daylight hours avoiding any tiger he saw, and when that was not possible, standing perfectly still until it had passed and gone, before continuing on his way. And I think of him on one occasion stalking half a dozen jungle fowl that were feeding in the open, and, on creeping up to a plum-bush and standing up to peer over, the bush heaving and a tiger walking out on the far side and, on clearing the bush, turning round and looking at the boy with an expression on its face which said as clearly as any words, 'Hello, kid, what are you doing here?' and, receiving no answer, turning round and walking away very slowly without once looking back. And then again I think of the tens of thousands of men, women, and children who, while working in the forests or cutting grass or collecting dry sticks, pass day after day close to where tigers are lying up and who, when they return safely to their homes, do not even know that they have been under the observation of this so-called 'cruel' and 'bloodthirsty' animal.

Half a century has rolled by since the day the tiger walked out of the plum-bush, the latter thirty-two years of which have been spent in the more or less regular pursuit of man-eaters, and though sights have been seen which would have caused a stone to weep, I have not seen a case where a tiger has been deliberately cruel or where it has been bloodthirsty to the extent that it has killed, without provocation, more than it has needed to satisfy its hunger or the hunger of its cubs.

A tiger's function in the scheme of things is to help maintain the balance in nature and if, on rare occasions when driven by dire necessity, he kills a human being, or when his natural food has been ruthlessly exterminated by man he kills two per cent of the cattle he is alleged to have killed, it is not fair that for these acts a whole species should be branded as being cruel and bloodthirsty.

Sportsmen are admittedly conservative, the reason being that it has taken them years to form their opinions, and as each individual has a different point of view, it is only natural that opinions should differ on minor, or even in some cases on major points, and for this reason I do not flatter myself that all the opinions I have expressed will meet with universal agreement.

There is, however, one point on which I am convinced that all sportsmen—no matter whether their point of view has been a platform on a tree, the back of an elephant, or their own feet—will agree with me, and that is, that a tiger is a large-hearted gentleman with boundless courage and that when he is exterminated—as exterminated he will be unless public opinion rallies to his support—India will be the poorer by having lost the finest of her fauna.

Leopards, unlike tigers, are to a certain extent scavengers, and become man-eaters by acquiring a taste for human flesh when unrestricted slaughter of game has deprived them of their natural food.

The dwellers in our hills are predominantly Hindu, and as such cremate their dead. The cremation invariably takes place on the bank of a stream or river in order that the ashes may be washed down into the Ganges, and eventually into the sea. As most of the villages are situated high up on the hills, while the streams or rivers are in many cases miles away down in the valleys, it will be realized that a funeral entails a considerable tax on the man-power of a small community when, in addition to the carrying party, labour has to be provided to collect and carry the fuel needed for the cremation. In normal times these rites are carried out very effectively; but when disease in epidemic form sweeps through the hills and the inhabitants die faster than they can be disposed of, a very simple rite, which consists of placing a live coal in the mouth of the deceased, is performed in the village and the body is then carried to the edge of the hill and cast into the valley below.

A leopard, in an area in which his natural food is scarce, finding these bodies very soon acquires a taste for human flesh, and when the disease dies down and normal conditions are established, he very naturally, on finding his food supply cut off, takes to killing human beings.

Of the two man-eating leopards of Kumaon, which between them killed five hundred and twenty-five human beings, one followed on the heels of a very severe outbreak of cholera, while the other followed the mysterious disease which swept through India in 1918 and was called 'war fever.'

The
MAN-EATING
LEOPARD
of
RUDRAPRAYAG

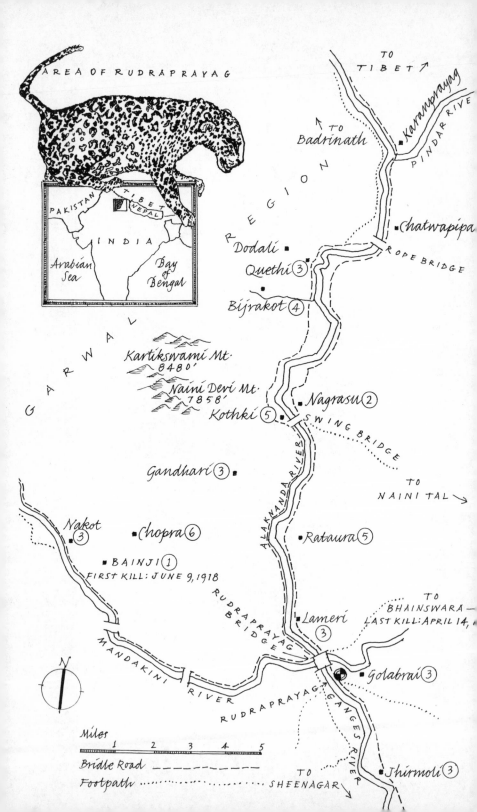

AREA OF RUDRAPRAYAG

PAKISTAN
TIBET
NEPAL
INDIA
Arabian Sea
Bay of Bengal

TO TIBET

Karanprayag

PINDAR RIVER

TO Badrinath

Chatwapipa

ROPE BRIDGE

REGION

GARWAL

Dodali

Quethi ③

Bijrakot ④

Kartikswami Mt. 8480'

Naini Devi Mt. 7858'

Kothki ⑤

Nagrasu ②

SWING BRIDGE

Gandhari ③

ALAKNANDA RIVER

TO NAINI TAL

Nakot ③

Chopra ⑥

Rataura ⑤

BAINJI ①
FIRST KILL: JUNE 9, 1918

RUDRAPRAYAG BRIDGE

Lameri ③

TO BHAINSWARA —
LAST KILL: APRIL 14,

MANDAKINI RIVER

RUDRAPRAYAG

GANGES RIVER

Golabrai ③

N

Jhirmoli ③

Miles
1 2 3 4 5

Bridle Road ———
Footpath ·········

TO SHEENAGAR

1

The Pilgrim Road

If you are a Hindu, from the sun-scorched plains of India, and you desire—as all good Hindus do—to perform the pilgrimage to the age-old shrines of Kedarnath and Badrinath, you must start on your pilgrimage from Hardwar and, in order to acquire a full measure of the merits vouchsafed to you for the correct performance of the pilgrimage, you must walk every step of the way from Hardwar to Kedarnath, and thence over the mountain track to Badrinath, barefoot.

Having purified yourself by immersion in the sacred Har-ki-pauri pool, and done *darshan* at the many shrines and temples in Hardwar and added your mite to their coffers, you must not fail to toss a coin within reach of the festering stumps—which once were hands—of the lepers who line the narrowest part of the pilgrim road above the sacred pool, for if you make this omission, they will call down curses on your head. What matter if these unfortunate ones have wealth beyond your dreams secreted in their filthy rags, or in the rock caves they call their homes? The curses of such as they are best avoided, and immunity will cost you but a few coppers.

You have now done all that custom and religion require of a good Hindu and are at liberty to start on your long and hard pilgrimage.

The first place of interest you will reach after leaving Hardwar is Rikikesh. Here you will make your first acquaintance with the 'Kalakamli Wallahas'—so called because of the black blanket their founder wore, and which many of his disciples still wear, in the form of a habit or loose cloak bound round the middle with a cord of goat's hair—who are renowned throughout the land for their good deeds. I do not know if any of the other religious brotherhoods you will meet on your pilgrimage have any claim to renown, but the 'Kalakamli Wallahas' have such a claim, and justly so, for out of the offerings they receive at their many shrines and temples they have built—and they maintain—hospitals, dispensaries, and pilgrim shelters, and feed the poor and the needy.

With Rikikesh behind you, you will come next to Lachman Jhula, where the pilgrim road crosses from the right to the left bank of the Ganges on a suspension bridge. Here beware of the red monkeys who infest the bridge, for they are even more importunate than the lepers of Hardwar, and unless you propitiate them with offerings of sweets or parched gram, your passage across the long and narrow bridge is likely to be both difficult and painful.

Three days' journey up the left bank of the Ganges and you have reached the ancient capital of Garhwal, Shreenagar, a historic, religious, and trading center of considerable importance and of great beauty, nestling in a wide open valley, surrounded by high mountains. It was here, in the year 1805, that the forebears of the Garhwali soldiers who have fought so gallantly in two world wars made their last, and unsuccessful, stand against the Gurkha invaders, and it is a matter of great regret to the people of Garhwal that their ancient city of Shreenagar, together with the palaces of their kings, was swept away, to the last stone, by the bursting of the Gohna Lake dam in 1894.

This dam, caused by a landslide in the valley of the Birehi Ganga, a tributary of the Ganges, was 11,000 feet wide at the base, 2,000 feet wide at the summit, and 900 feet high, and when it burst, ten billion cubic feet of water were released in the short space of six hours. So well was the bursting of the dam timed that though the flood devastated the valley of the Ganges right down to Hardwar and swept away every bridge, only one family was lost, the members of which returned to the danger zone after having been forcibly removed.

From Shreenagar you have to face a stiff climb to Chatikhal, which is compensated for by the magnificent views you will get of the Ganges valley, and of the eternal snows above Kedarnath.

A day's march from Chatikhal and you see in front of you Golabrai, with its row of grass-thatched pilgrim shelters, a one-room stone-built house, and its drinking trough. This big and imposing drinking trough is fed by a tiny crystal-clear stream, which in summer is sedately conducted down the mountainside by a series of channels roughhewn from pine saplings and at other seasons of the year cascades unfettered and merrily over rocks draped with moss and maiden-hair fern, through luxuriant beds of vivid green watercress and sky-blue strobilanthes.

A hundred yards beyond the pilgrim shelters, and on the right-hand side of the road, stands a mango tree. This tree and the two-story house above it, which is the home of the Pundit who owns the Golabrai pilgrim shelters, are worthy of note, for they play an important part in the tale I have to tell.

Another two miles, along the last flat bit of ground you will see for many a day, and you have reached Rudraprayag, where you and I, my pilgrim friend, must part, for your way lies across the Alaknanda and up the left bank of the Mandakini to Kedarnath, while mine lies over the mountains to my home in Naini Tal.

The road in front of you, which has been trodden by the feet of millions of pilgrims like you, is excessively steep and incredibly rough; and you, whose lungs have never breathed air above sea level, who have never climbed anything higher than the roof of your house, and whose feet have never trodden anything harder than yielding sand, will suffer greatly. Times there will be, and many, when gasping for breath you toil up the face of steep mountains on feet torn and bleeding by passage over rough rocks, sharp shale, and frozen ground, when you will question whether the prospective reward you seek is worth the present price you pay, but—being a good Hindu—you will toil on, comforting yourself with the thought that merit is not gained without suffering, and the greater the suffering in this world, the greater the reward in the next.

2

The Man-eater

The Hindi word for 'confluence' is *prayag*. At Rudraprayag two rivers—the Mandakini coming down from Kedarnath, and the Alaknanda from Badrinath—meet, and from here onwards the combined waters of the two rivers are known to all Hindus as Ganga Mai, and to the rest of the world as the Ganges.

When an animal, be it a leopard or be it a tiger, becomes a man-eater, it is given a place name for purposes of identification. The name so given does not necessarily imply that the animal began its man-eating career at that particular place, or that all its kills were

confined to it. It was quite natural, therefore, for the leopard that started his man-eating career at a small village twelve miles from Rudraprayag on the Kedarnath pilgrim route, to have been given the name of Rudraprayag, and to have been known for the rest of its career as the 'Man-Eating Leopard of Rudraprayag.'

Leopards do not become man-eaters for the same reasons that tigers do. Though I hate to admit it, our leopards—the most beautiful and the most graceful of all the animals in our jungles, and who when cornered or wounded are second to none in courage—are scavengers to the extent that they will, when driven by hunger, eat any dead thing they find in the jungle, just as lions will in the African bush.

The people of Garhwal are Hindus and, as such, cremate their dead. The cremation invariably takes place on the bank of a stream or river, in order that the ashes may be washed down into the Ganges and eventually into the sea. As most of the villages are situated high up on the hills, while the streams or rivers are in many cases miles away down in the valleys, a funeral entails a considerable tax on the manpower of a small community when, in addition to the carrying party, labor has to be provided to collect and carry the fuel needed for the cremation. In normal times these rites are carried out very effectively; but when disease in epidemic form sweeps through the hills, and the inhabitants die faster than they can be disposed of, a very simple rite, which consists of placing a live coal in the mouth of the deceased, is performed in the village, and the body is then carried to the edge of the hill and cast into the valley below.

A leopard in an area in which his natural food is scarce, when he finds these bodies, very soon acquires a taste for human flesh, and when the disease dies down and normal conditions are re-established, he very naturally, on discovering his food supply has been cut off, takes to killing human beings. In the wave of epidemic influenza that swept through the country in 1918 and cost India over

a million lives, Garhwal suffered very severely, and it was at the end
of this epidemic that the Garhwal man-eater made his appearance.

The first human kill credited to the Man-Eating Leopard of
Rudraprayag is recorded as having taken place at Bainji village on 9
June 1918, and the last kill for which he was responsible took place
at Bhainswara village on 14 April 1926. Between these two dates the
number of human kills recorded by the Government was 125.

While I do not think that this figure is out to the extent claimed
by government officials who served in Garhwal at that time, and by
the residents in the area in which the man-eater was operating, I do
know that it is not correct, for some kills that took place while I was
on the ground have not been shown in the records.

In crediting the man-eater with fewer kills than he was actually
responsible for, I do not wish to minimize in any way the sufferings
endured by the people of Garhwal for eight long years, nor do I wish
to detract in any way from the reputation of the animal that the
people of Garhwal claim as having been the most famous man-
eating leopard of all time.

However, be the number of human kills what they may, Garhwal
can claim that this leopard was the most publicized animal that has
ever lived, for he was mentioned—to my knowledge—in the press
of the United Kingdom, America, Canada, South Africa, Kenya,
Malaya, Hong Kong, Australia, New Zealand, and in most of the
dailies and weeklies in India.

In addition to this paper publicity, tales of the man-eater were
carried to every part of India by the sixty thousand pilgrims who annually visit the shrines of Kedarnath and Badrinath.

The procedure laid down by the Government in all cases of
human beings alleged to have been killed by man-eaters is for the
relatives, or friends, of the deceased to file a report with the *Patwari*
(official in charge of a group of villages) as soon after the occurrence
as possible. On receipt of the report the *Patwari* proceeds to the

spot, and if the body of the victim has not been found he organizes a search party, with the aid of which he endeavors to find it. If the body was found before his arrival, or if the search party finds it, the *Patwari* holds an inquiry on the spot, and if he is satisfied that it is a genuine kill by a man-eater—and not a case of murder—he gives the relatives permission to remove the remains for cremation or burial, according to the caste or creed of the victim, and the kill is duly recorded in his register against the man-eater operating in that area, and a full report of the occurrence is submitted to the administrative head of the district—the Deputy Commissioner—who also keeps a register in which all the man-eater's kills are recorded. In the event, however, that the body, or any portion of it, is not found—as sometimes happens, for man-eaters have an annoying habit of carrying their victims for long distances—the case is held over for further inquiry, and the man-eater is not credited with the kill. Again, when people are mauled by a man-eater and subsequently die from their injuries, the man-eater concerned is not credited with their deaths.

It will thus be seen that though the system adopted for recording the kills of man-eaters is as good as it can be, it is possible for one of these abnormal animals to be responsible for more human kills than he is finally credited with, especially when his operations extend over a long period of years.

3

Terror

The word 'terror' is so generally and universally used in connection with everyday trivial matters that it often fails to convey, when intended to do so, its real meaning. I should like, therefore, to give you some idea of what terror—real terror—meant to the fifty thousand inhabitants living in the five hundred square miles of Garhwal in which the man-eater was operating, and to the sixty thousand pilgrims who annually passed through that area, between the years 1918 to 1926. And I shall give a few instances to show you what grounds the inhabitants, and the pilgrims, had for that terror.

No curfew order has ever been more strictly enforced or more implicitly obeyed than the curfew imposed by the Man-Eating Leopard of Rudraprayag.

During the hours of sunlight, life in that area carried on in a normal way. Men went long distances to the bazaars to transact business, or to outlying villages to visit relatives or friends. Women went up the mountainsides to cut grass for thatching or for cattle fodder. Children went to school or into the jungles to graze goats or to collect dry sticks. And, if it was summer, pilgrims either singly or in large numbers toiled along the pilgrim routes on their way to, or from, the sacred shrines of Kedarnath and Badrinath.

As the sun approached the western horizon and the shadows lengthened, the behavior of the entire population of the area underwent a very sudden and a very noticeable change. Men who had sauntered to the bazaars or to outlying villages were hurrying home; women carrying great bundles of grass were stumbling down the steep mountainsides; children who had loitered on their way from school, or who were late in bringing in their flocks of goats or the dry sticks they had been sent out to collect, were being called by anxious mothers; and the weary pilgrims were being urged by any local inhabitant who passed them to hurry to shelter.

When night came an ominous silence brooded over the whole area: no movement, no sound anywhere. The entire local population was behind fast-closed doors—in many cases, for further protection, with additional doors to the existing outer ones—and those pilgrims who had not been fortunate enough to find accommodation in houses were huddled close together in pilgrim shelters. Whether in house or in shelter all were silent, for fear of attracting the dreaded man-eater.

This is what terror meant to the people of Garhwal, and to the pilgrims, for eight long years.

Following are a few instances that show what grounds there were for that terror.

A boy, a fourteen-year-old orphan, was employed to look after a flock of forty goats. He was of the depressed—untouchable—class and each evening when he returned with his charges he was given his food and then shut into a small room with the goats. The room was on the ground floor of a long row of two-story buildings and was immediately below the room occupied by the boy's master, the owner of the goats. To prevent the goats' crowding in on him as he slept, the boy had fenced off the far left-hand corner of the room.

This room had no windows and only the one door, and when the boy and the goats were safely inside, the boy's master pulled the door to and fastened it by passing the hasp, which was attached by a short length of chain to the door, over the staple fixed in the lintel. A piece of wood was then inserted in the staple to keep the hasp in place, and on his side of the door the boy, for his better safety, rolled a stone against it.

On the night the orphan was gathered to his fathers, his master asserts the door was fastened as usual, and I have no reason to question the truth of his assertion, for the door showed many deep claw marks. It is possible that in his attempts to claw open the door the leopard displaced the piece of wood that was keeping the hasp in place, after which it would have been easy for him to push the stone aside and enter the room.

Forty goats packed into a small room, one corner of which was fenced off, could not have left the intruder much space in which to maneuver, and it is left to conjecture whether the leopard covered the distance from the door to the boy's corner of the room over the backs of the goats or under their bellies, for at this stage of the proceedings all the goats must have been on their feet.

The assumption is that the boy slept through all the noise that must have been made by the leopard when trying to force open the door, and by the goats when the leopard had entered the room, and that he did not cry for help to deaf ears, only screened from him and the danger that menaced him by a thin plank.

After killing the boy in the fenced-off corner, the leopard carried him across the room—now empty of goats, which had escaped into the night—down a steep hillside and then over some terraced fields to a deep boulder-strewn ravine. It was here after the sun had been up a few hours that the master found all that the leopard had left of his servant.

Incredible as it may seem, not one of the forty goats had received so much as a scratch.

A neighbor had dropped in to spend the period of a long smoke with a friend. The room was L-shaped and the only door in it was not visible from where the two men sat on the floor smoking, with their backs to the wall. The door was shut but not fastened, for up to that night there had been no human kills in the village.

The room was in darkness and the owner of it had just passed the hookah (Indian pipe with a large clay bowl varying in diameter from four to six inches) to his friend when the hookah fell to the ground, scattering a shower of burning charcoal and tobacco. Telling his friend to be more careful or he would set on fire the blanket on which they were sitting, as well as their clothes, the man bent forward to gather up the burning embers, and as he did so, the door came into view. A young moon was near setting, and silhouetted against it the man saw a leopard carrying his friend through the door.

When recounting the incident to me a few days later the man said, 'I am speaking the truth, Sahib, when I tell you I never heard even so much as the intake of a breath, or any other sound, from my friend who was sitting only an arm's length from me, either when the leopard was killing him, or when it was carrying him away. There was nothing I could do for my friend, so I waited until the leopard had been gone some little while, and then—I crept up to the door and hastily shut and secured it.'

The wife of the headman of a village was ill of a fever, and two friends had been called in to nurse her.

There were two rooms in the house. The outer room had two doors, one opening onto a small flagged courtyard, and the other leading into the inner room. This outer room also had a narrow slip of a window set some four feet above floor level, and in this window, which was open, stood a large brass vessel containing drinking water for the sick woman.

Except for the one door giving access to the outer room, the inner room had no other opening in any of its four walls. The door leading out onto the courtyard was shut and securely fastened, and the door between the two rooms was wide open.

The three women in the inner room were lying on the ground, the sick woman in the middle with a friend on either side of her. The husband was on a bed in the outer room, on the side of the room nearest the window, and on the floor beside his bed, where its light would shine into the inner room, was a lantern, turned low to conserve oil.

Round about midnight, when the occupants of both rooms were asleep, the leopard entered by way of the narrow slip of a window, avoiding in some miraculous way the brass vessel that nearly filled it; he skirted round the man's low bed and, entering the inner room, killed the sick woman. It was only when the heavy brass vessel crashed to the floor as the leopard attempted to lift his victim through the window that the sleepers awoke.

When the lantern had been turned up, the woman who had been sick was discovered lying huddled up under the window, and in her throat were four great teeth marks.

A neighbor whose wife had been one of the nurses on that night, when relating the occurrence to me, said, 'The woman was very ill of her fever and was like to have died in any case, so it was fortunate that the leopard selected her.'

Two *Gujars,* who were brothers, were moving their herd of thirty buffalos from one grazing ground to another, and accompanying them was the twelve-year-old daughter of the elder of the two men.

They were strangers to the locality and either had not heard of the man-eater or, which is more probable, thought the buffalos would give them all the protection they needed.

Near the road and at an elevation of eight thousand feet was a narrow strip of flat ground below which was a sickle-shaped terraced field, some quarter of an acre in extent which had long been out of cultivation. The men selected this site for their camp and, cutting stakes in the jungle that surrounded them on all sides, they drove them deep into the field and tethered their buffalos to them in a long row.

After the evening meal, which the girl prepared, had been eaten, the party of three laid their blankets on the narrow strip of ground between the road and the buffalos and went to sleep.

It was a dark night, and some time towards the early hours of the morning the men were awakened by the booming of their buffalo bells and the snorting of the frightened animals. Knowing from long experience that these sounds indicated the presence of carnivora, the men lit a lantern and went among the buffalos to quiet them, and to see that none had broken the ropes tethering them to the stakes.

The men were absent only a few minutes and when they returned to their sleeping place they found that the girl, whom they had left asleep, was missing. On the blanket on which she had been lying were big splashes of blood.

When daylight came, the father and the uncle followed the blood trail, which, after skirting round the row of tethered buffalos, went across the narrow field and down the steep hillside for a few yards, to the place where the leopard had eaten his kill.

'My brother was born under an unlucky star, Sahib, for he has no son, and he had only this one daughter who was to have been married shortly, and to whom he looked in the fullness of time to provide him with an heir, and now—the leopard has come and eaten her.'

I could go on and on, for there were many kills, and each one has its own tragic story, but I think I have said enough to convince you that the people of Garhwal had ample reason to be terrified of the Man-Eating Leopard of Rudraprayag. Garhwalis as a whole are intensely superstitious and added to their fear of physical contact with the leopard was their even greater fear of the supernatural, of which I shall give you an example.

I set out from the small one-room Rudraprayag Inspection Bungalow one morning just as day was breaking, and as I stepped off the veranda I saw in the dust where the ground had been worn away by human feet, the pug marks of the man-eater.

The pug marks were perfectly fresh and showed that the leopard had stepped out of the veranda only a few minutes before me, and

from the direction in which they were pointing it was evident that the leopard, after his fruitless visit to the bungalow, was making for the pilgrim road some fifty yards away.

Tracking between the bungalow and the road was not possible, owing to the hard surface of the ground, but as I reached the gate I saw the pug marks were heading in the direction of Golabrai. A large flock of sheep and goats had gone down the road the previous evening, and in the dust they had kicked up the leopard's tracks showed as clearly as they would have on freshly fallen snow.

I had, by then, become quite familiar with the man-eater's pug marks and could with little difficulty have distinguished them from the pug marks of any hundred leopards.

A lot can be learned from the pug marks of carnivora, as, for instance, sex, age, size, and so on. I had examined the pug marks of the man-eater very carefully the first time I had seen them, and I knew he was an outsized male leopard, long past his prime.

As I followed the tracks of the man-eater on this morning I could see that he was only a few minutes ahead of me, and that he was moving at a slow even pace.

The road, which had no traffic on it at this early hour of the morning, wound in and out of a number of small ravines, and as it was possible that the leopard might on this occasion break his rule of never being out after daylight, I crept round each corner with the utmost care until I found, a mile further on, where he had left the road and gone up a goat track into dense scrub and tree jungle.

A hundred yards from where the leopard left the road there was a small field, in the center of which was a thorn enclosure, erected by the owner of the field to encourage packmen to camp there, in order to fertilize the field. In this enclosure was the flock of sheep and goats that had come down the road the previous evening.

The owner of the flock, a rugged fellow who, by the looks of him, had been packing trade commodities up and down the pilgrim road for nigh on half a century, was just removing the thorn bush closing the entrance to the enclosure when I came up. In reply to my inquiries he informed me that he had seen nothing of the leopard but that just as dawn was breaking his two sheep dogs had given tongue, and a few minutes later a kakar had barked in the jungle above the road.

I asked the old packman if he would sell me one of his goats, and he asked for what purpose I wanted it. When I told him I wanted it to tie up for the man-eater, he walked through the opening in the fence, replaced the bush, and, accepting one of my cigarettes, sat down on a rock by the side of the road.

We sat smoking for a while—with my question still unanswered—and then the man told the following story:

'You, Sahib, are undoubtedly he whom I have heard tell of on my way down from my village near Badrinath, and it grieves me that you should have come all this long way from your home on a fruit-less errand. The Evil Spirit that is responsible for all the human deaths in this area is not an animal, as you think it is, which can be killed by ball or shot, or by any of the other means that you have tried and that others have tried before you, and in proof of what I say, I will tell you a story while I smoke this second cigarette. The story was told to me by my father who, as everyone knows, had never been heard to tell a lie.

'My father was a young man then—and I unborn—when an evil spirit, like the one that is now troubling this land, made its appear-ance in our village, and all said it was a leopard. Men, women, and children were killed in their homes and every effort was made, as has been made here, to kill the animal. Traps were set, and renowned marksmen sat in trees and fired ball and shot at the leopard. When all these attempts to kill it had failed, a great terror seized the peo-ple and none dared leave the shelter of their homes between the hours of sunset and sunrise.

'And then the *Padhans* [headmen] of my father's village, and of the surrounding villages, bade all the men attend a *panchayat* [pub-lic meeting] and when everyone was assembled the Panch [chair-man] addressed the meeting and said they were assembled to devise some other means, in place of those that had already been tried, to rid themselves of this man-eating leopard. And then an old man fresh back from the burning ghat, whose grandson had been killed the previous night, arose and said it was no leopard that had entered his house and killed his grandson as he lay asleep by his side, but one from among their community who, when he craved for human flesh and blood, assumed the semblance of a leopard, and that such a one could not be killed by the methods already tried, as had been amply proved, and could only be killed by fire, and that his suspicions fell on the fat *sadhu* [holy man] who lived in the hut near the ruined temple.

'At this saying there was a great uproar at the meeting, some saying that the old man's sorrow at the loss of his grandson had demented him, while others said he was right. These latter recalled that the *sadhu* had arrived at the village at about the time the killing had started, and it was further recalled that on the day succeeding a killing the *sadhu* had been wont to sleep all day, stretched on his bed in the sun.

'When order had been restored, the matter was long debated and the *panchayat* eventually decided that no immediate action would be taken, but that the *sadhu*'s movements should in future be watched. The assembled men were then divided into three parties, the first party to start its watch from the night the next kill could be expected; for the kills had taken place at more or less regular intervals.

'During the nights the first and the second party were on watch, the *sadhu* did not leave his hut.

'My father was with the third party and at nightfall they silently took up their positions, and shortly thereafter, the door of the hut slowly opened, and the *sadhu* emerged and vanished into the night. Some hours later an agonized scream came floating down on the night air from the direction of a charcoal burner's hut far up the mountainside, and thereafter there was silence.

'No man of my father's party closed an eye that night, and, as the gray dawn was being born in the east, they saw the *sadhu* hurrying home, and his hands and his mouth were dripping blood.

'When the *sadhu* had gone inside his hut and had closed the door, the watchers went up to it, and fastened it from the outside by passing the chain that was dangling from it over the staple in the lintel. They then went each to his haystack and returned with a big bundle of straw, and when the sun rose that morning, there was nothing but smouldering ash where the hut had been. From that day the killing stopped.

'Suspicion has not yet fallen on any of the many *sadhus* in these parts, but when it does, the method employed in my father's time will be adopted in mine, and until that day comes the people of Garhwal must suffer.

'You have asked if I will sell you a goat. I will not sell you a goat, Sahib, for I have none to spare, but if, after hearing my story, you still want an animal to tie up for what you think is a man-eating leopard, I will lend you one of my sheep. If it is killed you shall pay me its price, and if it is not killed no money shall pass between us. Today and tonight I rest here and tomorrow at the rising of the *Bhootia* star [a star that rises at about 4 a.m. and by which all packmen throughout Garhwal time the start of their journeys] I must be on my way.'

Near sundown that evening I returned to the thorn enclosure and my packman friend very cheerfully let me select from his flock a fat sheep I considered was heavy enough to give the leopard two nights' feed. This sheep I tied in the scrub jungle close to the path up which the leopard had gone some twelve hours earlier.

Next morning I was up betimes. As I left the bungalow I again saw the pug marks of the man-eater where he had stepped off the veranda and at the gate I found he had come up the road from the direction of Golabrai and, after calling at the bungalow, had gone away towards the Rudraprayag bazaar.

The fact that the leopard was trying to secure a human kill was proof that he had no interest in the sheep I had provided for him, and I was not surprised therefore to find that he had not eaten any portion of the sheep, which he had apparently killed shortly after I had tied it up.

'Go back to your home, Sahib, and save your time and your money,' was the parting advice of the old packman as he whistled to his flock and headed down the road for Hardwar.

A parallel case—happily without as tragic an ending—occurred a few years previously near Rudraprayag.

Incensed at the killing of their relatives and friends, and convinced that a human being was responsible for their deaths, an angry crowd of men seized an unfortunate *sadhu* of village Kothgi, Dasyula Patti, but before they were able to wreak their vengeance on him, Philip Mason, then Deputy Commissioner of Garhwal, who was camping in the vicinity, arrived on the scene. Seeing the temper of the crowd—and being a man of great experience—Mason said he had no doubt that the real culprit had been apprehended, but that before the *sadhu* was lynched justice demanded that his guilt should be established. To this end he suggested that the *sadhu* should be placed under arrest and closely guarded, night and day. To this suggestion the crowd agreed, and for seven days and seven nights the *sadhu* was carefully guarded by the police, and as carefully watched by the populace. On the eighth morning, when the guard and the watchers were being changed, word was brought that a house in a village some miles away had been broken into the previous night and a man carried off.

The populace raised no objection to the *sadhu's* being released that day, contenting themselves by saying that on this occasion the wrong man had been apprehended, but that next time no mistake would be made.

In Garhwal all kills by man-eaters are attributed to sadhus, and in the Naini Tal and Almora districts all such kills are attributed to *Bokhsars* (a tribe inhabiting the unhealthy belt of grass at the foot of the hills called the Terai, who live chiefly on game).

The *sadhus* are believed to kill for the lust of human flesh and blood, and the *Bokhsars* are believed to kill for the jewelry their victims are wearing or for other valuables they have on their person. More women than men have been killed by man-eaters in the Naini Tal and Almora districts, but for this there is a better reason than the one given.

I have lived too long in silent places to be imaginative; even so, there were times a-many, during the months I spent at Rudraprayag, when sitting night after night—on one occasion for twenty-eight nights in succession—watching bridges, or crossroads, or approaches to villages, or over animal or human kills, when I could imagine the man-eater as being a big light-colored animal; for so he had appeared to me the first time I saw him—with the body of a leopard and the head of a fiend.

A fiend who, while watching me through the long night hours, rocked and rolled with silent baleful laughter at my vain attempt to outwit him, and licked his lips in anticipation of the time when, finding me off my guard for one brief moment, he would get the opportunity he was waiting for, to bury his teeth in my throat!

It may be questioned what the Government was doing all the years the Rudraprayag man-eater was menacing the people of Garhwal. I hold no brief for government, but after having spent ten weeks on the ground, during which period I walked many hundreds of miles and visited most of the villages in the affected area, I assert that the Government did everything in its power to remove the menace. Rewards were offered, believed by the local population to amount to ten thousand rupees in cash and the gift of two villages, sufficient inducement to make every one of the four thousand licensed gun holders of Garhwal a prospective slayer of the man-eater. Picked *shikaris* were employed at liberal wages and were promised special rewards if their efforts to shoot the man-eater were successful. Over three hundred special gun licenses—over and above the four thousand in force—were granted for the specific purpose of shooting the man-eater. Men of the Garhwal regiments stationed in Lansdowne when going home on leave were permitted to take their rifles with them, or were provided with sporting arms by their officers. Appeals were made through the press to sportsmen all over India to assist in the destruction of the leopard. Scores of traps of the drop-door type, with goats as bait, were erected on approaches to villages and on roads frequented by the man-eater. *Patwaris* and other government officials were supplied with poison for the purpose of poisoning human kills; and, last but not least, government servants, often at great personal risk, spent all the time they could spare from their official duties in pursuit of the man-eater.

The sum total results from all these many and combined efforts were a slight gunshot wound that creased the pad of the leopard's left hind foot and shot away a small piece of skin from one of its toes, and an entry in government records by the Deputy Commissioner of Garhwal that, far from suffering any ill effects, the leopard appeared to thrive on, and be stimulated by, the poison he absorbed *via* human kills.

In a government report, three interesting incidents are recorded in connection with the man-eater; they are:

1. In response to the press appeal to sportsmen, two young British officers arrived at Rudraprayag in 1921, with the avowed object of shooting the man-eater. What reason they had for thinking that the leopard crossed from bank to bank of the Alaknanda River by the Rudraprayag suspension bridge, I do not know; anyway, they decided to confine their efforts to this bridge and shoot the leopard as he was crossing it at night. To this end, while one of the young sportsmen sat on the tower carrying the cables of the suspension bridge on the left bank of

the river, his companion sat on the tower on the right bank. After they had been sitting on these towers for two months— so the report says—the man on the tower on the left bank saw the leopard walk out onto the bridge from the archway below him. Waiting until the leopard had got well onto the bridge, the officer fired at him, and as the animal dashed across the bridge, the man on the tower on the right bank emptied the six chambers of his revolver at him. Next morning blood was found on the bridge and on the hill up which the leopard had gone, and as it was thought that the wound, or wounds, must be fatal, a search was kept up for many days. The report goes on to say that for six months after he was wounded, the leopard did not kill any human beings.

I was told about this incident by men who had heard the seven shots, and who had assisted in trying to recover the wounded animal. It was thought by the two sportsmen, and also by my informants, that the leopard had been hit in the back by the first bullet and possibly in the head by some of the subsequent bullets, and it was for this reason that a diligent and prolonged search had been made for him. From the particulars given me of the blood trail, I was of the opinion that the sportsmen were wrong in thinking that they had inflicted a body and a head wound on the leopard, for the blood trail as described to me could only have been made by a foot wound, and I was very gratified to find later that my deductions were correct and that the bullet fired by the man on the tower on the left bank had only creased the pad of the leopard's left hind foot and shot away a portion of one of his toes, and that the man on the right bank had missed all his shots.

2. After some twenty leopards had been caught and killed in traps of the drop-door type, a leopard, which everyone thought was the man-eater, was caught in one of them and as

the Hindu population was unwilling to kill him for fear the spirits of the people whom he had killed would torment them, an Indian Christian was sent for. This Christian was living in a village thirty miles away, and before he could arrive on the scene the leopard dug his way out of the trap and escaped.

3. The leopard, after killing a man, lay up with his kill in a small isolated patch of jungle. Next morning, when a search was being made for the victim, the leopard was detected leaving the jungle. After being chased for a short distance it was seen to enter a cave, the mouth of which was promptly closed with thorn bushes heaped over with big rocks. Every day a crowd of men, which grew in numbers, visited the spot. On the fifth day, when some five hundred men were assembled, a man whose name is not given but whom the report describes as a man of influence came, and to quote the report, 'said scornfully there is no leopard in this cave and took the thorns off the cave. As he took the thorns up, the leopard suddenly rushed out of the cave and made his way safely through a crowd of some five hundred persons who had gathered there.'

These incidents took place shortly after the leopard had become a man-eater, and had he been killed on the bridge, shot in the trap, or sealed up in the cave, a few hundred people need not have died, and Garhwal would have been saved many years of suffering.

4

Arrival

It was during one of the intervals of Gilbert and Sullivan's *Yeoman of the Guard*, which was showing at the Chalet Theatre in Naini Tal in 1925, that I first had any definite news of the Rudraprayag man-eater.

I had heard casually that there was a man-eating leopard in Garhwal and had read articles in the press about the animal, but knowing that there were over four thousand licensed gun holders in Garhwal, and a host of keen sportsmen in Lansdowne, only some seventy miles from Rudraprayag, I imagined that people were falling over each other in their eagerness to shoot the leopard and that in these circumstances a stranger would not be welcome.

It was with no little surprise, therefore, that, as I stood at the Chalet bar that night having a drink with a friend, I heard Michael Keene—then Chief Secretary to the Government of the United Provinces and later Governor of Assam—telling a group of men about the man-eater, and trying to persuade them to go after it. His appeal, judging from the remark of one of the group and endorsed by the others, was not received with any enthusiasm. The remark was, 'Go after a man-eater that has killed a hundred people? Not on your life.'

Next morning I paid Michael Keene a visit and got all the particulars I wanted. He was not able to tell me exactly where the man-eater was operating, and suggested my going to Rudraprayag and getting in touch with Ibbotson. On my return home I found a letter from Ibbotson on my table.

Ibbotson—now Sir William Ibbotson, and lately Adviser to His Excellency the Governor of the United Provinces—had very recently been posted to Garhwal as Deputy Commissioner, and one of his first acts had been to try and rid his district of the man-eater. It was in this connection that he had written to me.

My preparations were soon made and, traveling *via* Ranikhet, Adbadri, and Karanprayag, I arrived on the evening of the tenth day at a road-inspection bungalow near Nagrasu. When leaving Naini Tal I did not know it was necessary to provide myself with a permit to occupy this bungalow, and as the caretaker had orders not to allow anyone to occupy it unless so provided, the six Garhwalis carrying my kit, and my servant and I toiled on for another two miles down the Rudraprayag road until we found a suitable place on which to camp for the night.

While my men busied themselves getting water and dry sticks, and my servant collected stones for a *chula* (an open cooking place), I picked up an axe and set out to cut down thorn bushes to make an enclosure to protect us during the night, for we had been warned ten miles further up the road that we had entered the man-eater's territory.

Shortly after the fires to cook our evening meal had been lit, a very agitated call came down to us from a village far up the mountainside, asking us what we were doing out in the open, and warning us that if we remained where we were one or more of us would surely be killed by the man-eater. When the Good Samaritan had delivered his warning, to do which he had possibly taken a great risk—for it was then dark—Madho Singh, whom you have met elsewhere,[1] expressed the wishes of all present when he said, 'We will stay here, Sahib, for there is sufficient oil in the lantern to keep it alight all night, and you have your rifle.'

There was sufficient oil in the lantern to keep it alight all night, for I found it burning when I awoke in the morning, and my loaded rifle lay across my bed. But the thorn enclosure was very flimsy and we were dead tired after our ten days' march, and, if the leopard had paid us a visit that night, he would have secured a very easy victim.

Next day we arrived at Rudraprayag and were given a warm welcome by the men whom Ibbotson had instructed to meet us.

[1] See 'The Chowgarh Tigers' in *Man-Eaters of Kumaon.*

5

Investigation

I shall not attempt to give you a day-to-day account of my activities during the ten weeks I spent at Rudraprayag, for it would be difficult—after this lapse of time—to write such an account and, if written, would be boring for you to read. I shall therefore confine myself to relating a few of my experiences, at times while I was alone and at other times when in company with Ibbotson. But before doing so I should like to give you some idea of the country over which the leopard ranged for eight years, and in which I hunted him for ten weeks.

If you were to climb the hill to the east of Rudraprayag, you would be able to see the greater portion of the five hundred square miles of country over which the Rudraprayag man-eater ranged. This area is divided into two more or less equal parts by the Alaknanda River, which, after passing Karanprayag, flows south to Rudraprayag, where it is met by the Mandakini coming down from the northwest. The triangular bit of country between the two rivers is less steep than the country along the left bank of the Alaknanda, and there are consequently more villages in the former area than in the latter.

From your elevated position, the cultivated land in the distance shows up as a series of lines drawn across the face of the steep mountains. These lines are terraced fields, which vary in width from a yard to, in some cases, fifty or more yards. The village buildings are invariably set at the upper end of the cultivated land; this is done with the object of overlooking and protecting the cultivation from stray cattle and wild animals, for except in very rare cases there are no hedges or fences around the fields. The brown and the green patches that make up most of the landscape are respectively grassland and forests. Some of the villages, you will observe, are entirely surrounded by grasslands, while others are surrounded by forests. The whole country as you look down on it is rugged and rough and is cut up by innumerable deep ravines and rock cliffs. In this area there are only two roads, one starting from Rudraprayag and going up to Kedarnath, and the other being the main pilgrim road to Badrinath. Both roads, up to the time I am writing about, were narrow and rough and had never had a wheel of any kind on them.

If you look at the map at the end of the book you will see many circles on it. These mark the number of human beings killed in each village by the Rudraprayag man-eater. The number of human beings killed in each of these marked villages between 1918 and 1926 is shown on the tables on page 33.

It would be reasonable to assume that more human beings would have been killed in villages surrounded by forests than in those surrounded by cultivated land. Had the man-eater been a tiger, this would undoubtedly have been the case, but to a man-eating leopard, which only operates at night, the presence or absence of cover made no difference, and the only reason why there were more kills in one village than in another was due in the one case to lack of precautions and, in the other, to observance of them.

I have mentioned that the man-eater was an outsized male leopard long past his prime, but though old, he was enormously strong. The ability of carnivora to carry their kill to a place where they can feed undisturbed determines, to a great extent, the place selected in which to do their killing. To the Rudraprayag man-eater all places were alike, for he was capable of carrying the heaviest of his human victims for distances up to—on one occasion that I know of—four miles. On that occasion, the leopard, after killing a well-grown man in his house, carried the victim for two miles up the steep slope of a heavily wooded hill, and down the far side for another two miles through dense scrub jungle. This was done for no apparent reason, for the kill had taken place in the early hours of the night, and the leopard had not been followed up until noon of the next day.

Leopards—other than man-eaters—are the most easily killed of all our jungle animals, having but a poor sense of smell. More methods are employed in killing leopards than in killing any other animal. The methods vary according to whether the leopard is being killed for sport or for profit. The most exciting and the most interesting way of killing for sport is to track them down in the jungles and, when they are located, stalk and shoot them. The easiest and the most cruel method of killing them for profit is to insert a small and very highly explosive bomb, which the locals have learned to make, in the flesh of an animal that has been killed by a leopard. When one of these bombs comes in contact with the leopard's teeth, it explodes and blows the leopard's jaws off. Death in some cases is instantaneous, but more often than not the unfortunate animal crawls away to die a lingering and very painful death, for the people who use the bombs have not the courage to follow the blood trail left by the leopard, and despatch it.

CASUALTY LIST (by villages), 1918-26

Six kills
CHOPRA
Five kills
KOTHKI, RATAURA
Four kills
BIJRAKOT
Three kills
NAKOT, GANDHARI, KOKHANDI, DADOLI, QUETHI, JHIRMOLI, GOLABRAI, LAMERI
Two kills
BAJADU, RAMPUR, MAIKOTI, CHHATOLI, KOTI, MADOLA, RAUTA, KANDE (JOGI), BAWRUN, SARI, RANAU, PUNAR, TILANI, BAUN-THA, NAGRASU, GWAR, MARWARA
One kill
ASON, PILU, BHAUNSAL, MANGU, BAINJI, BHATWARI, KHAMOLI, SWANRI, PHALSI, KANDA DHARKOT, DANGI, GUNAUN, BHAT-GAON, BAWAL, BARSIL, BHAINSGAON, NARI, SANDAR, TAMEND, KHATYANA, SEOPURI, SAN, SYUND, KAMERA, DARMARI, BELA, BELA-KUND, SAUR, BHAINSARI, BAJNU, QUILI, DHARKOT, BHAIN-GAON, CHHINKA, DHUNG KIURI, BAMAN KANDAI, POKHTA, THAPALOGAON, BANSU, NAG, BAISANI, RUDRAPRAYAG, GWAR, KALNA, BHUNKA, SAIL, PABO, BHAINSWARA.

Annual Totals

1918	1
1919	3
1920	6
1921	23
1922	24
1923	26
1924	20
1925	8
1926	14
	125

The tracking, locating, and stalking of leopards, besides being exciting and interesting, is comparatively easy. Leopards have tender pads and keep to footpaths and game tracks as far as possible; they are not hard to locate for practically every bird and animal in the jungle assists the hunter, and they are easy to stalk, for though they are blessed with keen sight and hearing, they are handicapped by having no keen sense of smell. The sportsman can therefore select the line of approach that best suits him, irrespective of the direction in which the wind is blowing.

Having tracked, located, and stalked a leopard, far more pleasure is got from pressing the button of a camera than is ever got from pressing the trigger of a rifle. In the one case the leopard can be watched for hours—and there is no more graceful and interesting animal in the jungles to watch—and the button of the camera can be pressed as fancy dictates and a record secured that never loses its interest. In the other case a fleeting glimpse, one press of the trigger and—if the aim has been true—the acquisition of a trophy that soon loses its beauty and its interest.

6

The First Kill

Shortly before my arrival at Rudraprayag, Ibbotson organized a beat for the man-eater, which—if it had been successful—would have saved the lives of fifteen human beings. The beat and the circumstances leading up to it are worthy of record.

Twenty pilgrims toiling up the road to Badrinath arrived towards evening at a small roadside shop. After the shopkeeper had met their wants, he urged them to be on their way, telling them there was only just sufficient daylight left for them to reach the pilgrim shelters four miles further up the road, where they would get food and safe shelter. The pilgrims were unwilling to accept this advice; they said they had done a long march that day and were too tired to walk another four miles, and that all they wanted were facilities to prepare and cook their evening meal, and permission to sleep on the platform adjoining the shop. To this proposal the shopkeeper vigorously objected. He told the pilgrims that his house was frequently visited by the man-eater, and to sleep out in the open would be to court death.

While the argument was at its height, a *sadhu* on his way from Muttra to Badrinath arrived on the scene and championed the cause of the pilgrims. He said that if the shopkeeper would give shelter to the women of the party he would sleep on the platform with the men, and if any leopard—man-eater or otherwise—dared molest them he would take it by the mouth and tear it in half.

To this proposal the shopkeeper had perforce to agree. So while the ten women of the party took shelter in the one-room shop behind a locked door, the ten men lay down in a row on the platform, with the *sadhu* in the middle.

When the pilgrims on the platform awoke in the morning they found the *sadhu* missing, the blanket on which he had slept rumpled, and the sheet he had used to cover himself with partly dragged off the platform and spotted with blood. On hearing the excited chattering of the men, the shopkeeper opened the door and at a glance saw what had happened. When the sun had risen the shopkeeper, accompanied by the men, followed the blood trail down the hill and across three terraced fields to a low boundary wall; here lying across the wall, with the lower portion of his body eaten away, they found the *sadhu*.

Ibbotson was staying at Rudraprayag at this time, trying to get in touch with the man-eater. There had been no kills during his stay so he decided to beat, on 'speck,' a very likely-looking bit of cover on the far side of the Alaknanda, which the locals suspected was used by the man-eater as a lying-up place during the hours of daylight. So while the twenty pilgrims were toiling up the road towards the little shop, the *Patwaris* and other members of Ibbotson's staff were going round the near-by villages warning men to be ready for the beat, which was to take place on the morrow.

After an early breakfast next morning Ibbotson, accompanied by Jean (Lady) Ibbotson and a friend whose name I have forgotten, and followed by some members of his staff and two hundred beaters, crossed the Alaknanda by the suspension bridge and, going up the hill on the far side for a mile or so, took up positions for the beat.

While the beat was still in progress, word was brought by runner of the killing of the *sadhu*.

The beat, which proved to be a blank, was completed and a hurried council held, the upshot of which was that while Ibbotson, his party, and the two hundred beaters set off up the right bank to cross the river four miles further up by a *jhula* (swing) bridge and make their way up the left bank to the scene of the kill, the staff dispersed themselves over the countryside to collect as many men as possible and assemble them at the shop.

By late afternoon two thousand beaters and several additional guns were assembled at the shop, and the high rugged hill above the shop was beaten from top to bottom. If you know Ibbotson, there is no need for me to tell you that the beat was very efficiently organized and as efficiently carried out, and the only reason why it failed in its object was that the leopard was not in that area.

When a leopard, or a tiger, leaves—of his own accord—a kill out in the open in an exposed spot, it is an indication that the animal has no further interest in the kill, and after his feed he invariably removes himself to a distance perhaps of only two or three miles, or—in the case of man-eaters—perhaps of ten or more miles. So it is quite possible that while the hill was being beaten, the man-eater was peacefully slumbering ten miles away.

7

Locating the Leopard

Man-eating leopards are of rare occurrence, and for this reason very little is known about them.

My own experience of these animals was very limited, amounting to no more than a brief encounter with one many years previously, and though I suspected that the change-over from animal to human-and-animal diet would affect the habits of a leopard as much as it does those of a tiger, I did not know to what extent, and until I did, I decided to try and kill the man-eater by the methods usually employed for killing leopards.

The most common method of killing leopards is to sit up for them, either over a kill or over live bait in the form of a goat or a sheep. To carry out either method it is necessary in the one case to find a kill, and in the other to locate the quarry.

My object in going to Rudraprayag was to try and prevent further loss of human life, and I had no intention of waiting for another human kill to occur, over which I could sit; therefore, the obvious thing to do was to locate the man-eater and shoot him over live bait.

Here a formidable difficulty presented itself, which I hoped in time partly to overcome. From the maps I had been supplied with,

I found that the man-eater was operating over an area of roughly five hundred square miles. Five hundred square miles of country anywhere would have been a considerable area in which to find and shoot any animal, and in this mountainous and rugged part of Garhwal the task of finding an animal that only operated at night appeared, at first glance, to be well-nigh impossible—until I took the Alaknanda River, which divided the area into two more or less equal parts, into consideration.

It was generally believed that the Alaknanda offered no obstacle to the man-eater and that when he found it difficult to obtain a human kill on one bank, he crossed over to the other bank by swimming the river.

I discounted this belief. In my opinion no leopard would in any circumstances voluntarily commit itself to the swift flowing ice-cold waters of the Alaknanda, and I was convinced that when the man-eater crossed from one bank to the other, he did so by one of the suspension bridges.

There were two suspension bridges in the area, one at Rudraprayag, and the other about twelve miles further up the river, at Chatwapipal. Between these two bridges there was a *jhula* bridge—the one by which Ibbotson, his party, and the two hundred men had crossed the river on the day of the beat. This swing bridge, which no animal, excepting a rat, could possibly have crossed, was the most fear-compelling structure of its kind that I have ever seen. The two hand-twisted grass cables, blackened by age and mouldy from the mists rising from the river, spanned some two hundred feet of foaming white water, which a hundred yards further down surged with a roar like thunder between two walls of rock, where a kakar driven by wild dogs is credited with having leaped across the Alaknanda. Between the cables, and forming the footway, were odd bits of sticks an inch and a half to two inches in diameter, set about two feet apart and loosely tied to the cables with wisps of grass. To add to the difficulty in crossing this cobweb structure, one of the cables had sagged, with the result that the sticks, on which one had to place one's feet, were at an angle of forty-five degrees. The first time I met this fearsome *jhula* I was foolish enough to ask the toll collector, who for the payment of one pice permitted me to risk my life on it, whether the bridge was ever tested or repaired. His answer, given as he ran a speculative eye over me, that the bridge was replaced when it broke under the weight of someone who was trying to cross it, gave me a cold feeling down my spine that remained with me long after I had safely reached the other side.

As this *jhula* was beyond the powers of the man-eater to cross, there remained the two suspension bridges, and I felt sure that if I could close them against the leopard I should be able to confine him to one side of the Alaknanda, and so reduce by half the area in which to look for him.

The first thing, therefore, was to try and find out on which bank of the river the leopard was. The last kill, that of the *sadhu*, had taken place on the left bank of the river a few miles from the Chatwapipal suspension bridge, and I felt sure that the leopard, after abandoning his kill, had crossed this bridge, for no matter what precautions the locals and the pilgrims may have taken before a kill, these precautions were redoubled immediately after one, making it almost impossible for the leopard to secure two or more consecutive kills in the same area. You will ask why, if this was so, as many as six kills have been attributed to a single village. I can only answer that an effort cannot be sustained indefinitely, and that on hearing that the man-eater was operating at a village ten, fifteen, or twenty miles away, people living in small houses without any conveniences or means of sanitation might, at the urgent dictate of nature, have opened a door for a brief minute, thus giving the leopard the chance he had possibly been awaiting for many nights.

8

The Second Kill

No photographs or other means by which I could identify the man-eater by his pug marks were available and, until I had been given an opportunity of acquiring this information for myself, I decided to treat all leopards in the vicinity of Rudraprayag as suspect, and shoot any that gave me a chance.

The day I arrived at Rudraprayag I purchased two goats. One of these goats I tied up the following evening, a mile up the pilgrim road; the other I took across the Alaknanda and tied up on a path running through some heavy scrub jungle, where I found the old pug marks of a big male leopard. On visiting the goats the following morning I found the one across the river had been killed, and a small portion of it eaten. It had unquestionably been killed by a leopard, but had been eaten by a small animal, possibly a pine marten.

I received no news about the man-eater during the day, so decided to sit up over the dead goat, and at 3 p.m. took up my position in the branches of a small tree about fifty yards from the kill. During the three hours I sat in the tree I had no indication, from either animals or birds, that the leopard was anywhere in the vicinity, and as dusk was falling I slipped off the tree, cut the cord tethering the goat—which the leopard had made no attempt to break the previous night—and set off for the bungalow.

As I have already admitted I had very little previous experience of man-eating leopards, but I had met a few man-eating tigers, and from the time I left the tree until I reached the bungalow, I took every precaution to guard against a sudden attack—and it was fortunate that I did so.

I made an early start next morning and near the gate of the bungalow I picked up the tracks of a big male leopard. These tracks I followed back to a densely wooded ravine that crossed the path close to where the goat was lying. The goat had not been touched during the night.

The leopard that had followed me could only have been the maneater, and for the rest of the day I walked as many miles as my legs would carry me, telling all the people in the villages I visited, and all whom I met on the roads, that the man-eater was on our side of the river, and warning them to be careful.

Nothing happened that day, but next day just as I was finishing breakfast, after a long morning spent in prospecting the jungles beyond Golabrai, a very agitated man dashed into the bungalow to tell me that a woman had been killed by the man-eater the previous night in a village on the hill above the bungalow—the same hill and almost at the exact spot from where you obtained a bird's-eye view of the five hundred square miles of country in which the man-eater was operating.

Within a few minutes I collected all the things that I needed—a spare rifle and shotgun, cartridges, rope, and a length of fishing line—and set off up the steep hill accompanied by the villager and two of my men. It was a sultry day and though the distance was not great—three miles at the most—the climb of four thousand feet in the hot sun was very trying and I arrived at the village in a bath of sweat.

The story of the husband of the woman who had been killed was soon told. After their evening meal, which had been eaten by the light of the fire, the woman collected the metal pots and pans that had been used for the meal and carried them to the door to wash, while the man sat down to have a smoke. On reaching the door the woman sat down on the doorstep and as she did so the utensils clattered to the ground. There was not sufficient light for the man to see what had happened and when he received no answer to his urgent call, he dashed forward and shut and barred the door. 'Of what use,' he said, 'would it have been for me to risk my life in trying to recover a dead body?' His logic was sound, though heartless; and I gathered that the grief he showed was occasioned not so much by the loss of his wife as by the loss of that son and heir—exposed to view by the leopard—whom he had expected to see born within the next few days.

The doorway from which the woman had been seized opened onto a four-foot-wide lane that ran for fifty yards between two rows of houses. On hearing the clatter of the falling pots and pans, followed by the urgent call of the man to his wife, every door in the lane had been instantaneously shut. The marks on the ground showed that the leopard had dragged the unfortunate woman the length of the lane, then killed her, and carried her down the hill for a hundred yards into a small ravine that bordered some terraced fields. Here he ate his meal, and here he left the pitiful remains.

The body lay in the ravine at one end of a narrow terraced field, at the other end of which, some forty yards away, was a leafless and stunted walnut tree in whose branches a hayrick had been built, some four feet from the ground and about six feet tall. In this hayrick I decided to sit.

Starting near the body, a narrow path ran down into the ravine. On this path were the pug marks of the leopard, and they were identical with the pug marks of the leopard that had followed me two nights previously from the goat kill to the Rudraprayag bungalow. The pug marks were of an outsized male leopard long past his prime, with a slight defect where a bullet fired four years previously had creased the pad of his left hind paw.

Procuring two stout eight-foot-long bamboos from the village, I drove them into the ground close to the perpendicular bank that divided the field in which the body was lying from the field below, and tied my spare rifle and shotgun securely to them. To the triggers I tied lengths of dressed-silk fishing line and, looping the lines back over the trigger guards, fastened them to two stakes driven into the hillside on the far side of and a little above the path. If the leopard came along the path he had used the previous night, there was a reasonable chance of his pulling on the lines and shooting himself; on the other hand, if he avoided them or came by any other way, and I fired at him while he was on the kill, he would be almost certain to run into the trap, for that was his most natural line of retreat. Both the leopard, because of his protective coloring, and the body, which had been stripped of all clothing by the leopard, would be invisible in the dark; so to give me an idea of the direction in which to fire I took a slab of white rock from the ravine and put it on the edge of the field, about a foot from the near side of the body.

My ground arrangements completed to my satisfaction, I made myself a comfortable seat on the rick, throwing out some of the straw and heaping some behind me and up to my waist in front. As I was facing the kill and had my back to the tree, there was little chance of the leopard's seeing me, no matter at what time he came; and that he would come during the night, in spite of his reputation of not returning to his kills, I was firmly convinced. All clothes were still wet after the stiff climb, but a comparatively dry jacket kept out the chill wind; so, settling down into my soft and comfortable seat and prepared for an all-night vigil, I sent my men away, telling them to remain in the headman's house until I came for them, or until the sun was well up next morning. (I had stepped from the bank onto the rick, and there was nothing to prevent the man-eater from doing the same.)

The sun was near setting, and the view of the Ganges valley, with the snowy Himalayas in the background showing blush pink under the level rays of the setting sun, was a feast for the eyes; and almost before I realized it, daylight had faded out of the sky and night had come.

Darkness, when used in connection with night, is a relative term and has no fixed standard; what to one man would be pitch dark, to another would be dark, and to a third be moderately dark. To me, who have spent so much of my life in the open, the night is never dark, unless the sky is overcast with heavy clouds. I do not wish to imply that I can see as well by night as by day; but I can see quite well enough to find my way through any jungle, or, for that matter, over any ground. I had placed the white stone near the body only as a precaution, for I hoped that the starlight, with the added reflection from the snowy range, would give me sufficient light by which to shoot. But my luck was out—or rather, the luck of the people of Garhwal—for night had hardly fallen when there was a flash of lightning, followed by distant thunder, and in a few minutes the sky was heavily overcast. Just as the first big drops of a deluge began to fall, I heard a stone roll into the ravine, and a minute later the loose straw on the ground below me was being scratched up. The leopard had arrived; and while I sat in torrential rain with the ice cold wind whistling through my wet clothes, he lay dry and snug in the straw below. The storm was one of the worst I have ever experienced, and while it was at its height I saw a lantern being carried towards the village, and marveled at the courage of the man who carried it. It was not until some hours later that I learned that the man who so gallantly braved both the leopard and the storm had done a forced march of over thirty miles from Pauri to bring me the electric night-shooting light that the Government had promised me; the arrival of this light three short hours earlier might—But regrets are vain, and who can say that the fourteen people who died later would have had a longer span of life if the leopard had not buried his teeth in their throats? Again, even if the light had arrived in time, there is no certainty that I should have killed the leopard that night.

The rain was soon over—leaving me chilled to the bone—and the clouds were breaking up, when the white stone was suddenly obscured, and a little later I heard the leopard eating. The night before he had lain in the ravine and eaten from that side; so, expecting him to do the same this night, I had placed the stone on the near side of the kill. Obviously, the rain had formed little pools in the ravine, and to avoid them the leopard had taken up a new position and in doing so had obscured my mark. This was something I had not foreseen; however, knowing the habits of leopards, I knew I should not have to wait long before the stone showed up again. Ten minutes later the stone was visible, and almost immediately thereafter I heard a sound below me, and saw the leopard as a light-yellowish object disappearing under the rick. His light color could be accounted for by old age, but the sound he made when walking I could not then, nor can I now, account for; it was like the soft rustle of a woman's silk dress, and could not be explained by stubble in the field—for there was none—or by the loose straw lying about.

Waiting a suitable length of time, I raised the rifle and covered the stone, intending to fire the moment it was again obscured; but there is a limit to the time a heavy rise can be held to the shoulder, and when the limit had been reached I lowered the rifle to ease my aching muscles. I had hardly done so when the stone for the second time disappeared from view. Three times within the next two hours the same thing happened, and in desperation as I heard the leopard approaching the rick for the fourth time, I leaned over and fired at the indistinct object below me.

The narrow terrace to which I have given the usual name of 'field' was only about two feet wide at this point, and when I examined the ground next morning I found my bullet hole in the center of the two-foot-wide space, with a little hair, cut from the leopard's neck, scattered round it.

I saw no more of the leopard that night, and at sunrise I collected my men and set off down the steep hill to Rudraprayag, while the husband and his friends carried away the woman's—and the infant's—remains for cremation.

9

Preparations

My thoughts as I walked, cold and stiff, down the hill to Rudra-prayag from the scene of my night's failure were very bitter, for, from whatever angle it was viewed, there was no question that the fickle jade Chance had played both Garhwal and myself a scurvy trick we did not deserve.

However little I merit it, the people of our hills credit me with supernatural powers where man-eaters are concerned. News that I was on my way to try and rid Garhwal of the man-eater had preceded me, and while I was still many days march from Rudrapra-yag the men I met on the roads, and those who from their fields or village homes saw me passing, greeted me with a faith in the accomplishment of my mission that was as touching as it was embarrassing, and which increased in intensity the nearer I approached my destination. Had any been there to witness my entry into Rudraprayag he would have found it hard to believe that the man whom the populace thronged around was no hero returning from the wars, but a man, very sensible of his limitations, who greatly feared that the task he had undertaken was beyond his powers of accomplishment.

Five hundred square miles, much of which was clothed with dense scrub jungle and all of which was rugged and mountainous, was an enormous area in which to find and shoot one particular leopard out of possibly fifty that inhabited it, and the more I saw of the grand and beautiful country the less I liked it from the point of view of the task I had undertaken. The populace quite naturally did not share my misgivings; to them I was one who had rid others of man-eaters and who had now come among them to rid them of the menace they had lived under for eight long years. And then, with incredible good luck, I had within a few hours of my arrival got the animal to kill one of my goats and, by staying out a little after dark, to follow me to that side of the Alaknanda where I believed it would be less difficult to deal with him than it would have been on the other side. Following up this initial success had been the kill of the unfortunate woman; I had tried to prevent the further loss of human life and had failed, and my failure had presented me with an opportunity of shooting the leopard that I might otherwise have not got for many months.

As I had climbed uphill the previous day in the wake of my guide I had weighed up my chances of killing the leopard and assessed them at two-to-one—this despite the fact that the animal had in recent years earned the reputation of never returning to a kill, that it was a dark night, and that I had no aid to night shooting. The day I had visited Michael Keene and told him I would go to Garhwal he asked me if I had everything I wanted, and when I told him I only lacked a night-shooting light and that I would telegraph to Calcutta for one, he said the least the Government could do for me was to provide me with one, and he promised to have the best one procurable waiting for me at Rudraprayag. The light had not arrived and, though my disappointment was great, it was to a certain extent mitigated by my ability to see in the dark, and on this ability I assessed my chance at two-to-one. As so much depended on the success of that night's venture, however, I had armed myself with a spare rifle and shotgun, and when from my concealed position on the hayrick I viewed the scene in front of me—the short range at which I would get my shot, and the perfectly camouflaged gun trap into which the leopard would of a certainty run, if I missed or wounded him—my hopes rose high and I put my chances of success at ten-to-one. And then had come the storm, and with visibility reduced to practically nil and lacking the electric light, I had failed, and my failure would in a few hours be known throughout the stricken area.

Exercise, warm water, and food have a wonderfully soothing effect on bitter thoughts, and by the time I had picked my way down the steep hillside, and had a hot bath and breakfast, I had ceased to rail at fate and was able to take a more reasonable view of my night's failure. Regret over a bullet fired into the ground was as profitless as regret over milk spilled on sand, and if the leopard had not crossed the Alaknanda my chances of killing him had improved, for I now had the electric shooting light, which the runner had braved both the leopard and the storm to bring me.

The first thing to do was to find out if the leopard had crossed the Alaknanda, and as I was firm in my conviction that the only way he could do this was by way of the suspension bridges, I set out after breakfast to glean this information. I discounted the possibility of the leopard's having crossed the Chatwapipal bridge, for no matter how great the shock he had received by the discharge of my heavy rifle a few feet from his head, it was not possible that he would have covered the fourteen miles that separated the kill from the bridge in the few hours that remained between the firing of my shot and daylight; so I decided to confine my search to the Rudra-prayag bridge.

There were three approaches to the bridge: one from the north, one from the south, and between these two a well-beaten footpath from the Rudraprayag bazaar. After examining these approaches very carefully, I crossed the bridge and examined the Kedarnath pilgrim road for half a mile, and then the footpath on which three nights previously my goat had been killed. Satisfied that the leopard had not crossed the river, I determined to put into operation my plan for closing the two bridges at night and thus confine the leopard to my side of the river. The plan was a simple one and, given the co-operation of the caretakers of the bridges, both of whom lived on the left bank and close to the bridge abutments, was certain of success.

To close the only means of communication between the two banks of the river over a stretch of some thirty miles would appear to be a very high-handed proceeding, but actually it was not so, for no human being dared to use the bridges between sunset and sunrise, owing to the curfew imposed by the leopard.

The bridges were closed by wedging thorn bushes in the four-foot-wide archway in the towers carrying the steel cables from which the plank footway was suspended, and during the whole period that the bridges were closed with thorn, or were guarded by me, no human being demanded passage across them.

I spent in all some twenty nights on the tower on the left bank of the Rudraprayag bridge, and those nights will never be forgotten. The tower was built out on a projecting rock and was twenty feet high, and the platform on the top of it, which had been worn smooth by the wind, was about four feet wide and eight feet long. There were two means of reaching this platform, one by swarming along the cables, which ran through holes near the top of the tower and were anchored in the hillside some fifty feet from the tower, and the other by climbing up a very rickety bamboo ladder. I chose the latter way, for the cables were coated over with some black and very evil-smelling matter, which clung to the hands and permanently stained one's clothes.

The ladder—two uneven lengths of bamboo connected with thin sticks loosely held in position with string—only reached to within four feet of the platform. As I was standing on the top rung of the ladder and dependent for a hand-hold on the friction of the palms of my hands on the smooth masonry, the safe gaining of the platform was an acrobatic feat that had less appeal the oftener it was tried.

All the rivers in this part of the Himalayas flow from north to south, and in the valleys through which they flow a wind blows that changes direction with the rising and the setting of the sun. During daylight hours the wind—locally called *Dadu*—blows from the south, and during the hours of night it blows from the north.

During the hour at which I took up my position on the platform there was usually a lull in the wind, but shortly thereafter it started blowing as a light zephyr, gaining in strength as daylight faded, and amounting by midnight to a raging gale. With no hand-hold on the platform, and even when lying flat on my stomach to increase friction and reduce wind pressure, there was imminent risk of being blown off the platform onto the rocks sixty feet below, off which I would have bounced into the ice-cold Alaknanda. Not that the temperature of the water would have been of any interest after a fall of sixty feet onto sharp and jagged rocks; yet strangely enough, whenever I felt in fear of falling, it was always the water, and never the rocks, that I thought of. Added to the discomfort of the wind, I suffered torment from a multitude of small ants, which, entering my clothes, ate away patches of skin. During the twenty nights I guarded the bridge, the thorn bushes were not placed in position, and in all that long period the bridge was only crossed by one living thing—a jackal.

10

Magic

Each evening when I went to the bridge to take up my position on the tower, I was accompanied by two men who carried the ladder that enabled me to climb to the platform, and which they removed, after handing me my rifle.

On the second day as we arrived at the bridge, we saw a man dressed in flowing white robes, with something glinting on his head and breast. He carried a six-foot silver cross, and was approaching the bridge from the direction of Kedarnath. On reaching the bridge the man knelt down, and holding the cross in front of him bowed his head; after remaining in this position for a little while, he raised the cross on high and, getting to his feet, took a few steps forward and again knelt down, bowed his head, and again raised the cross. This he continued to do at short intervals all the way across the long bridge.

As he passed me the man raised his hand in salutation, but as he appeared to be deep in prayer, I did not speak to him; the glint I had seen on his headdress and breast were, I perceived, silver crosses.

My men had been as interested in this strange apparition as had I, and as he climbed the steep footpath to the Rudraprayag bazaar, they asked me what manner of man he was and from what country he had come. That he was a Christian was apparent, but as I had not heard him speak I could only assume from his long hair, jet-black luxuriant beard, and what I could see of his features, that he was from northern India.

The following morning when with the help of the ladder I had climbed down from the tower and was proceeding to the Inspection Bungalow, where I spent that portion of the daylight hours that I was not visiting both near and distant villages in search of news of the man-eater, I saw the tall white-robed figure standing on a great slab of rock near the road, surveying the river. At my approach he left the rock and greeted me, and on my asking him what had brought him to these parts he said he had come from a distant land to free the people of Garhwal from the evil spirit that was torment-ing them. When I asked how he proposed to accomplish this feat, he said he would make an effigy of a tiger and after he had, by prayer, induced the evil spirit to enter it, he would set the effigy afloat on the Ganges and the river would convey it down to the sea whence it could not return, and where it would do no further harm to human beings.

However much I doubted the man's ability to accomplish the task he had set himself, I could not help admiring his faith and his in-dustry. He arrived each morning before I left the tower and was still at work when I returned in the evening, laboring with split bam-boos, string, paper, and cheap colored cloth on his 'tiger.' When the effigy was nearing completion, a heavy rainstorm one night made the whole structure come unstuck; nothing daunted, he cheerfully started on it again next morning, singing as he worked.

Came at last the great day when the 'tiger'—about the size of a horse, and resembling no known animal—was fashioned to his satisfaction.

Who is there among our hill folk who does not wholeheartedly enjoy taking part in a *tamasba*? When the effigy, tied to a long pole, was carried down a steep path to a small sandy beach, it had an escort of over a hundred men, many of whom were beating gongs and blowing long trumpets.

At the edge of the river the effigy was unlashed from the pole. The white-robed man, with silver crosses on his headgear and breast and holding his six-foot cross in his hands, knelt on the sand and with earnest prayer induced the evil spirit to enter his handiwork. Then the effigy, with a crash of gongs and a blare of trumpets, was consigned to the Ganges, and sped on its way to the sea by a liberal offering of sweets and flowers.

Next morning the now-familiar figure was absent from the rock, and on my asking some men, who were on their way to have an early dip in the river, where my friend of the flowing robes had come from and where he had gone, they answered, 'Who can tell whence a Holy Man has come, and who dare question whither he has departed?'

These men, with sandalwood-paste caste marks on their foreheads, who spoke of the man as 'holy,' were Hindus, as were all those others who had taken part in the launching ceremony.

I believe that in India, where there are no passports or identity discs, and where religion counts for so much—except among those few who have crossed the 'black water'—a man wearing a saffron robe, or carrying a beggar's bowl, or with silver crosses on his headgear and chest, could walk from the Khyber Pass to Cape Comorin without once being questioned about his destination, or the object of his journey.

11

A Near Escape

While I was still guarding the bridge Ibbotson and his wife Jean
arrived from Pauri, and as the accommodation in the Inspection
Bungalow was very limited, I moved out to make room for them,
and set up my forty-pound tent on the hill on the far side of the pilgrim road.

As a tent afforded little protection against an animal that had left
his claw marks on every door and window for miles around, I
helped my men to put up a thorn fence round the ground we intended to camp on. Overhanging this plot of ground was a giant
prickly-pear tree and, as its branches interfered with the erection of
my tent, I told the men to cut it down. After the tree had been
partly cut through, I changed my mind, for I saw that I would be
without shade during the heat of the day; so instead of felling the
tree I told them to lop the overhanging branches. This tree, which
was leaning over the camp at an angle of forty-five degrees, was on
the far side of the fence.

There were eight of us in the little camp. When we had eaten our
evening meal, I wedged a thorn bush securely into the opening in

the fence we had entered by, and as I did so I noticed that it would be very easy for the man-eater to climb the tree and drop down on our side of the fence; however, it was too late then to do anything about it, and if the leopard left us alone for that one night, the tree could be cut down and removed in the morning.

I had no tents for my men, and had intended that they should sleep with Ibbotson's men in the outbuildings of the Inspection Bungalow; but this they had refused to do, asserting that there was no more danger for them than there was for me in the open tent. My cook—who I discovered was a very noisy sleeper—was lying next to me, about a yard away, and beyond him, packed like sardines in the little enclosure, were the six Garhwalis I had brought from Naini Tall.

The weak spot in our defence was the tree, and I went to sleep thinking of it.

It was a brilliant moonlit night, and round about midnight I was suddenly awakened by hearing the leopard climbing the tree. Picking up the rifle, which was lying ready loaded on the bed, I swung my legs off the bed and had just slipped my feet into my slippers —to avoid the thorns that were scattered all round—when there was an ominous crack from the partly cut-through tree, followed by a yell from the cook of 'Sahib, *bagh, bagh!*' In one jump I was outside the tent, and swinging round was just too late to get the rifle to bear on the leopard as he sprang up the bank onto a terraced field. Pulling the bush out of the gap I dashed up to the field, which was about forty yards in width and bare of crops, and as I stood scanning the hillside dotted over with thorn bushes and a few big rocks, the alarm call of a jackal far up the hill informed me that the leopard had gone beyond my reach.

The cook informed me later that he had been lying on his back— a fact of which I had long been aware—and on hearing the tree crack he had opened his eyes and looked straight into the leopard's face just as the animal was preparing to jump down.

The tree was cut down next day and the fence strengthened, and though we stayed in that camp for several weeks our slumbers were not again disturbed.

12

The Gin-trap

From reports received from near-by villages where unsuccessful attempts had been made to break into houses, and from the pug marks I had seen on the roads, I knew that the man-eater was still in the vicinity, and a few days after the arrival of the Ibbotsons, news was brought that a cow had been killed in a village two miles from Rudraprayag and about half a mile from the village where I had sat on a hayrick in a walnut tree.

Arriving at the village, we found that a leopard had broken down the door of a small one-room house and had killed and dragged to the door one of the several cows that were in it, and, not being able to drag it through the door, had left it on the threshold, after eating a good meal.

The house was in the heart of the village, and on prospecting around, we found that, by making a hole in the wall of a house a few yards away, we could overlook the kill.

The owner of this house, who was also the owner of the dead cow, was only too willing to fall in with our plans, and as evening closed down we locked ourselves very securely into the room, and after eating our sandwiches and drinking the tea we had brought with us, we mounted guard in turns over the hole in the wall throughout the long night, without either seeing or hearing anything of the leopard.

When we emerged from the house in the morning, the villagers took us round the village, which was of considerable size, and showed us the claw marks on doors and windows made by the man-eater in the course of years in his attempts to get at the inmates. One door in particular had more and deeper claw marks than any other—it was the door the leopard had forced to enter the room in which the forty goats and the boy had been secured.

A day or two later, another cow was reported to have been killed in a small village on the hill a few hundred yards from the bungalow. Here again we found that the cow had been killed inside a house, dragged as far as the door, and partly eaten. Facing the door, and about ten yards distant from it, was a newly built hayrick, sixteen feet tall and built on a wooden platform two feet above ground.

News of the kill was brought to us early in the morning, so we had the whole day before us, and the *machan* we built by evening was, I am sure, not only the most effective but also the most artistic that has ever been constructed for a similar purpose.

To start with, the rick was dismantled, and a scaffolding of poles was set around the platform. With these poles to support it, a second and smaller platform was built four feet above the lower one. Two-inch-mesh wire netting was then wound round the whole structure, leaving bare only the space between the lower platform and the ground. Wisps of straw were then looped into the meshes of the netting, and a little straw was spread round the rick and under the platform, just as it had been before we started work. One of the joint owners of the hayrick, who had been absent from the village for a day or two and who returned just as we had finished our task, would not believe that the rick had been disturbed until he felt it all round, and had been shown the second rick we had built with the spare hay from an adjoining field.

As the sun was setting, we crawled through the hole we had left in the netting and entered the *machan*, securely closing the entrance behind us. Ibbotson is a little shorter than I, so he took the upper platform, and when we had made ourselves comfortable we each made a small hole in the straw to shoot through. As it would not be possible for us to communicate with each other once the leopard arrived, we agreed that whoever saw him first was to fire. It was a bright moonlight night, so there was no need for either of us to use the electric light.

Sounds in the village quieted down after the evening meal had been eaten, and at about 10 p.m. I heard the leopard coming down the hill behind us. On arriving at the rick he paused for a few minutes and then started to crawl under the platform on which I was sitting. When immediately below me, and with only the thickness of a plank between my seat and his head, he paused for a long minute and then started to crawl forward. Just as I was expecting him to emerge from under the platform and give me an easy shot at a range of three or four feet, there was a loud creak in the platform above me. The leopard dashed out to the right, where I could not see him, and went up the hill. The creaking of the planks at the critical moment had resulted from Ibbotson's changing his position to relieve a very painful cramp in both legs. The leopard, after the fright he had got, abandoned the kill and did not return that night or the next.

Two nights later another cow was killed a few hundred yards above the Rudraprayag bazaar.

The owner of the cow was living alone in an isolated house, which contained only one room divided by a rough partition, made of odd bits of plank, into a kitchen and living room. Sometime during the night a noise in the kitchen—the door of which he had forgotten to shut—awakened the man, and a little later, in the dim moonlight the open door was admitting, he saw the leopard through the wide chinks in the partition, trying to tear one of the planks out.

For a long time the man lay and sweated, while the leopard tried plank after plank. Eventually being unable to find a weak place in the partition, the leopard left the kitchen and killed the man's cow, which was tethered in a grass lean-to against the side of the house. After killing the cow the leopard broke the rope by which it was tethered, dragged it a short distance from the lean-to, and left it out in the open after partaking of a good meal.

On the very edge of the hill, and about twenty yards from where the dead cow was lying, there was a fair-sized tree, in the upper branches of which a hayrick had been built; on this natural *machan*—from which there was a sheer drop of several hundred feet into the valley below—Ibbotson and I decided to sit.

To assist in killing the man-eater, the Government a few days previously had sent us a gin-trap. This trap, which was five feet long and weighed eighty pounds, was the most fearsome thing of its kind I have ever seen. Its jaws, armed with sharp teeth three inches long, had a spread of twenty-four inches and were actuated by two powerful springs, which needed two men to compress them.

When leaving the kill the leopard had followed a footpath across a field about forty yards wide, up a three-foot bank, and across another field bordered by a densely scrub covered hill. At this three-foot step from the upper to the lower field, we set the trap and, to insure the leopard's stepping on to it, we planted a few thorn twigs on either side of the path. To one end of the trap was attached a short length of half-inch-thick chain, terminating in a ring three inches in diameter; through this ring we drove a stout peg, chaining the trap to the ground.

When these arrangements had been completed, Jean Ibbotson returned to the bungalow with our men, and Ibbotson and I climbed up to the hayrick. After tying a stick in front of us and looping a little hay over it to act as a screen, we made ourselves comfortable and waited for the leopard, which we felt sure would not escape us on this occasion.

As evening closed in, heavy clouds spread over the sky, and as the moon was not due to rise until 9 p.m. we had of necessity to depend on the electric light for the accuracy of our shooting. This light was a heavy and cumbersome affair, and as Ibbotson insisted on my taking the shot, I attached it to my rifle with some little difficulty.

An hour after dark a succession of angry roars apprised us of the fact that the leopard was in the trap. Switching on the electric light, I saw the leopard rearing up with the trap dangling from his forelegs, and taking a hurried shot, my .450 bullet struck a link in the chain and severed it.

Freed from the peg, the leopard went along the field in a series of great leaps, carrying the trap in front of him, followed up by the bullet from my left barrel and two lethal bullets from Ibbotson's shotgun, all of which missed him. In trying to reload my rifle, I displaced some part of the light, after which it refused to function.

Hearing the roars of the leopard and our four shots, the people in the Rudraprayag bazaar and in nearby villages swarmed out of their houses, carrying lanterns and pine torches, and converged from all sides on the isolated house. Shouting to them to keep clear was of no avail, for they were making so much noise that they could not hear us. So while I climbed down the tree, taking my rifle with me—a hazardous proceeding in the dark—Ibbotson lit and pumped up the gasoline lamp we had taken into the *machan* with us. Letting the lamp down to me on the end of a length of rope, Ibbotson joined me on the ground, and together we went in the direction the leopard had taken. Halfway along the field there was a hump caused by an outcrop of rock; this hump we approached with Ibbotson holding the heavy lamp high above his head, while I walked by his side with rifle to shoulder. Beyond the hump was a little depression, and crouching down in this depression, and facing us and growling, was the leopard. Within a few minutes of my bullet's crashing into his head, we were surrounded by an excited crowd, who literally danced with joy round their long-dreaded enemy.

The animal that lay dead before me was an outsized male leopard, who the previous night had tried to tear down a partition to get at a human being, who had been shot in an area in which dozens of human beings had been killed—all good and sufficient reasons for assuming that he was the man-eater. But I could not make myself believe that he was the same animal I had seen the night I sat over the body of the woman. True, it had been a dark night and I had only vaguely seen the outline of the leopard. Even so, I was convinced that the animal that was now being lashed to a pole by willing hands was not the man-eater.

With the Ibbotsons leading the way, followed by the men carrying the leopard and a crowd of several hundred men, we set off via the bazaar for the bungalow.

As I stumbled down the hill in the wake of the procession—the only one in all that throng who did not believe that the Man-Eating Leopard of Rudraprayag was dead—my thoughts went back to an occurrence that had taken place not far from our winter home when I was a small boy, and which I saw recounted many years later in a book entitled *Brave Deeds,* or it may have been *Bravest Deeds.* The occurrence concerned two men: Smeaton of the Indian Civil Service, and Braidwood of the Forest Department. One dark stormy night, in pre-railway days, these two men were traveling in a *dak-gharry* from Moradabad to Kaladhungi, and on going round a bend in the road they ran into a rogue elephant. In killing the dri-

ver and the two horses, the elephant overturned the *gharry*. Braidwood had a rifle, and, while he got it out of its case, put it together,
and loaded it, Smeaton climbed onto the *gharry* and released the
one unbroken lamp from its socket. Then Smeaton, holding over
his head the oil lamp, which only gave a glimmer of light, advanced
up to the elephant and shone the light on the elephant's forehead,
to enable Braidwood to get in a killing shot. Admittedly there was
a great difference between a rogue elephant and a leopard; even so,
there are few who would care to walk up to a pain-maddened leopard—which we later found had practically torn its paw free and was
only held by a thin strip of skin—holding a lamp above his head
and depending for safety on a companion's bullet.

For the first night in many years every house in the bazaar was
open, with women and children standing in the doorways. Progress
was slow, for every few yards the leopard was put down to let the
children cluster round and get a better view of it. At the further end
of the long street our escort left us, and the leopard was carried in
triumph to the bungalow by our men.

Returning to the bungalow after a wash at my camp, the Ibbotsons and I, both during dinner and long after it, put forward our ar-
guments for and against the dead leopard being the man-eater;
eventually without either side convincing the other, we decided that
as Ibbotson had to get back to his work at Pauri, and I was tired out
after my long stay at Rudraprayag, we would spend the next day in
skinning the leopard and drying the skin, and on the day after
would break camp and make for Pauri.

From early morning to late evening, relays of men kept coming
in from near and distant villages to see the leopard, and as most of
these men asserted that they recognized the animal as the man-eater,
Ibbotson's conviction grew, that they were right and I was wrong.
Two concessions Ibbotson made at my request: he added his warning to the people to mine, not to relax precautions against the

man-eater; and he refrained from telegraphing to the Government that we had shot the man-eater.

We went to bed early that night, for we were to start at daybreak next morning. I was up while it was still dark and was having *chota hazri*, when I heard voices on the road. As this was very unusual, I called out to ask what men were doing on the road at that hour; on seeing me, four men climbed up the path to my camp and informed me they had been sent by the *Patwari* to tell me that a woman had been killed by the man-eater on the far side of the river, about a mile from the Chatwapipal bridge.

13

The Hunters Hunted

Ibbotson was just unbolting the door to admit his man with early tea when I arrived, and, after he had countermanded his move to Pauri, we sat on Jean's bed with a large-scale map between us, drinking tea and discussing our plans.

Ibbotson's work at his headquarters at Pauri was pressing, and at most he could spare only two more days and nights. I had telegraphed to Naini Tal the previous day that I was returning home *via* Pauri and Kotdwara; this telegram I would cancel, and, instead of going by rail, would return on foot the way I had come. These details settled, and the village where the woman had been killed found on the map, I returned to camp to tell my men of our change of plans, and to instruct them to pack up and follow us, accompanied by the four men who had brought news of the kill.

Jean was to remain at Rudraprayag, and after breakfast Ibbotson and I set off on two of his horses, a Gulf Arab and an English mare—two of the most surefooted animals I have ever had the good fortune to ride.

We took our rifles, a blue-flame stove, a gasoline lamp, and some provisions with us, and were accompanied by one of Ibbotson's *syces* (grooms) on a borrowed horse carrying food for our horses.

We left the horses at Chatwapipal bridge. This bridge had not been closed the night we shot the leopard, with the result that the man-eater had got across the river and secured a kill at the first village he visited.

A guide waiting for us at the bridge took us up a very steep ridge and along a grassy hillside, and then down into a deep and densely wooded ravine with a small stream flowing through it. Here we found the *Patwari* and some twenty men guarding the kill.

The kill was a very robust and fair girl, some eighteen or twenty years of age. She was lying on her face with her hands by her sides; every vestige of clothing had been stripped from her, and she had been licked by the leopard, from the soles of her feet to her neck, in which were four great teeth marks; only a few pounds of flesh had been eaten from the upper portion of her body, and a few pounds from the lower portion.

The drums we had heard as we came up the hill were being beaten by the men who were guarding the kill, and as it was then about 2 p.m. and there was no chance of the leopard's being anywhere in the vicinity, we went up to the village to brew ourselves some tea, taking the *Patwari* and the guard with us.

After tea we went and had a look at the house where the girl had been killed. This one-room stone house was situated in the midst of terraced fields some two or three acres in extent, and was occupied by the girl, her husband, and their six-month-old child.

Two days previous to the kill, the husband had gone to Pauri to give evidence in a land-dispute case, and had left his father in charge of the house. On the night of the kill, after the girl and her father-in-law had partaken of their evening meal and it was getting near time to retire for the night, the girl, who had been nursing her child, handed it over to her father-in-law and, unlatching the door, stepped outside and squatted down—I have already mentioned that there are no sanitary conveniences in the houses of our hill folk.

When the child was transferred from the mother to the grandfather, it started crying, so even if there had been any sound from outside—and I am sure there was none—he would not have heard it. It was a dark night and after waiting for a few minutes the man called to the girl, and receiving no answer called again, and then got up and hurriedly closed and latched the door.

It had rained earlier in the evening and it was easy to reconstruct the scene. Shortly after the rain had stopped, the leopard, coming from the direction of the village, had crouched down behind a rock in the field, about thirty yards to the left front of the door. Here the leopard had lain for some time—possibly listening to the man and the girl talking. When the girl opened the door she squatted down on the right-hand side of it, partly turning her back on the leopard. Creeping round the far side of the rock, he had covered the twenty yards separating him from the corner of the house with belly to ground, and creeping along close to the wall of the house, had caught the girl from behind and dragged her to the rock. Here, when she was dead, or possibly when the man called out in alarm, the leopard had picked her up, and holding her high, so that no mark of hand or foot showed on the soft newly plowed ground, had carried her across one field, down a three-foot bank, and across another field, which ended in a twelve-foot drop onto a well-used footpath. Down this drop the leopard had sprung with the girl —who weighed about 150 pounds—in his mouth, and some idea of his strength will be realized from the fact that when he landed on the footpath he did not let any portion of her body come in contact with the ground.

Crossing the footpath he had gone straight down the hill for half a mile, to the spot where he had undressed the girl, and, after eating a little of her, had left her lying in a little glade of emerald-green grass, under the shade of a tree roofed over with dense creepers.

At about four o'clock we went down to sit over the kill, taking the gasoline lamp and night-shooting light with us.

It was reasonable to assume that the leopard had heard the noise the villagers made when searching for the girl and later when guarding the body, and that if he returned to the kill he would do so with great caution; so we decided not to sit near the kill, and selected a tree about sixty yards away on the hill overlooking the glade.

This tree—a stunted oak—was growing out of the hill at almost a right angle, and, after we had hidden the gasoline lamp in a little hollow and covered it over with pine needles, Ibbotson took his seat in a fork of the tree from which he had a clear view of the kill, while I sat on the trunk with my back to him and facing the hill; Ibbotson was to take the shot, while I saw to our safety. As the shooting light was not functioning—possibly because the battery had faded out—our plan was to sit up as long as Ibbotson could see to shoot, and then, with the help of the gasoline lamp, get back to the village, where we hoped to find that our men had arrived from Rudraprayag.

We had not had time to prospect the ground, but the villagers had informed us that there was heavy jungle to the east, to which they felt sure the leopard had retired when they drove him off the kill. If the leopard came from this direction, Ibbotson would see him long before the animal got to the glade and would get an easy shot, for his rifle was fitted with a telescopic sight; this not only made for accurate shooting, but also added—as we had found from tests—half an hour to the light factor, which on an occasion like this was very important—a minute of daylight, more or less, may make the difference between success and failure.

The sun was setting behind the high hills to the west, and we had been in shadow for some minutes, when a kakar dashed down the hill, barking, from the direction in which we had been told there was heavy jungle. On the shoulder of the hill the animal pulled up, and, after barking in one spot for some time, went away on the far side of the hill, and the sound died away in the distance.

The kakar had undoubtedly been alarmed by a leopard, and though it was quite possible that there were other leopards in that area, my hopes had been raised. When I looked round at Ibbotson, I saw that he too was keyed up, and that he had both hands on his rifle.

Light was beginning to fade, but was good enough to shoot by even without the aid of the telescopic sight, when a pine cone dislodged from behind some low bushes, about thirty yards immediately above us, came rolling down the hill and struck the tree close to my feet. The leopard had arrived and, possibly suspecting danger, had taken a line that would enable him to prospect from a safe place on the hill all the ground in the vicinity of his kill. Unfortunately, in doing so he had got our tree in a direct line with the kill, and though I, who was showing no outline, might escape observation, he would be certain to see Ibbotson, who was sitting in a fork of the tree.

When sufficient light for me to shoot by had long since gone, and Ibbotson's telescopic sight was no longer of any use to him, we heard the leopard coming stealthily down towards the tree. It was then time to take action, so I asked Ibbotson to take my place, while I retrieved the lamp. This lamp was of German make and was called a petromax. It gave a brilliant light but, with its long body and longer handle, was not designed to be used as a lantern in a jungle.

I am a little taller than Ibbotson, and suggested that I should carry the lamp, but Ibbotson said he could manage all right, and, further, he would rather depend on my rifle than his own. So we set off, Ibbotson leading and I following, with both hands on my rifle.

Fifty yards from the tree, while climbing over a rock, Ibbotson slipped—the base of the lamp came in violent contact with the rock—and the mantle fell in dust to the bottom of the lamp. The streak of blue flame, directed from the nozzle onto the gasoline reservoir, gave sufficient light for us to see where to put our feet, but it was a question how long we would have even this much light. Ibbotson was of the opinion that he could carry the lamp for three minutes before it burst; three minutes to do a stiff climb of half a mile, over ground on which it was necessary to change direction every few steps to avoid huge rocks and thorn bushes, and possibly followed—actually followed, as we found later—by a man-eater, was a terrifying prospect.

There are events in one's life that, no matter how remote, never fade from memory; the climb up that hill in the dark was, for me, one of them. When we eventually reached the footpath our troubles were not ended, for the path was a series of buffalo wallows, and, further, we did not know where our men were. Alternately slipping on wet ground and stumbling over unseen rocks, we at last came to some stone steps, which took off from the path and went up to the right. Climbing these steps we found a small courtyard, on the far side of which was a door. Kicking the door, I shouted to the inmates—we had heard the gurgling of a *hookah* as we came up the steps—to open it; receiving no answer I took out a box of matches and, shaking it, said that if the door was not opened in a minute I would set the thatch alight. On this an agitated voice came from inside the house, begging me not to set the house on fire, and saying that the door was being opened. A minute later, first the inner door in the wall and then the outer door was opened, and in two strides Ibbotson and I were in the house and, shutting the inner door, put our backs to it.

There were some twelve or fourteen men, women, and children of all ages in the room. When the men had regained their wits after our unceremonious entry, they begged us to forgive them for not having opened the doors sooner, adding that they and their families had lived so long in terror of the man-eater that their courage had gone and, not knowing what form the man-eater might take, they suspected every sound they heard at night. In their fear they had our full sympathy, for from the time Ibbotson had slipped and broken the mantle, and a few minutes later had extinguished the lamp—which was red hot—to prevent its bursting, I had been convinced that one and possibly both of us would not live to reach the village.

We were told that our men had arrived about sundown, and that they had been housed in a block of buildings further along the hill. The two able-bodied men in the room offered to show us the way, but as we knew it would be murder to let them return to their homes alone, we declined their offer—which had been made with the full realization of the risk it would entail—and asked if they could provide us with a light of some kind. After rummaging about in a corner of the room, they produced an old and decrepit lantern with a cracked globe and, when vigorous shaking had revealed that it contained a few drops of oil, lit it; and with the combined good wishes of the inmates we left the house—the two doors being shut and bolted on our heels.

More buffalo wallows and more sunken rocks, but with the glimmer of light to help us, we made good progress, and, finding the second lot of steps we had been instructed to climb, we mounted them and found ourselves in a long courtyard facing a row of two-story buildings extending to the right and to the left, every door of which was fast shut, and not a glimmer of light showed anywhere.

After calls to our men a door was opened, and climbing a short flight of stone steps we gained the veranda of the upper story, where we found two adjoining rooms had been placed at the disposal of our men and ourselves. While the men were relieving us of the lamp and our rifles, a dog arrived from nowhere. He was just a friendly village pye, and after sniffing around our legs and wagging his tail, he went towards the steps up which we had just come. The next second, with a scream of fear followed by hysterical barking, he backed towards us with all his hair on end.

The lantern we had been lent had died on us as we reached the courtyard, but our men had procured its twin brother, and though Ibbotson held it at all angles while I hurriedly reloaded my rifle, he could not get its light to illuminate the ground eight feet below.

By watching the dog, it was possible to follow the movements of the leopard, and when the leopard had crossed the yard and gone down the steps leading to the footpath, the dog gradually stopped barking and lay down, intently watching in that direction, and growling at intervals.

The room that had been vacated for us had no windows, and as the only way in which we could have occupied it in safety would have been by closing the solid door and excluding all air and light, we decided to spend the night in the veranda. The dog quite evidently belonged to the late occupant of the room and had been accustomed to sleeping on the veranda, for he lay contentedly at our feet, giving us a feeling of safety as we watched in turn through the long hours of the night.

14

At daybreak next morning we very carefully stalked the kill, and were disappointed to find that the leopard had not returned to it, which we felt sure he would do after his failure to bag one of us the previous evening.

During the day, while Ibbotson dealt with some office work that had been sent out to him, I took a rifle and went off to see if I could get a shot at the leopard. Tracking on the hard and pine-needle-covered ground was not possible, so I made for the shoulder of the hill beyond which the villagers had told us there was heavy jungle. Here I found the ground very difficult to negotiate, for, in addition to dense scrub jungle through which it was not possible to penetrate, there were a series of rock cliffs on which it was impossible for a human being to find foothold. In this area there was a surprisingly large head of game, and on the paths that intersected it I found the tracks of kakar, ghooral, pig, and a solitary serow. Of the leopard—except for a few old scratch-marks—I found no trace.

The gin-trap that had been sent off from Rudraprayag the previous day arrived while we were having lunch, and in the early evening we took it down to the glade and, after setting it, poisoned the kill with cyanide. I had no experience of poisons, nor had Ibbotson, but in a conversation with a doctor friend before leaving Naini Tal I had mentioned that Government wanted me to try every means to kill the man-eater, and that there was little use in my trying poison, as the records showed that the leopard throve on it. I told him what poisons had hitherto been tried, and he then recommended my using cyanide, which was the best poison for the cat family. I had passed this information on to Ibbotson, and a few days previously a supply had arrived, with capsules with which to use it. We inserted a few of these capsules in the kill at the places where the leopard had eaten.

There was every hope of the leopard returning to the kill this second night, and as he had seen us on the tree the previous evening we decided not to sit up, but to leave him to the gin-trap and to the poison.

In a big pine-tree near the footpath we built a machan, which we padded with hay and on which we took up our position after we had eaten the dinner which Ibbotson cooked on the blue-flame stove. Here on the comfortable machan we were able to lie at full stretch and talk and smoke, for our only reason for being there was to listen for sounds from the direction of the kill. We watched and slept by turns, hoping to hear the angry roar of the leopard if by accident it walked into the trap, for here there was no well-used track along which to direct the leopard to it.

Once during the night a kakar barked, but in the opposite direction to that from which we expected the leopard to come.

At the first streak of dawn we climbed out of the tree and, after brewing ourselves a cup of tea, visited the kill, which we found lying just as we had left it.

Ibbotson left for Rudraprayag after an early breakfast, and I was packing my things and having a final word with the villagers before starting on my fifteen-day journey back to Naini Tal when a party

of men arrived to give the news that a cow had been killed by a leopard in a village four miles away. They suspected that the cow had been killed by the man-eater, for the previous night—the night the leopard had followed Ibbotson and myself from the tree to the veranda—and towards the small hours of the morning, the leopard had made a determined attempt to break down the door of the headman's house; late the following evening, the cow had been killed in the jungle three hundred yards from this house. At the urgent request of these men I postponed my departure to Naini Tal and accompanied them back to their village, taking the gin-trap and a supply of poison with me.

The headman's house was on a little knoll surrounded by cultivated land, and was approached by a footpath which for a short distance ran over soft and boggy ground; here I found the pug marks of the man-eater.

The headman had seen me approaching across the valley and had a steaming dish of tea brewed in fresh milk and sweetened with jaggery, waiting for me. While I drank this rich and over-sweetened liquid on the courtyard, sitting on a reed couch upholstered with ghooral skins, he drew my attention to the condition of the door which two nights previously the leopard had attempted to break down, in which attempt it would undoubtedly have succeeded if he had not fortunately had some sawn timber in the house—intended for repairing the roof—which he had used to shore up the door from inside.

The headman was old and crippled with rheumatism, so he sent his son to show me the kill while he made room in the house for myself and my men.

I found the kill—a young cow in grand condition—lying on a flat bit of ground just above the cattle track, in an ideal position for setting up the gin-trap. Its back was against a tangle of wild rose-bushes, and its hooves were against a foot-high bank; while eating, the leopard had sat on the bank with its forepaws between the cow's legs.

Having dug away the ground between the cow's legs and removed it to a distance, I set the trap where the leopard had placed his paws and covered it over with big green leaves. Then, after sprinkling on a layer of earth, I replaced the dead leaves, bits of dry sticks, and splinters of bone in the exact position between the cow's legs in which I had found them. Not one of a hundred human beings going to the kill would have noticed that the ground had in any way been disturbed, and a deadly trap set.

My arrangements made to my satisfaction I retraced my steps and climbed a tree half-way between the kill and the headman's house, where I would be handy if needed at the trap.

Near sundown a pair of kaleege pheasants and their brood of five chicks, which I had been watching for some time, suddenly took alarm and went scuttling down the hill, and a few seconds later a kakar came dashing towards me and after barking under my tree for a little while, went off up the hill on tiptoes. Nothing happened after that, and when it was getting too dark under the shade of the trees for me to see the sights of my rifle, I slipped off the tree and myself tiptoed away on rubber-shod feet towards the village.

A hundred yards from the headman's house the track ran across an open glade, some thirty yards long and twenty yards wide. On the upper, hill side of the glade was a big rock. As I reached this open ground I felt I was being followed, and, determined to exploit the situation, I left the track and, taking two long steps over soft and spongy ground, lay down behind the rock, with only one eye showing in the direction of the kill.

For ten minutes I lay on the wet ground. When daylight had all but gone I regained the path and, taking every precaution, covered the remaining distance to the headman's house.

Once during the night the headman roused me from a sound sleep to tell me he had heard the leopard scratching on the door, and when I opened the door next morning I saw the pug marks of the man-eater in the dust in front of it. These pug marks I followed back to the glade, and found that the leopard had done just what I had done the previous evening. He had left the track where I had; had crossed the soft ground to the rock and, after regaining the track, had followed me to the house, round which he had walked several times.

On leaving the house the leopard had gone back along the track, and as I followed his pug marks towards the kill my hopes rose high, for up to that time I had not fully realized the degree of cunning that a man-eating leopard can acquire after eight years of close association with human beings.

I left the track and approached from the high ground, and from a little distance away saw that the kill had gone, and that the ground where the trap had been buried was, except for two pug marks, undisturbed.

Sitting on the foot-high bank, as he had done the first night, the leopard had put both front paws between the cow's legs, but on this occasion he had spread them wide apart and rested them on the buried levers of the trap which, released, would have closed the great jaws. Here, safe from the trap, he had eaten his meal, and when he had done, he skirted round the flat ground and, getting hold of the cow by the head, had dragged it through the rose-thorns and rolled it down the hill, where fifty yards lower down it had fetched up against an oak sapling. Content with his night's work, the leopard had then gone along the cattle track, and after following him for a mile I lost his tracks on hard ground.

There was no hope of the leopard returning to the kill. However, to salve my conscience for not having done so the previous night, I put a liberal dose of cyanide in the carcass of the cow. Truth to tell I hated the very thought of using poison then, and I hate it no less now.

I visited the kill in the morning and found that a leopard had eaten all that portion of the cow that I had poisoned. So sure was I that the poison had been eaten by a leopard that had accidentally come across the kill, and not by the man-eater, that on my return to the village I told the headman that I would not stay to recover the leopard, though I would pay a hundred rupees to anyone who found it and took its skin to the *Patwari*. A month later the reward was claimed, and the skin of a leopard which had been dead many days was buried by the *Patwari*.

It did not take my men long to pack up, and shortly after mid-day we started on our long journey back to Naini Tal. As we went down a narrow footpath to the Chatwapipal bridge a big dhamin (rat snake) leisurely crossed the path, and as I stood and watched it slip away Madho Singh, who, was behind me, said, 'There goes the evil spirit that has been responsible for your failure.'

My action in leaving Garhwal to the tender mercies of the man-eater may appear heartless to you—it did so to me—and was adversely criticized in the press, for the leopard at that time was daily mentioned in the Indian papers. In extenuation—I would urge that an effort entailing great strain cannot be indefinitely sustained. There were twenty-four hours in every day of the many weeks I spent in Garhwal, and time and time again after sitting up all night, I walked endless miles next day, visiting distant villages, from which reports had come of unsuccessful attacks by the man-eater. On many moonlit nights, when sitting in an uncomfortable position physical endurance had reached its limit, and when sitting where it would have been easy for the leopard to have got at me I had no longer been able to keep my eyes open. I had for hours walked the roads which were alone open to me and to the leopard, trying every trick I knew of to outwit my adversary, and the man-eater had, with luck beyond his deserts or with devilish cunning, avoided the bullet that a press of my finger would have sent into him, for on retracing my steps in the morning after these night excursions I had found from the pug marks on the road that I was right in assuming I had been closely followed. To know that one is being followed at night—no matter how bright the moon may be—by a man-eater intent on securing a victim, gives one an inferiority complex that is very unnerving, and that is not mitigated by repetition.

Tired out in mind and in body, my longer stay at Rudraprayag would not have profited the people of Garhwal, and it might have cost me my own life. Knowing that the temporary abandonment of my self-imposed task would be severely criticized by the press, but that what I was now doing was right, I plodded on towards my distant home, having assured the people of Garhwal that I would return to help them as soon as it was possible for me to do so.

15

Fishing Interlude

I left the scene of my failure, weary and dispirited, in the late autumn of 1925, and returned to continue my labours, refrained and full of hope, in the early spring of 1926.

On this my second visit to Garhwal in pursuit of the man-eater, I travelled by train to Kotdwara and went from there by foot to Pauri, thus saving eight days on the journey. At Pauri Ibbotson joined me and accompanied me to Rudraprayag.

During my three months' absence from Garhwal the man-eater had killed ten human beings, and during these three month, no attempt had been made by the terror-stricken inhabitants to kill the leopard.

The last of these ten kills—the victim was a small boy—had taken place on the left bank of the Alaknanda, two days before our arrival at Rudraprayag. We had received telegraphic news of this kill at Pauri, and though we had travelled as fast as it was possible for us to do, we were disappointed to learn from the *Patwari*, who was awaiting our arrival at the Inspection Bungalow, that the leopard disposed of the entire kill the previous night, leaving nothing of its small victim over which we could sit.

The boy had been killed at midnight in a village four miles from Rudraprayag, and as it was unlikely that the leopard had crossed the river after his undisturbed feed, we took steps immediately on our arrival to close the two suspension bridges.

During the winter Ibbotson had organized a very efficient intelligence service throughout the area in which the man-eater was operating. If in this area a dog, goat, cow, or human being was killed, or an attempt made to force open a door, news of the occurrence was conveyed to us by the service, and in this way we were able to keep in constant touch with the man-eater. Hundreds of false rumours of alleged attacks by the man-eater were brought to us, entailing endless miles of walking, but this was only to be expected, for in an area in which an established man-eater is operating everyone suspects their own shadows, and every sound heard at night is attributed to the man-eater.

One of these rumours concerned a man by the name of Galtu, a resident of Kunda, a village seven miles from Rudraprayag on the right bank of the Alaknanda. Galtu left the village in the evening to spend the night in his cattle shed a mile away from the village, and when his son went to the shed next morning he found his father's blanket half in and half out of the door of the shed, and in a patch of soft ground nearby he found what he thought was a drag mark, and near it the pug marks of the man-eater. Returning to the village he raised an alarm, and while sixty men went off to search for the body, four men were dispatched to Rudraprayag to inform us. Ibbotson and I were beating a hillside on the left bank of the river for the man-eater when the men arrived, and as I was convinced that the leopard was on our side of the river, and that there was no truth in the rumour that Galtu had been killed, Ibbotson sent a *Patwari* back to Kunda with the four men, with instructions to make a personal search and report back to us. Next evening we received the *Patwari*'s report, with a sketch of the pug marks in the soft earth near the door of the shed. The report stated that an all day search of the surrounding country, with two hundred men, had not resulted in finding Galtu's remains, and that the search would be continued. The sketch showed six circles, the inner one as large as a plate, with five equally spaced circles round it, each the size of a tea cup; all the circles had been made with a compass. Five days later, and just as Ibbotson and I were setting out to sit up on the tower of the bridge, a procession came up to the bungalow led by an irate man who was protesting loudly that he had committed no offence that justified his being arrested and brought to Rudraprayag. The irate man was Galtu. After we had pacified him, he gave us his story. It appeared that just as he was leaving his house on the night he was alleged to have been carried off by the man-eater, his son arrived and informed him that he had paid Rs 100 for a pair of bullocks which Galtu asserted were not worth more than Rs 70. The wanton waste of good money had so angered him that, after sleeping the night in the cattle shed, he had got up early next morning and gone to a village ten miles away, where a married daughter of his was living. On his return to his village that morning, he had been arrested by the *Patwari*, and he wanted to know what crime he had committed that justified his arrest. It was some little time before he saw the humour of the situation, but once having done so, he laughed as heartily as any of the assembled throng at the thought of an important person like a *Patwari*, and two hundred of his friends, searching for five days for his remains, what time he was cooling off in a village ten miles away.

Ibbotson was averse to lying all night on the wind-swept tower of the Rudraprayag suspension bridge, and as wood and carpenters were available, he had a platform built in the arch of the tower, and on this platform we sat for the five nights Ibbotson was able to spend at Rudraprayag.

After Ibbotson's departure the leopard killed one dog, four goats, and two cows. The dog and goats had been eaten out on the nights on which they had been killed, but I sat over each of the cows for two nights. On the second night on which I was sitting up over the first cow, the leopard came, but just as I was raising my rifle and preparing to switch on the torch I had provided myself with, a woman in the house adjoining the one I was sitting in, thumped on the door preparatory to opening it, and unfortunately frightened the leopard away.

No human beings had been killed during this period, but a woman and her baby had been badly mauled. The leopard had forced open the door of the room in which she was sleeping with her baby, and seizing her arm had attempted to drag her out of the room. The woman fortunately was stout of heart, and had not fainted or lost her wits, and after the leopard—dragging her along the floor—had backed out of the room, she shut the door on it, and escaped with a badly lacerated arm and several deep wounds on her breast, while the baby escaped with one head wound. I sat in this room for the following two nights, but the leopard did not return.

I was returning one day towards the latter end of March, after visiting a village on the Kedarnath pilgrim route, when, as I approached a spot where the road runs close alongside the Mandakini river, and where there is a waterfall ten to twelve feet high, I saw a number of men sitting on the rock at the head of the fall on the far side of the river, armed with a triangular net attached to a long bamboo pole. The roar of the water prevented conversation, so leaving the road I sat down on the rocks on my side of the fall, to have a rest and a smoke—for I had walked far that day—and to see what the men were doing.

Presently one of the men got to his feet, and as he pointed down excitedly into the foaming white water at the foot of the fall, two of his companions manning the long pole held the triangular net close to the fall. A large shoal of mahseer fish, varying in size from five to fifty pounds, were attempting to leap the fall. One of these fish, about ten pounds in weight, leapt clear of the fall and when falling back was expertly caught in the net. After the fish had been extracted and placed in a basket, the net was again held out close to the fall. I watched the sport for about an hour, during which time the men caught four fish, all about the same size—ten pounds.

On my previous visit to Rudraprayag I had been informed by the *Chowkidar* in charge of the Inspection Bungalow that there was good fishing in the spring—before the snow-water came down—in both the Alaknanda and Mandakini rivers, so I had come armed on this my second visit with a fourteen-foot split cane salmon rod, a silex reel with two hundred and fifty yards of line, a few stout traces, and an assortment of home-made brass spoons varying in size from one to two inches.

The following morning—as no news had come in of the man-eater—I set off for the waterfall with my rod and tackle.

No fish were leaping the fall as they had been doing the previous day, and the men on the far side of the river were sitting in a group round a small fire smoking a hookah which was passing from hand to hand. They watched me with interest.

Below the waterfall was a pool thirty to forty yards wide, flanked on both sides by a wall of rock, and about two hundred yards long, one hundred yards of which was visible from where I stood at the head of the pool. The water in this beautiful and imposing pool was crystal-clear.

The rock face at the head of the pool rose sheer up out of the water to a height of twelve feet, and after keeping at this height for twenty yards, sloped gradually upwards to a height of a hundred feet. It was not possible to get down to water level anywhere on my side of the pool, nor would it be possible, or profitable, to follow a fish—assuming that I hooked one—along the bank, for at the top of the high ground there were trees and bushes, and at the tail of the pool the river cascaded down in a foaming torrent to its junction with the Alaknanda. To land a fish in this pool would be a difficult and a hazardous task, but the crossing of that bridge could be deferred until the fish had been hooked—and I had not yet put together my rod.

On my side of the pool the water—shot through with millions of small bubbles—was deep, and from about halfway across a shingle bottom was showing, over which four to six feet of water was flowing. Above this shingle bottom, every stone and pebble of which was visible in the clear water, a number of fish, ranging in size from three to ten pounds, were slowly moving upstream.

As I watched these fish, standing on the rocks twelve feet above the water with a two-inch spoon mounted with a single strong treble hook in my hand, a flight of fingerlings flashed out of the deep water and went skimming over the shingle bottom, hotly pursued by three big mahseer. Using the good salmon rod as friend Hardy had never intended that it should be used—and as it had been used on many previous occasions—I slung the spoon out, and in my eagerness over-estimated the distance, with the result that the spoon struck the rock on the far side of the pool, about two feet above the water. The falling of the spoon into the water coincided with the arrival of the fingerlings at the rock, and the spoon had hardly touched the water, when it was taken by the leading mahseer.

Striking with a long line from an elevated position entails a very heavy strain, but my good rod stood the strain, and the strong treble hook was firmly fixed in the mahseer's mouth. For a moment or two the fish did not appear to realize what had happened as, standing perpendicularly in the water with his white belly towards me, he shook his head from side to side, and then, possibly frightened by the dangling spoon striking against his head, he gave a mighty splash and went tearing downstream, scattering in all directions the smaller fish that were lying on the shingle bottom.

In his first run the mahseer ripped a hundred yards of line off the reel, and after a moment's check carried on for another fifty yards. There was plenty of line still on the reel, but the fish had now gone round the bend and was getting dangerously near the tail of the pool. Alternately easing and tightening the strain on the line, I eventually succeeded in turning his head upstream, and having done so, very gently pulled him round the bend, into the hundred yards of water I was overlooking.

Just below me a projection of rock had formed a backwater, and into this backwater the fish, after half an hour's game fight, permitted himself to be drawn.

I had now very definitely reached my bridge and had just regretfully decided that, as there was no way of crossing it, the fish would have to be cut adrift, when a shadow fell across the rock beside me. Peering over the rock into the backwater, the new arrival remarked that it was a very big fish, and in the same breath asked what I was going to do about it. When I told him that it would not be possible to draw the fish up the face of the rock, and that therefore the only thing to do was to cut it free, he said, 'Wait, sahib, I will fetch my brother.' His brother—a long and lanky stripling with dancing eyes—had quite evidently been cleaning out a cow shed when summoned, so telling him to go upstream and wash himself lest he should slip on the smooth rock, I held council with the elder man.

Starting from where we were standing, a crack, a few inches wide, ran irregularly down the face of the rock, ending a foot above the water in a ledge some six inches wide. The plan we finally agreed on was that the stripling—who presently returned with his arms and legs glistening with water—should go down to the ledge, while the elder brother went down the crack far enough to get hold of the stripling's left hand, while I lay on the rock holding the elder brother's other hand. Before embarking on the plan I asked the brothers whether they knew how to handle a fish and whether they could swim, and received the laughing answer that they had handled fish and swum in the river from childhood.

The snag in the plan was that I could not hold the rod and at the same time make a link in the chain. However, some risk had to be taken, so I put the rod down and held the line in my hand, and when the brothers had taken up position I sprawled on the rock and, reaching down, got hold of the elder brother's hand. Then very gently I drew the fish towards the rock, holding the line alternately with my left hand and with my teeth. There was no question that the stripling knew how to handle a fish, for before the fish had touched the rock, he had inserted his thumb into one side of the gills and his fingers into the other, getting a firm grip on the fish's throat. Up to this point the fish had been quite amenable, but on having its throat seized, it lashed out, and for seconds it appeared that the three of us would go headlong into the river.

Both brothers were barefooted, and when I had been relieved of the necessity of holding the line and was able to help with both hands, they turned and, facing the rock, worked their way up with their toes, while I pulled lustily from on top.

When the fish at last had been safely landed, I asked the brothers if they ate fish, and on receiving their eager answer that they most certainly did, when they could get any, I told them I would give them the fish we had just landed—a mahseer in grand condition weighing a little over thirty pounds—if they would help me to land another fish for my men. To this they very readily agreed.

The treble had bitten deep into the leathery-underlip of the mahseer, and as I cut it out, the brothers watched interestedly. When the hook was free, they asked if they might have a look at it. Three hooks in one, such a thing had never been seen in their village. The bit of bent brass of course acted as a sinker. With what were the hooks baited ? Why should fish want to eat brass? And was it really brass, or some kind of hardened bait? When the spoon, and the trace with its three swivels, had been commented on and marvelled at, I made the brothers sit down and watch while I set about catching the second fish.

The biggest fish in the pool were at the foot of the fall, but here in the foaming white water, in addition to mahseer were some very big goonch, a fish that takes a spoon or dead bait very readily, and which is responsible for 90 per cent of the tackle lost in our hill rivers through its annoying habit of diving to the bottom of the pool when hooked and getting its head under a rock from where it is always difficult, and often impossible, to dislodge it.

No better spot than the place from where I had made my first cast was available, so here I again took up my position, with rod in hand and spoon held ready for casting.

The fish on the shingle bottom had been disturbed while I was playing the mahseer and by our subsequent movements on the face of the rock but were now beginning to return, and presently an exclamation from the brothers, and an excited pointing of fingers, drew my attention to a big fish downstream where the shingle bottom ended and the deep water began. Before I was able to make a cast the fish turned and disappeared in the deep water, but a little later it reappeared, and as it came into the shallow water I made a cast, but owing to the line being wet the cast fell short. The second cast was beautifully placed and beautifully timed, the spoon striking the water exactly where I wanted it to. Waiting for a second to give the spoon time to sink, I started to wind in the line, giving the spoon just the right amount of spin, and as I drew it along in little jerks, the mahseer shot forward, and next moment with the hook firmly fixed in his mouth, jumped clean out of the water, fell back with a great splash, and went madly downstream, much to the excitement of the spectators, for the men on the far bank had been watching the proceedings as intently as the brothers.

As the reel spun round and the line paid out, the brothers—now standing one on either side of me—urged me not to let the fish go down the run at the tail of the pool. Easier said than done, for it is not possible to stop the first mad rush of a mahseer of any size without risking certain break or the tearing away of the hook-hold. Our luck was in, or else the fish feared the run, for when there was less than fifty yards of line on the reel he checked, and though he continued to fight gamely he was eventually drawn round the bend, and into the little backwater at the foot of the rock.

The landing of this second fish was not as difficult as the landing of the first had been, for we each knew our places on the rock and exactly what to do.

Both fish were the same length, but the second was a little heavier than the first, and while the elder brother set off in triumph for his village with his fish carried over his shoulder—threaded on a grass cable he had made—the stripling begged to be allowed to accompany me back to the Inspection Bungalow, and to carry both my fish and my rod. Having in the days of long ago been a boy myself; and having had a brother who fished, there was no need for the stripling when making his request to have said, 'If you will let me carry both the fish and the rod, and will walk a little distance behind me, sahib, all the people who see me on the road, and in the bazaar, will think that I have caught this great fish, the like of which they have never seen.'

16

Death of a Goat

Ibbotson returned from Pauri on the last day of March, and the following morning, while we were having breakfast, we received a report that a leopard had called very persistently the previous night near a village to the northwest of Rudraprayag, about a mile from the place where we had killed the leopard in the gin-trap.

Half a mile to the north of the village, and on the shoulder of the great mountain, there was a considerable area of rough and broken ground where there were enormous rocks and caves, and deep holes in which the locals said their forefathers had quarried copper. Over the whole of this area there was scrub jungle, heavy in some places and light in others, extending down the hillside to within half a mile of the terraced fields above the village.

I had long suspected that the man-eater used this ground as a hide-out when he was in the vicinity of Rudraprayag, and I had frequently climbed to a commanding position above the broken ground in the hope of finding him basking on the rocks in the early morning sun, for leopards are very fond of doing this in a cold climate, and it is a very common way of shooting them, for all that is needed is a little patience, and accuracy of aim.

After an early lunch Ibbotson and I set out armed with our .275 rifles, and accompanied by one of Ibbotson's men carrying a short length of rope. At the village we purchased a young male goat—the leopard having killed all the goats that I had purchased from time to time.

From the village, a rough goat track ran straight up the hill to the edge of the broken ground, where it turned left, and after running across the face of the hill for a hundred yards carried on round the shoulder of the mountain. The track where it ran across the hill was bordered on the upper side by scattered bushes, and on the steep lower side by short grass.

Having tied the goat to a peg firmly driven into the ground at the bend in the track, about ten yards below the scrub jungle, we went down the hill for a hundred and fifty yards to where there were some big rocks, behind which we concealed ourselves. The goat was one of the best callers I have ever heard, and while his shrill and piercing bleat continued there was no necessity for us to watch him, for he had been very securely tied and there was no possibility of the leopard carrying him away.

The sun—a fiery red ball—was a hand's breadth from the snow mountains above Kedarnath when we took up our position behind the rocks, and half an hour later, when we had been in shadow for a few minutes, the goat suddenly stopped calling. Creeping to the side of the rock and looking through a screen of grass, I saw the goat with ears cocked, looking up towards the bushes; as I watched, the goat shook his head, and backed to the full length of the rope.

The leopard had undoubtedly come, attracted by the calling of the goat, and that he had not pounced before the goat became aware of his presence was proof that he was suspicious. Ibbotson's aim would be more accurate than mine, for his rifle was fitted with a telescopic sight, so I made room for him, and as he lay down and raised his rifle I whispered to him to examine carefully the bushes in the direction in which the goat was looking, for I felt sure that if the goat could see the leopard—and all the indications were that it could—Ibbotson should also be able to see it through his powerful telescope. For minutes Ibbotson kept his eye to the telescope and then shook his head, laid down the rifle, and made room for me.

The goat was standing in exactly the same position in which I had last seen it, and taking direction from it I fixed the telescope on the same bush at which it was looking. The flicker of an eyelid, or the very least movement of ear or even whiskers, would have been visible through the telescope, but though I also watched for minutes I too could see nothing.

When I took my eye away from the telescope I noted that the light was rapidly fading, and that the goat now showed as a red-and-white blur on the hillside. We had a long way to go and waiting longer would be both useless and dangerous, so getting to my feet I told Ibbotson it was time for us to make a move.

Going up to the goat—who from the time he had stopped bleating had not made a sound—we freed it from the peg, and with the man leading it we set off for the village. The goat quite evidently had never had a rope round its neck before and objected violently to being led, so I told the man to take the rope off—my experience being that when a goat is freed after having been tied up in the jungle, through fear or for want of companionship it follows at heel like a dog. This goat, however, had ideas of its own, and no sooner had the man removed the rope from its neck, than it turned and ran up the track.

It was too good a calling goat to abandon—it had attracted the leopard once, and might do so again. Moreover, we had only a few hours previously paid good money for it, so we in turn ran up the track in hot pursuit. At the bend, the goat turned to the left, and we lost sight of it. Keeping to the track, as the goat had done, we went to the shoulder of the hill where a considerable extent of the hill, clothed in short grass, was visible, and as the goat was nowhere in sight we decided it had taken a short cut back to the village, and started to retrace our steps. I was leading, and as we got half-way along the hundred yards of track, bordered on the upper side by scattered bushes and on the steep lower side by short grass, I saw something white on the track in front of me. The light had nearly gone, and on cautiously approaching the white object I found it was the goat laid head and tail on the narrow track, in the only position in which it could have been laid to prevent it from rolling down the steep hillside. Blood was oozing from its throat, and when I placed my hand on it the muscles were still twitching.

It was as though the man-eater—for no other leopard would have killed the goat and laid it on the track—had said, 'Here, if you want your goat so badly, take it; and as it is now dark and you have a long way to go, we will see which of you live to reach the village.'

I do not think all three of us would have reached the village alive if I had not, very fortunately, had a full box of matches with me (Ibbotson at that time was a nonsmoker). Striking a match and casting an anxious look all round and taking a few hurried steps, and then again striking another match, we stumbled down the rough track until we got to within calling distance of the village. Then, at our urgent summons, men with lanterns and pine torches came up to meet us.

We had left the goat lying where the leopard had placed it, and when I returned at daybreak next morning I found the pug marks of the man-eater where he had followed us down to the village, and I found the goat untouched and lying just as we had left it.

17

Cyanide Poisoning

As I was returning to the Inspection Bungalow after visiting the goat that had been killed the previous night, I was informed in the village that my presence was urgently needed at Rudraprayag, for news had just been received that the man-eater had killed a human being the previous night. My informants were unable to give me any particulars as to where the kill had taken place, but as the pug marks of the man-eater showed that, after following us to the village, it had gone back up the goat track and turned right at the bend, I assumed—rightly, as I later found—that the leopard, after failing to bag one of us, had secured a victim farther up the mountainside.

At the bungalow I found Ibbotson in conversation with a man by the name of Nand Ram. Nand Ram's village was about four miles from where we had sat the previous evening. Half a mile above this village and on the far side of a deep ravine, a man of the depressed class, named Gawiya, had cleared a small area of forest land and built himself a house in which he lived with his mother, wife, and three children. At daybreak that morning, Nand Ram had heard the wailing of women from the direction of Gawiya's house and, on his shouting out and asking what was wrong, he had been informed that 'the man of the house' had been carried off by the man-eater half an hour previously. With this information Nand Ram had come hot-foot to the Inspection Bungalow.

Ibbotson had had the Arab and the English mare saddled, and after we had eaten a good meal we set out, with Nand Ram to show us the way. There were no roads on the hill, only goat and cattle tracks, and as the big English mare found the hairpin bends on these tracks difficult to negotiate we sent the horses back and did the rest of the hot and steep climb on foot.

Arrived at the little isolated clearing in the forest, the two distracted women—who appeared to be nursing the hope that the 'man of the house' might still be alive—showed us where Gawiya had been sitting near the door of the house when the leopard had seized him. The leopard had caught the unfortunate man by the throat, thus preventing him from making any sound, and after dragging him for a hundred yards had killed him. Then he had carried him for four hundred yards to a little hollow surrounded by dense brushwood. The wailing of the women and the shouting of Nand Ram had evidently disturbed the leopard at his meal, for he had only eaten the throat and jaw, and a small portion of one shoulder and thigh.

There were no trees within sight of the kill on which we could sit, so we poisoned the kill with cyanide at the three places where the leopard had eaten, and as it was now getting towards evening we took up position on a hill several hundred yards away, from where we could overlook the hollow in which the kill was lying. The leopard was undoubtedly in the dense brushwood, but though we lay in our concealed position and watched for two hours, we saw nothing of him. At dusk we lit the lantern we had provided ourselves with, and went back to the bungalow.

We were up very early next morning, and it was just getting light when we again sat down on the hill overlooking the hollow. We saw and heard nothing, and when the sun had been up an hour, we went to the kill; the leopard had not touched the three places where we had buried the poison, but had eaten the other shoulder and leg, and had then carried the body away for a short distance and hidden it under some bushes.

Again there were no trees overlooking the kill on which we could sit, and after a prolonged discussion we eventually decided that while Ibbotson went down the hill for a mile to a village where there was a big mango-tree, in which he could make himself a *machan* and spend the night, I would sit about four hundred yards from the kill, over a village path on which the previous day we had seen the pug marks of the man-eater.

The tree I selected to sit in was a rhododendron which many years previously had been cut about fifteen feet above ground. Stout branches had grown out from the cut, and sitting on the old stump surrounded by the branches I had a perfect seat and perfect concealment.

Facing me was a steep well-wooded hill with a dense under-growth of bracken and dwarf bamboo. Running across the face of the hill east and west was a well-used footpath; the rhododen-dron-tree was growing about ten feet below this footpath.

From my seat in the tree I had an uninterrupted view of a length of about ten yards of the path, which to my left crossed a ravine and carried on at the same level on the far side, and to my right, and some three hundred yards farther on, passed a little below the bushes where the kill was lying. There was no water in the ravine where the path crossed it, but thirty yards lower down and immediately below, and three or four yards from, the root of my tree, there were several small pools—the start of a little spring which lower down became a stream providing drinking water to the villagers and irrigation for their crops.

The ten yards of path of which I had an uninterrupted view was joined at right-angles by a path coming down the hill from the house three hundred yards above me where Gawiya had been killed. Thirty yards up this path there was a bend, and from this point a small depression ran down to the lower path—the points where the depression started on the upper path and ended on the lower were not in my view.

There was no need for a torch, for it was a brilliant moonlight night, and if the leopard came along the level path or down the path from the house—as its pug marks showed it had done the previous day—I should get an easy shot at a range of from twenty to forty feet.

I had gone down the hill a short distance with Ibbotson, and then a little before sunset had taken up my position on the tree. A few minutes later three kaleege pheasants—a cock and two hens —came down the hill, and after drinking at the spring went back the way they had come. On both occasions they had passed under my tree, and that they had not seen me was proof that my hide was a good one.

The early part of the night was silent, but at eight o'clock a kakar started barking in the direction of the kill. The leopard had arrived, and I was convinced he had not gone to the kill along either of the paths I was watching. After barking for a few minutes the kakar stopped, and thereafter the night was again silent up to ten o'clock, when the kakar again barked. The leopard had been at the kill for two hours—sufficient time for him to have had a good meal, and for him to have poisoned himself several times over. And there was a good chance of his having done so, for on this second night the kill had been very effectively poisoned, the cyanide having been buried deep in the victim's flesh.

Without closing an eye I sat watching the hill in front of me, where the moonlight was so brilliant that I could clearly see every blade of grass, and at 2 a.m. I heard the leopard coming down the path from the direction of the house. I had scattered dry leaves on this path, and also on the lower path, with the object of getting some warning of the leopard's approach, and that he was now walking carelessly over these leaves, and not making any attempt at silence, filled me with hope—though I expected within the next few seconds to put a bullet into him—that all was not well with him.

At the bend in the path the leopard made a short pause, and then leaving the path entered the little depression and followed it down to the lower path, on reaching which he again paused.

I had sat without movement for hours with my hands on the rifle lying across my knees, and as I was convinced that he would come along the path, I decided to let him pass in front of me, and when there was no longer any danger of his seeing the movement raise the rifle to my shoulder, and hit him where I wanted to. For seconds I watched the path, expecting to see his head appear from behind the screen of branches, and then, when tension was becoming unbearable, I heard him jump down off the path and come diagonally across the hill towards my tree. For a moment I thought he had in some mysterious way become aware of my presence on the tree and, not liking the flavour of his last kill, was intent on securing another human victim. His object, however, in leaving the path was not to try to get at me but to take a short cut down to the spring, for he passed the foot of the tree without a pause, and next second I heard him eagerly and noisily lapping water.

From the leopard's behaviour on the hill, and from the way he was now drinking, I was convinced he had poisoned himself, but not having had any previous experience of the effect of cyanide, I did not know how long the poison would take to act. For ten minutes after the leopard had stopped drinking, and just as I was beginning to hope that he had died at the spring, I heard him going up the hill on the far side of the ravine, all sound ceasing when he regained the path which carried on round the shoulder of the hill.

At no time, either when the leopard was coming down the path, coming down the depression, coming across the hill to the foot of my tree, when drinking, or going up the hill on the far side of the ravine, had I seen him, for either by accident or intent he had kept under cover to which not a glint of moonlight had penetrated.

There was now no hope of my getting a shot, but this was not of much account if the poison was as potent as the doctor in Naini Tal had claimed that it was.

I sat on for the rest of the night, watching the path and listening for sounds. At daylight Ibbotson returned, and while we brewed ourselves a very welcome cup of tea I told him of the night's happenings.

On visiting the kill we found that the leopard had eaten the leg from which he had taken a small portion two nights previously, and in which we had buried a full dose of poison, and that he had in addition eaten two other doses of poison, one from the left shoulder and the other from the back.

It was now necessary to make a search for the leopard, and for this purpose the *Patwari*, who had returned with Ibbotson, set off to collect men. At about midday the *Patwari* returned with two hundred men, and with these we made a line and beat the whole side of the hill in the direction in which the leopard had gone.

Half a mile from where the leopard had quenched his thirst, and in the direct line in which I had heard him going away, there were some big rocks at the foot of which there was a cave extending far into the hill, with an opening large enough to admit a leopard. Near the mouth of this cave the leopard had scratched up the ground, and rid himself of his victim's toes—which he had swallowed whole.

Willing hands brought loose stones from the hillside, and when we left the cave we had sealed it beyond all possibility of any leopard that might be lurking in it escaping.

Next morning I returned with a roll of one-inch wire netting and a number of iron tent-pegs, and, after removing the stones, very effectively wired up the mouth of the cave. Thereafter for the following ten days I visited the cave morning and evening, and as during this period no news of the man-eater came in from any village on the left bank of the Alaknanda, my hopes each day grew stronger that on my next visit I would surely get some indication that the leopard had died in the cave.

On the tenth morning, when I returned from my visit to the cave—where I had found the netting undisturbed—Ibbotson greeted me with the news that a woman had been killed the previous night in a village five miles away, and about a mile above the Rudraprayag-Badrinath pilgrim road.

Quite evidently cyanide was not the right poison for an animal that had the reputation of thriving on, and being stimulated by, arsenic and strychnine. That the leopard had eaten the cyanide there could be no doubt whatever, nor was there any doubt that he had entered the cave, for his hairs were adhering to the rock where his back had come in contact with it when entering the cave.

An overdose might account for the poison not having had the desired effect and a second opening somewhere farther up the hill might account for his escape from the cave. Even so, it was no longer any matter of surprise to me—who had only been acquainted with the leopard for a few short months—that the people of Garhwal, who had lived in close and intimate association with him for eight long years, should credit him—animal or spirit—with supernatural powers, and that they should cling to the belief that nothing but fire would rid them of this evil spirit.

18

Touch and Go

News that is of importance to every individual travels fast, and during the past ten days everyone in Garhwal had heard of the poisoning of the man-eater, and of our hope that we had sealed it up in a cave. It was natural therefore for risks to have been taken, and quite evidently the leopard, having recovered from the effects of the poison and found a way out of the cave, had found the first person who was taking a risk.

We had the day before us, for I had returned early from my visit to the cave, and after breakfast, mounted on Ibbotson's surefooted horses and carrying our rifles, we set out for the village where the woman was reported to have been killed.

After a fast ride up the pilgrim road we took a track that went diagonally across the hill, and a mile along this track, where the path from the village joined it, there were signs of a struggle and a big pool of blood.

The headman, and relatives of the victim, were waiting for us at the village, and they showed us where the leopard had seized the woman as she was in the act of closing the door of her house behind her. From this point the leopard had dragged the woman along on her back for a hundred yards to the junction of the track, where he had released his hold, and after a violent struggle had killed her. The people in the village had heard the woman's screams as she was being dragged along the ground and as she was struggling for her life with the leopard, but had been too frightened to render any help.

When the woman was dead, the leopard had picked her up and carried her over some waste land, across an open ravine a hundred yards wide, and up the hill on the far side for another two hundred yards. There were no drag marks, but the blood trail was easy to follow, and it led us to a flat bit of ground, four feet wide and twenty feet long. On the upper side of this narrow strip of ground there was a perpendicular bank eight feet high with a stunted medlar-tree growing on it, and on the lower side of the narrow strip the hill fell steeply away, and growing on it was a wild rose-bush, which had reached up and smothered the medlar-tree. Lying huddled up between the steep bank and the rose-bush, with her head against the bank, with every vestige of clothing stripped from her, and with her naked body flecked with white rose-petals that had fallen from above, was the kill—an old greyhaired lady, seventy years of age.

For this pitiful kill the leopard would have to pay with his life, and after a short council of war, Ibbotson, leading the spare horse, returned to Rudraprayag for the things we needed, while I set off with my ride to see whether it was possible to make contact with the man-eater in daylight.

This part of the country was new to me, and the first thing to do was to reconnoitre the ground. I had already noted while at the village that the hill went steeply up from the ravine to a height of four to five thousand feet; that about two thousand feet of the top of the hill was clothed with dense oak and pine forest, below which was an open stretch of short grass about half a mile wide, and that below the grass was scrub jungle.

Keeping now to the edge of the grass and scrub jungle I went round the shoulder of the hill, and found in front of me a wide depression, extending for half a mile down to the pilgrim road, and evidently caused in the days of long ago by a landslide. Beyond this depression, which was about a hundred yards wide at the upper end and about three hundred yards wide where it met the road, the ground was open. The ground in the depression was damp, and growing on this damp ground were a number of big trees, and under the tree a dense growth of scrub jungle. At the upper end of the depression was a cliff of overhanging rock, varying in height from twenty to forty feet, and about a hundred yards long; half-way along the cliff was a deep cleft a few feet wide, down which a tiny stream was trickling. Above the rocks was a narrow belt of scrub jungle, and above that again, open grassland.

I had reconnoitered the ground with care, for I did not want the leopard—which I was convinced was lying up in the depression—to be aware of my presence before it suited me. It was now necessary to find, approximately, where the leopard was most likely to be lying up, and to gain this information I went back to the kill.

We had been told in the village that it had got light shortly after the woman had been killed, and as it must have taken the leopard some little time to effect the kill, carry his victim four hundred yards, and eat a portion of it, it was reasonable to assume that he had left the spot where he had hidden the kill when day was fully established. The hill on which the kill was lying was in full view of the village, in which at this hour there must have been considerable movement; the leopard therefore on leaving the kill would very naturally have kept to cover as far as was possible, and working on this assumption, and also because the ground was too hard to show pug marks, I set out to follow him along the line I assumed he had taken.

When I had covered half a mile and was out of view of the village and was approaching the depression, I was gratified to find that I had followed on the leopard's tracks foot by foot, for in the lee of a bush where there was some loose earth, I found where he had been lying for several hours. His pug marks when leaving this spot showed that he had entered the depression about fifty yards below the cliff of rock.

For half an hour I lay where the leopard had lain, watching the small area of tree and scrub jungle in front of me in the hope that the leopard would make some slight movement and give away his position.

After I had been watching for a few minutes a movement among the dead leaves attracted my attention, and presently two scimitar babblers came into view industriously turning over the leaves, looking for grubs. Where carnivora are concerned, these birds are among the most reliable informants in the jungle, and I hoped later to make use of this pair to help in locating the leopard.

No movement had been visible and no sound had come to indicate that the leopard was in the depression; but that he was there I was still convinced, and having failed to get a shot in one way I decided to try another way.

Without coming out into the open, there were two natural lines of retreat for the leopard, one down the hill towards the pilgrim road, and the other up the hill. To move him down the hill would not profit me, but if I moved him up the hill he would to a certainty go up the cleft in the rock cliff to gain the shelter of the bushes above the cliff, and while he was doing so, there was a reasonable chance of my getting a shot.

Entering the depression a little below where I thought the leopard was, I started to zigzag very slowly across it, gaining a few feet in height at each turn. There was as yet no need for me to keep an eye on the cleft, for the babblers were on the ground a few feet below it, and they would let me know when the leopard was on the move. I had gained about forty yards in height in my movements forward and backward across the depression and was about ten yards from, and a little to the left of the cleft, when the babblers rose in alarm and, flying into a small oak-tree and hopping about excitedly on the branches, started to give their clear and ringing alarm call, which can in the hills be heard for a distance of half a mile. Holding the rifle ready to take a snap shot, I stood perfectly still for a minute, and then started slowly moving forward.

The ground here was wet and slippery and, with my eyes fixed on the cleft, I had only taken two steps when my rubber-soled shoes slipped on the wet surface; and while I was endeavouring to regain my balance, the leopard sprang up the cleft, and in the bushes above put up a covey of kaleege pheasants, which came sailing down over my head.

My second attempt had failed, and though it would have been quite easy for me to have moved the leopard back to where he had started from, it would have been of no use for me to do so, for, from above, the cleft in the rock was not visible until one was right up to it, and long before I gained the position the leopard would have been far down the depression.

Ibbotson and I had arranged to meet in the open ravine at 2 p.m., and a little before that hour he returned from Rudraprayag, accompanied by several men carrying the things he had gone to fetch. These consisted of food, and drink—in the way of tea—our old friend the petromax lamp—which this occasion I decided I would carry myself, if the necessity arose—two spare rifles and ammunition, my fishing-reel, a liberal supply of cyanide, and the gin-trap.

Sitting in the ravine by a clear stream of water, we had our lunch and brewed ourselves a cup of tea, and then went over to the kill.

I will give a description of the position of the kill, to enable you to follow our movements and the subsequent happenings.

The kill was lying about five feet from the near or ravine end of the flat strip of ground, which was four feet wide and about twenty feet long. The upper side of this strip of ground was protected by a high bank, and the lower side by a steep drop and a spreading rose-bush. The stunted medlar-tree on the bank was too small to admit of a *machan* being made in it, so we decided to depend entirely on a gun-trap, poison, and the gin-trap; having come to this decision we set about our preparations.

First we poisoned the kill, of which the leopard had—for want of time—only eaten a small portion; hoping that on this occasion he would only consume sufficient to poison himself effectively. Then, while I bent over the kill in the position we anticipated the leopard would assume when eating, Ibbotson sighted and securely lashed his .256 Mannlicher—which had a hair trigger—and my .450 high-velocity rifle to two saplings, fifteen yards on our approach side of the kill.

There were no insuperable obstacles to the leopard getting at the kill from any side he might wish to, but his most natural line of approach from where I had left him was along the fifteen feet or so of flat ground, and on this strip of flat ground we proceeded to bury the huge gin-trap, first removing from the ground every dead leaf, bit of stick, and blade of grass that were lying on it.

After we had dug a hole sufficiently long, wide, and deep—removing the displaced earth to a distance—we put the gin-trap in it, and when the powerful springs that closed the jaws had been depressed, and the plate that constituted the trigger adjusted as delicately as we dared set it, we covered the whole trap with a layer of green leaves, over which we sprinkled earth, and finally we replaced the dead leaves, bits of stick, and blades of grass in the position we had found them. So carefully had the trap been set in the ground that we who had set it found it difficult to determine its exact position.

My fishing-reel was now produced and one end of the dressed silk line was tied to the trigger of one rifle, looped round the butt-end, and taken to within ten feet of the kill, from where it was taken back, looped round the butt-end of the second rifle, and tied to the trigger. The line was then cut—much to my regret, for it was a new and very good line—and after the end had been tied round the woman's waist, the line was passed through the loop, the lines to the triggers pulled taut, and a secure knot was tied. The line was then cut for the second time.

As we cast a final look over our handiwork—which appeared to us very good—it struck us that if the leopard was to wander round and approach the kill from our side, and not from the side we expected him to come, he *might* avoid both the guns and the gin-trap, and to prevent his doing so we sent to the village for a crowbar, while we cut five thornbushes from some little distance away. With the crowbar we made five holes a foot deep, on our side of the flat strip of ground, and into these holes we planted the bushes, stamping the earth round them and making them almost as secure and quite as natural to look at as when they were growing on the hillside. We were now quite satisfied that no animal bigger than a rat could approach the kill and eat any portion of it without meeting death in one form or another, so throwing off the safety-catch of the rifles, we returned to the village.

Fifty yards from the village, and close to where we had on our arrival found the pool of blood, there was a big wide-spreading mango-tree. In this tree we made a *machan* from planks procured from the village, and on it we piled a lot of sweet-smelling rice straw, for it was our intention to spend the night on it, in anticipation of having to finish off the leopard if he was caught in the gin-trap.

Near sundown we took our position on the *machan*, which was long enough for us to lie at length and wide enough for us to lie side by side. The distance from the *machan* to the kill across the ravine was two hundred yards, and the kill was on a higher level than the *machan* by about a hundred feet.

Ibbotson feared that his aim with the telescopic sight fitted to his rifle would not be quite accurate, so while he took a pair of powerful field-glasses from their case, I loaded my .275 rifle. Our plan was that while Ibbotson concentrated on the portion of the hill along which we expected the leopard to come, I would keep a general look-out all over the hill, and if we saw the leopard, I would risk taking a shot, even if the shot had to be taken at the extreme range to which my rifle was sighted, which was three hundred yards.

While Ibbotson dozed, I smoked and watched the shadows cast by the hills in the west slowly creep up the hill in front of us, and when the rays from the setting sun were gilding the crest of the hill red, Ibbotson awoke and picked up his field-glasses, and I picked up my rifle, for the time had now come when we could expect the leopard to make his appearance. There was still some forty-five minutes of daylight left, and during that time we intently scanned—I with a pair of eyes that few are blessed with, and Ibbotson with his field-glasses—every foot of the considerable expanse of hill visible from our *machan*, without seeing the movement of a bird or animal.

When there was no longer sufficient light to shoot by, I put down my rifle, and a little later Ibbotson returned his field-glasses to their case. One chance of killing the leopard had gone, but there were still three chances left, so we were not unduly depressed.

Shortly after dark it came on to rain, and I whispered to Ibbotson that I feared it would prove our undoing, for if the additional weight of rain-water on the delicately set gin-trap did not set it off, the contracting of the fishing-line due to getting wet, no matter how slight it might be, would to a certainty fire off his hair-trigger rifle. Some time later, and while it was still raining, Ibbotson asked me what time it was. I had a luminous wrist-watch, and I had just told him it was a quarter to eight when a succession of savage and angry roars came from the direction of the kill—the leopard, the much-famed man-eating leopard of Rudraprayag, was at long last in the gin-trap.

Ibbotson took a flying leap from the *machan* while I swung down from a branch, and that neither of us broke limbs in the descent can only be attributed to luck. The petromax lamp hidden in a nearby yam field was found, and while Ibbotson proceeded to light it, I gave expression to my fears and doubts, and admit I deserved Ibbotson's rejoinder, 'You are a rotten pessimist. First you think a few drops of rain are going to spring the trap and fire off my rifle, and now you think because the leopard is not making a noise that it has got out of the trap.' That was just what I was thinking, and fearing, for on that other occasion when we had trapped a leopard it had roared and growled continuously, whereas this one, after that one expression of rage which had brought us tumbling out of the *machan*, had been ominously silent.

Ibbotson is an expert with all makes of lamps and in a very short time he had the petromax lit and pumped up, and throwing our doubts to the winds—for Ibbotson was by now beginning to suspect the silence—we set off over the rough ground as hard as we could go, circling wide to avoid the fishing-lines, and a possible angry leopard, and approached the kill from above. When we got to the high bank and looked down we saw the hole in the ground, but no gin-trap, and as our hopes were bounding up, the brilliant light of the petromax revealed the trap; with its jaws closed and empty, ten yards down the hillside. The kill was no longer lying with its head against the bank, and a glance revealed that a considerable portion of it had been eaten.

Our thoughts were too bitter to give expression to as we went back to the mango-tree and climbed into the *machan*. There was no longer any need for us to keep awake, so heaping some of the straw over ourselves, for we had no bedding and the night was cold, we went to sleep.

At the first streak of dawn a fire was built near the mango-tree and water heated, and after we had drunk several cups of tea and warmed ourselves at the fire, we set off for the kill, accompanied by the *Patwari* and several of Ibbotson's and my men, together with a number of men from the village.

I mention the fact that there were two of us, and that we had the *Patwari* and a number of men with us, for had I been alone I would have hesitated to relate what I am now going to tell you.

Fiend or animal, had the slayer of the old woman been present and watched our overnight preparations it would even then have been difficult to understand how it had, on a dark and rainy night, avoided capture or death in one form or another. The rain, though light, had been sufficient to soften the ground, and we were able to reconstruct and to follow his every movement of the previous night.

The leopard had come from the direction from which we had expected him to come, and on arrival at the flat strip of ground, had skirted round and below it, and had then approached the kill from the side where we had firmly planted the thornbushes. Three of these bushes he had pulled up, making a sufficiently wide gap to go through, and then, getting hold of the kill, he had drawn it a foot or so towards the rifles, thus slackening off the fishing-lines. Having done this he had started to eat, avoiding while doing so contact with the fishing-line that was tied round the woman's body. We had not thought it necessary to poison either the head or the neck. These he had eaten first, and then—very carefully—he had eaten all that portion of the body between the many doses of poison we had inserted in different places.

After satisfying his hunger the leopard left the kill with the intention of seeking shelter from the rain and, while he was doing so, what I feared would happen actually happened. The weight of rain-water on the very finely set trap had depressed the plate that constituted the trigger, and released the springs just as the leopard was stepping over the trap, and the great jaws had met on either side of the stifle, or knee-joint, of his hind leg. And here was the greatest tragedy of all, for when bringing the trap up from Rudraprayag the men carrying it had let it fall, and one of the three-inch-long teeth had been broken off, and the stifle of the leopard's left hind leg had been caught by the jaws exactly where this missing tooth formed a gap in the otherwise perfectly fitting set of teeth. But for this missing tooth the leopard would have been fixed to the trap without any possibility of getting free, for the grip on his leg had been sufficiently good for him to lift the eighty-pound trap out of the hole in which we had buried it, and carry it ten yards down the hillside. And now, instead of the leopard, the jaws of the trap only held a tuft of hair and a small piece of skin, which we later—much later—had the great satisfaction of fitting back into position.

However unbelievable the actions of the leopard may appear to have been, they were in fact just what one would have expected from an animal that had been a man-eater for eight years. Avoiding the open ground, and approaching the kill under cover; removing the thorn obstruction we had erected across the blood trail he had left that morning; pulling the kill towards him into a convenient position for his meal, and rejecting those portions of the kill that we had poisoned—cyanide, of which he now had experience, has a very strong smell—were all quite normal and natural actions.

The explanation I have given for the springing of the trap is, I am convinced, correct. It was just a coincidence that the leopard happened to be directly over the trap the very moment that the additional weight of water set it off.

Having dismantled the gin-trap, and waited until the relatives had removed what remained of the old woman for cremation, we set out to walk back to Rudraprayag, leaving our men to follow us. Some time during the night the leopard had come to the mango-tree, for we found his pug marks near the tree where the pool of blood—now washed away by the rain—had been, and we followed these pug marks down the track to the pilgrim road and four miles along the road to the gate of the Inspection Bungalow where, after scratching up the ground at the base of one of the pillars of the gate, he had gone on down the road for another mile to where my old friend the packman was camped, one of whose goats he had wantonly killed.

I need not tell those of you who have carried a sporting rifle in any part of the world that all these many repeated failures and disappointments, so far from discouraging me, only strengthened my determination to carry on until that great day or night came when, having discarded poisons and traps, I would get an opportunity of using my rifle as rifles were intended to be used, to put a bullet truly and accurately into the man-eater's body.

19

A Lesson in Caution

I have never agreed with those sportsmen who attribute all their failures in big-game hunting to their being Jonahs.

The thoughts of a sportsman, whether they be pessimistic or whether they be optimistic, sitting waiting for an animal, cannot in any conceivable way influence the actions of the animal he is endeavouring to shoot or, maybe, to photograph.

We are apt to forget that the hearing and sight of wild animals, and especially of those animals that depend exclusively on these senses not only for food but also for self-preservation, are on a plane far and away above that of civilized human beings, and that there is no justification for us to assume that because we cannot hear or see the movements of our prospective quarry, our quarry cannot hear or see our movements. A wrong estimation of the intelligence of animals, and the inability to sit without making any sound or movement for the required length of time, is the cause of all failures when sitting up for animals. As an example of the acute sense of hearing of carnivora, and the care it is necessary to exercise when contact with one of them is desired, I will relate one of my recent experiences.

On a day in March, when the carpet of dry leaves on the ground recorded the falling of every dead leaf and the movements of the smallest of the birds that feed on the ground, I located in some very heavy undergrowth the exact position of a tiger I had long wished to photograph, by moving a troop of langurs in the direction in which I suspected the tiger to be lying up. Seventy yards from the tiger there was an open glade, fifty yards long and thirty yards wide. On the edge of the glade, away from the tiger, there was a big tree overgrown with creepers that extended right up to the topmost branches; twenty feet from the ground the tree forked in two. I knew that the tiger would cross the glade in the late afternoon, for the glade lay directly between him and his sambhur kill which I had found early that morning. There was no suitable cover near the kill for the tiger to lie up in during the day, so he had gone to the heavy undergrowth where the langurs had located him for me.

It is often necessary, when shooting or photographing tigers and leopards on foot, to know the exact position of one's quarry, whether it be a wounded animal that one desires to put out of its misery or an animal that one wants to photograph, and the best way of doing this is by enlisting the help of birds or animals. With patience, and with a knowledge of the habits of the bird or animal the sportsman desires to use, it is not difficult to get a particular bird or animal to go in the required direction. The birds most suitable for this purpose are red jungle fowl, peafowl, and white-capped babblers, and of animals the most suitable are kakars and langurs.

The tiger I am telling you about was unwounded, and it would have been quite easy for me to go into the undergrowth and find him myself, but in doing so I should have disturbed him and defeated my own purposes, whereas by using the troop of langurs and knowing what their reactions would be on sighting the tiger—if he happened to be in the undergrowth—I was able to get the information I wanted without disturbing the tiger.

Very carefully I stalked the tree I have referred to, and avoiding contact with the creepers, the upper tendrils and leaves of which might have been visible from where the tiger was lying, I climbed to the fork, where I had a comfortable seat and perfect concealment. Getting out my 16-mm. ciné-camera I made an opening in the screen of leaves in front of me just big enough to photograph through, and having accomplished all this without having made a sound, I sat still. My field of vision was confined to the glade and to the jungle immediately beyond it.

After I had been sitting for an hour, a pair of bronze-wing doves rose out of the jungle and went skimming over the low brushwood, and a minute or two later, and a little closer to me, a small flight of upland pipits rose off the ground and, after daintily tripping along the branches of a leafless tree, rose above the tree-tops and went off. Neither of these two species of birds has any alarm call, but I knew from their behaviour that the tiger was afoot and that they had been disturbed by him. Minutes later I was slowly turning my eyes from left to right scanning every foot of ground visible to me, when my

eyes came to rest on a small white object, possibly an inch or two square, immediately in front of me, and about ten feet from the edge of the glade. Focusing my eyes on this stationary object for a little while, I then continued to scan the bushes to the limit of my field of vision to the right, and then back again to the white object.

I was now convinced that this object had not been where it was for more than a minute or two before I had first caught sight of it, and that it could not be anything else than a white mark on the tiger's face. Quite evidently the tiger had heard me when I was approaching or climbing the tree, though I had done this in thin rubber shoes without making as far as I was aware any sound, and when the time had come for him to go to his kill he had stalked, for a distance of seventy yards over dry leaves, the spot he had pin-pointed as the source of some suspicious sound. After lying for half an hour without making any movement, he stood up, stretched himself, yawned, and, satisfied that he had nothing to fear, walked out into the glade. Here he stood, turning his head first to the right and then to the left, and then crossed the glade, passing right under my tree on his way to his kill.

When in my wanderings through the jungles I see the *machans* that have been put up for the purpose of shooting carnivora, and note the saplings that have been felled near by to make the platform, the branches that have been cut to give a clear view, and see the litter and debris left lying about, and consider the talking and noise that must have accompanied these operations, I am not surprised when I hear people say they have sat up hundreds of times for tigers and leopards without ever having seen one of these animals, and attribute their failures to their being Jonahs.

Our failure to bag the man-eater up to that date was not due to our having done anything we should not have done, or left undone anything we should have done. It could only be attributed to sheer bad luck. Bad luck, that had prevented my receiving the electric light in time; that had given Ibbotson cramps in both legs; that had made the leopard eat an overdose of cyanide; and, finally, that had made the men drop the gin-trap and break the one tooth that mattered. So when Ibbotson returned to Pauri, after our failure to kill the leopard over the body of his seventy-year-old victim, I was full of hope, for I considered my chances of shooting the leopard as good as they were on the first day I arrived at Rudraprayag, and in fact better than they had then been, for I now knew the capabilities of the animal I had to deal with.

One thing was causing me a lot of uneasiness and giving me much heart-searching, and that was confining the man-eater to one bank of the river. However I looked at it, it did not appear to be right that the people on the left bank of the Alaknanda should be exposed to attacks by the leopard, while the people on the right bank were free from the risk of such attacks. Including the boy killed two days before our arrival, three people had recently lost their lives on the left bank, and others might meet with a like fate, and yet to open the two bridges and let the leopard cross over to the right bank would add an hundredfold to my difficulties, which were already considerable, and would not benefit Garhwal as a whole, for the lives of the people on the right bank of the river were just as valuable as the lives of the people on the left bank; so, very reluctantly, I decided to keep the bridges closed. And here I should like to pay my tribute to the people—numbering many thousands—living on the left bank of the river who, knowing that the closing of the bridges was confining the activities of the dread man-eater to their area, never once, during the months I closed the bridges, removed the barriers themselves, or asked me to do so.

Having decided to keep the bridges closed, I sent a man to warn the villagers of their danger, and myself carried the warning to as many villages as time and my ability to walk permitted of my doing. No one whom I talked with on the roads and in the villages ever expressed one word of resentment at the leopard having been confined to their area, and everywhere I went I was offered hospitality and speeded on my way with blessings, and I was greatly encouraged by the assurances from both men and women—who did not know but what they might be the man-eater's next victim—that it was no matter for regret that the leopard had not died yesterday, for surely it would die today or, maybe, tomorrow.

20

A Wild Boar Hunt

The old packman had arrived at the thorn enclosure late the previous evening. He was packing salt and gur from the bazaar at Hardwar to the villages beyond Badrinath, and as his flock of sheep and goats were heavily laden and the last march had been a long one, he had arrived too late at the thorn enclosure to repair the weak places in it, with the result that several of the goats had strayed out of the enclosure and one of them the leopard had killed, close to the road, during the early hours of the morning. The barking of his dogs had awakened him, and when it got light, he saw his best goat—a beautiful steel-gray animal nearly as large as a Shetland pony—lying dead near the road, wantonly killed by the man-eater.

The behaviour of the man-eater during the previous night showed the extent to which the habits of a leopard change when it has become a man-eater and has lived in close association with human beings over a long period of years.

It was reasonable to assume that the man-eater had received a great shock, and a great fright, by being caught in the gin-trap; his having carried the heavy trap for ten yards and the angry way in which he had roared was in fact proof of this; and one would have expected him, the moment he got out of the trap, to have retired to some secluded spot as far removed from human habitation as possible, and to have remained there until he was again hungry, which he would not be for several days. But, so far from doing this, he had quite evidently remained in the vicinity of the kill, and after watching us climb into the *machan* and giving us time to go to sleep, had come to investigate; fortunately for us, Ibbotson had taken the precaution to protect the *machan* by putting wire netting all round it, for it is not an unheard-of thing for man-eating leopards to kill people who are sitting up trying to shoot them. At the present time there is a man-eating leopard in the Central Provinces that has—at different times—killed and eaten four Indian sportsmen who were trying to shoot him; up to the time I last heard of this animal he had killed forty human beings, and owing to his habit of eating his would-be slayers, he was living a very peaceful and undisturbed life, varying his human diet with game and domestic animals.

After his visit to the mango-tree, our man-eater went along the village path to its junction with the track. Here, where we had found the pool of blood, he had turned to the right and gone down the track for a mile, and then along the pilgrim road for another four miles and into the most densely populated part of the area in which he was operating. On arrival at Rudraprayag, he had gone through the main street of the bazaar, and half a mile farther on had scratched up the ground at the gate of the Inspection Bungalow. The rain of the previous night had softened the clay surface of the road, and on the soft clay the pug marks of the leopard showed up clearly, and from them it was possible to see that the leopard's encounter with the gin-trap had not resulted in injury to any of his limbs.

After breakfast I took up the tracks at the gate and followed them to the packman's camp. From a bend in the road, a hundred yards from the camp, the leopard had caught sight of the goats that had strayed from the enclosure, and crossing from the outer to the inner edge of the road and creeping along under shelter of the hill he had stalked the grazing animals and, after killing the steel-gray goat but without even troubling to drink its blood, had returned to the road.

In the thorn enclosure, guarding the dead goat and the neatly stacked pile of packs, were the packman's two sheep-dogs, tethered to stout pegs with short lengths of heavy chain. These big, black, and powerful dogs that are used by packmen throughout our hills are not accredited sheep-dogs in the same sense that sheep-dogs in Great Britain and in Europe are. On the march the dogs keep close to heel, and their duties—which they perform very efficiently—only start when camp is made. At night they guard the camp against wild animals—I have known two of them to kill a leopard—and during the day and while the packmen are away grazing the flock they guard the camp against all intruders. A case is on record of one of these dogs having killed a man who was attempting to remove a pack from the camp it had been left to guard.

I picked up the tracks of the leopard where he returned to the road after killing the goat, and followed them through Golabrai and for a mile farther on, to where a deep ravine crosses the road, up which he had gone. The distance the leopard had covered from the mango-tree to the ravine was about eight miles. This long and seemingly aimless walk away from a kill was in itself a thing no ordinary leopard would under any circumstances have undertaken, nor would an ordinary leopard have killed a goat when he was not hungry.

A quarter of a mile beyond the ravine the old packman was sitting on a rock by the side of the road, spinning wool and watching his flock, which were grazing on the open hillside. When he had dropped his spinning-stick and wool into the capacious pocket in his blanket robe and accepted a cigarette, he asked if I had come past his camp. When I told him I had done so and that I had seen what the evil spirit had done, and added that it would be wise to sell his dogs to camelmen on his next visit to Hardwar, for it was quite evident that they were lacking in courage, he nodded his head as one in what he heard. Then he said, 'Sahib, even we old hands are apt at times to make mistakes, and suffer for them, even as I have this night suffered by losing my best goat. My dogs have the courage of tigers, and are the best dogs in all Garhwal, and it is an insult to them for you to say they are only fit to be sold to camelmen. My camp, as you doubtless observed, is very close to the road, and I feared that if by chance anyone came along the road by night, my dogs might do them an injury, so I chained them up outside the thorn enclosure instead of leaving them loose, as is my wont. You have seen the result; but do not blame the dogs, sahib, for in their efforts to save my goat their collars have bitten deep into their necks, and made wounds that will take many days to heal.'

While we were talking, an animal appeared on the crest of the hill on the far side of the Ganges. From its colour and size, I at first thought it was a Himalayan bear, but when it started to come down the hill towards the river, I saw it was a big wild boar. The pig was followed by a pack of village pye dogs, who in turn were followed by a rabble of boys and men, all armed with sticks of varying size. Last of all came a man carrying a gun. As this man crested the hill he raised his piece and we saw a puff of smoke, and a little later heard the dull report of a muzzle-loading gun. The only living things within range of the gun were the boys and men, but as none of them dropped out of the race, the sportsman appeared to have missed them.

The pig had a long grassy slope before him, with an odd bush dotted here and there, and below the grass slope was some broken ground, and below that again a dense belt of brushwood which extended right down to the river.

On the rough broken ground the pig lost his lead, and pig and pye dogs disappeared into the brushwood together. Next minute all the dogs, with the exception of the big light-coloured animal that had been leading the pack, dashed back out of the brushwood. When the boys and men arrived they appeared to urge the dogs to reenter the cover, but this—after apparently having recently seen what the pig could do with his tusks—they were unwilling to do. The man with the gun then arrived, and was immediately surrounded by the boys and men.

To us sitting on our elevated grandstand with the river flowing between, the scene being enacted on the farther hill was a silent picture, for the noise of the water deadened sound and all we had heard was the dull report of the muzzle-loader.

The sportsman was apparently as reluctant to enter the cover as the dogs were, for presently he broke away from his companions and sat down on a rock, as if to say, 'I have done my bit, now you do yours.' Confronted with this double dilemma—for the dogs, even after some of them had been beaten, stoutly refused to face the pig—first the boys and then the men started to throw stones into the brushwood.

While this was going on, we saw the pig emerge from the lower end of the brushwood on to a narrow strip of sand. With a few quick steps he came out into the open, stood perfectly still for a few seconds, took a few more steps, stopped again, and then with a little run plunged into the river. Pigs—the wild variety—are exceptionally good swimmers, and they do not cut their throats with their hooves while swimming, as is generally believed.

The current in the river was strong, but there is no bigger-hearted animal than our wild pig, and when I last saw the old boar he had been washed down the river a quarter of a mile, but was swimming strongly and was nearing our bank, which I have no doubt he reached safely.

'Was the pig within range of your rifle, sahib?' asked the packman.

'Yes,' I replied, 'the pig was within range, but I have not brought a rifle to Garhwal to shoot pigs that are running for their lives, but to shoot what you think is an evil spirit, and what I know is a leopard.'

'Have it your own way,' he rejoined; 'and now, as you are going, and we may never meet again, take my blessings with you, and time will prove whether you or I am right.'

I regret I never saw the packman again, for he was a grand old man, as proud as Lucifer, and as happy as the day was long, when leopards were not killing his best goats and when the courage of his dogs was not being questioned.

21

Vigil on a Pine-tree

Ibbotson returned to Pauri next day, and the following morning, when I was visiting the villages on the hill to the east of Rudra-prayag, I found the tracks of the man-eater on a path leading out of a village in which the previous night he had tried to break open the door of a house in which there was a child suffering from a bad cough. On following the tracks for a couple of miles they led me to the shoulder of the mountain where, some days previously, Ibbotson and I had sat up over the calling goat which the leopard later had killed.

It was still quite early, and as there was a chance of finding the leopard basking on one of the rocks in this considerable area of broken ground, I lay on a projecting rock that commanded an extensive view. It had rained the previous evening—thus enabling me to track the leopard—and washed the haze out of the atmosphere. Visibility was at its best and the view from the projecting rock was as good as could be seen in any part of the world where mountains rise to a height of twenty-three thousand feet. Immediately below me was the beautiful valley of the Alaknanda, with the river showing as a gleaming silver ribbon winding in and out of it. On the hill beyond the river, villages were dotted about, some with only a single thatched hut, and others with long rows of slate-roofed houses. These rows of buildings are in fact individual homesteads, built one against the other to save expense and to economize space, for the people are poor, and every foot of workable land in Garhwal is needed for agriculture.

Beyond the hills were rugged rock cliffs, down which avalanches roar in winter and early spring, and beyond and above the cliffs were the eternal snows, showing up against the intense blue sky as clear as if cut out of white cardboard. No more beautiful or peaceful scene could be imagined, and yet when the sun, now shining on the back of my head, set on the far side of the snow mountains, terror—terror which it is not possible to imagine until experienced—would grip, as it had done for eight long years, the area I was now overlooking.

I had been lying on the rock for an hour when two men came down the hill, on their way to the bazaar. They were from a village about a mile farther up the hill that I had visited the previous day, and they informed me that a little before sunrise they had heard a leopard calling in this direction. We discussed the possibilities of my getting a shot at the leopard over a goat, and as at that time I had no goats of my own, they offered to bring me one from their village and promised to meet me where we were standing, two hours before sunset.

When the men had gone I looked round for a place where I could sit. The only tree on the whole of this part of the mountain was a solitary pine. It was growing on the ridge close to the path down which the men had come, and from under it a second path took off and ran across the face of the mountain skirting the upper edge of the broken ground, where I had recently been looking for the leopard. The tree commanded an extensive view, but it could be difficult to climb, and would afford little cover. However, as it was the only tree in the area, I had no choice, so decided I would try it.

The men were waiting for me with a goat when I returned at about 4 p.m., and when, in reply to their question where I intended sitting, I pointed to the pine, they started laughing. Without a rope ladder, they said, it would not be possible to climb the tree; and further, if I succeeded in climbing the tree without a ladder, and carried out my intention of remaining out all night, I should have no protection against the man-eater, to whom the tree would offer no obstacle. There were two white men in Garhwal—Ibbotson was one of them—who had collected birds' eggs when boys, and both of whom could climb the tree; and as there is no exact equivalent in Hindustani for 'waiting until you come to a bridge before crossing it,' I let the second part of the men's objection go unanswered, contenting myself by pointing to my rifle.

The pine was not easy to climb, for there were no branches for twenty feet, but once having reached the lowest branch, the rest was easy. I had provided myself with a long length of cotton cord, and when the men had tied my rifle to one end of it, I drew it up and climbed to the top of the tree, where the pine-needles afforded most cover.

The men had assured me that the goat was a good caller, and after they tied it to an exposed root of the tree they set off for their village promising to return early next morning. The goat watched the men out of sight, and then started to nibble the short grass at the foot of the tree. The fact that it had not up to then called once did not worry me, for I felt sure that it would presently feel lonely and that it would then do its share of the business of the evening, and if it did it while it was still night, from my elevated position I should be able to kill the leopard long before it got anywhere near the goat.

When I climbed the tree the shadows cast by the snow mountains had reached the Alaknanda. Slowly these shadows crept up the hill and passed me, until only the top of the mountain glowed with red light. As this glow faded, long streamers of light shot up from the snow mountains where the rays of the setting sun were caught and held on a bank of clouds as soft and as light as thistledown. Everyone who has eyes to see a sunset—and the number, as you might have observed, is regrettably few—thinks that the sunsets in his particular part of the world are the best ever. I am no exception, for I too think that there are no sunsets in all the world to compare with ours, and a good second are the sunsets in northern Tanganyika, where some quality in the atmosphere makes snow-capped Kilimanjaro, and the clouds that are invariably above it, glow like molten gold in the rays of the setting sun. Our sunsets in the Himalayas are mostly red, pink, or gold. The one I was looking at that evening from my seat on the pine-tree was rose pink, and the white shafts of light, starting as spear-points from valleys in the cardboard snows, shot through the pink clouds and, broadening, faded out in the sky overhead.

The goat, like many human beings, had no interest in sunsets, and after nibbling the grass within reach, scratched a shallow hole for itself, lay down, curled up, and went to sleep. Here was a dilemma. I had counted on the animal now placidly sleeping below me to call up the leopard, and not once since I had first seen it had it opened its mouth, except to nibble grass, and now, having made itself comfortable, it would probably sleep throughout the night. To have left the tree at that hour in an attempt to return to the bungalow would have added one more to the number who deliberately commit suicide, and as I had to be doing something to kill the man-eater, and as—in the absence of a kill—one place was as good as another, I decided to stay where I was, and try to call up the leopard myself.

If I were asked what had contributed most to my pleasure during all the years that I have spent in Indian jungles, I would unhesitatingly say that I had derived most pleasure from a knowledge of the language, and the habits, of the jungle-folk. There is no universal language in the jungles; each species has its own language, and though the vocabulary of some is limited, as in the case of porcupines and vultures, the language of each species is understood by all the jungle-folk. The vocal chords of human beings are more adaptable than the vocal chords of any of the jungle-folk, with the one exception of the crested wire-tailed drongo, and for this reason it is possible for human beings to hold commune with quite a big range of birds and animals. The ability to speak the language of the jungle-folk, apart from adding an hundredfold to one's pleasure in the jungle, can, if so desired, be put to great use. One example will suffice.

Lionel Fortescue—up till recently a housemaster at Eton—and I were on a photographing and fishing tour in the Himalayas shortly after 1918, and we arrived one evening at a Forest Bungalow at the foot of a great mountain, on the far side of which was our objective, the Vale of Kashmir. We had been marching over hard ground for many days, and as the men carrying our luggage needed a rest, we decided to halt for a day at the bungalow. Next day, while Fortescue wrote up his notes, I set out to explore the mountain and try for a Kashmir stag. I had been informed by friends who had shot in Kashmir that it was not possible to shoot one of these stags without the help of an experienced *shikari*, and this was confirmed by the *Chowkidar* in charge of the Forest Bungalow. With the whole day before me I set out alone, after breakfast, without having the least idea at what elevation the red deer lived, or the kind of ground on which they were likely to be found. The mountain, over which there is a pass into Kashmir, is about twelve thousand feet high, and after I had climbed to a height of eight thousand a storm came on.

From the colour of the clouds I knew I was in for a hailstorm, so I selected with care a tree under which to shelter. I have seen both human beings and animals killed by hail, and by the lightning that invariably accompanies hailstorms, so rejecting the big fir-trees with tapering tops I selected a small tree with a rounded top and dense foliage, and collecting a supply of dead wood and fir-cones, I built a fire, and for the hour that the thunder roared overhead and the hail lashed down, I sat at the foot of my tree safe and warm.

The moment the hail stopped the sun came out, and from the shelter of the tree I stepped into fairyland, for the hail that carpeted the ground gave off a million points of light to which every glistening leaf and blade of grass added its quota. Continuing up for another two or three thousand feet, I came on an outcrop of rock, at the foot of which was a bed of blue mountain poppies. The stalks of many of these, the most beautiful of all wild flowers in the Himalayas, were broken, even so these sky-blue flowers standing in a bed of spotless white were a never-to-be-forgotten sight.

The rocks were too slippery to climb, and there appeared to be no object in going to the top of the hill, so keeping to the contours I went to the left, and after half a mile through a forest of giant fir-trees I came to a grassy slope which, starting from the top of the hill, extended several thousand feet down into the forest. As I came through the trees towards this grassy slope I saw on the far side of it an animal standing on a little knoll, with its tail towards me. From illustrations seen in game books I knew the animal was a red Kashmir deer, and when it raised its head, I saw it was a hind.

On my side of the grassy slope, and about thirty yards from the edge of the forest, there was a big isolated rock some four feet high; the distance between this rock and the knoll was about forty yards. Moving only when the deer was cropping the grass, and remaining still each time she raised her head, I crept up to the shelter of the rock. The hind was quite obviously a sentinel, and from the way she looked to her right each time she raised her head, I knew she had companions, and the exact direction in which these companions were. To approach any nearer over the grass without being seen was not possible. To re-enter the forest and work down from above would not have been difficult but would have defeated my purpose, for the wind was blowing down the hill. There remained the alternative of re-entering the forest and skirting round the lower end of

the grass slope, but this would take time and entail a stiff climb. I therefore finally decided to remain where I was and see if these deer—which I was seeing for the first time—would react in the same way as chital and sambhur do to the call of a leopard, of which I knew there was at least one on the mountain, for I had seen its scratch-marks earlier in the day. With only one eye showing, I waited until the hind was cropping the grass, and then gave the call of a leopard.

At the first sound of my voice the hind swung round and, facing me, started to strike the ground with her forefeet. This was a warning to her companions to be on the alert, but those companions whom I wanted to see would not move until the hind called, and this she would not do until she saw the leopard. I was wearing a brown tweed coat, and projecting a few inches of my left shoulder beyond the rock I moved it up and down. The movement was immediately detected by the hind, who, taking a few quick steps forward, started to call; the danger she had warned her companions of was in sight, and it was now safe for them to join her. The first to come was a yearling, which, stepping daintily over the hail-covered ground, ranged itself along side the hind; the yearling was followed by three stags, who in turn were followed by an old hind. The entire herd, numbering six in all, were now in full view at a range of thirty-five yards. The hind was still calling, while the others, with ears alternately held rigid or feeling forward and backward for sound and wind direction, were standing perfectly still and gazing into the forest behind me. My seat on the melting hail was uncomfortable and wet, and to remain inactive longer would possibly result in a cold. I had seen a representative herd of the much-famed Kashmir deer, and I had heard a hind call, but there was one thing more that I wanted. That was, to hear a stag call; so I again projected a few inches of my shoulder beyond the rock, and had the satisfaction of hearing the stags, the hinds, and the yearling calling in different pitched keys.

My pass permitted me to shoot one stag, and for all I knew one of the stags might have carried a record head, but though I had set out that morning to look for a stag, and procure meat for the camp, I now realized that I was in no urgent need of a trophy. In any case the stag's meat would probably be tough so, instead of using the rifle, I stood up, and six of the most surprised deer in Kashmir vanished out of sight, and a moment later I heard them crashing through the undergrowth on the far side of the knoll.

It was now time for me to retrace my steps to the bungalow, and I decided to go down the grassy slope and work through the lighter forest at the foot of the mountain. The slope was at an angle that lent itself to an easy lope, provided care was taken to see that every step was correctly placed. I was running in the middle of the hundred-yard open ground and had gone about six hundred yards when I caught sight of a white object, standing on a rock at the edge of the forest on the left-hand side of the slope, and about three hundred yards below me. A hurried glance convinced me that the white object was a goat, that had probably been lost in the forest. We had been without meat for a fortnight and I had promised Fortescue that I would bring something back with me, and here was my opportunity. The goat had seen me, and if I could disarm suspicion would possibly let me pass close enough to catch it by the legs; so as I loped along I edged to the left, keeping the animal in sight out of the corner of my eyes. Provided the animal stayed where it was, no better place on all the mountain could have been found on which to catch it, for the flat rock, at the very edge of which it was standing, jutted out into the slope, and was about five feet high. Without looking directly at it, and keeping up a steady pace, I ran past the rock and, as I did so, made a sweep with my left hand for its forelegs. With a sneeze of alarm the animal reared up, avoiding my grasp, and when I pulled up clear of the rock and turned round, I saw to my amazement that the animal I had mistaken for a white goat was an albino musk-deer. With only some ten feet between us the game little animal was standing its ground and sneezing defiance at me. Turning away I walked down the hill for fifty yards, and when I looked back, the deer was still standing on the rock, possibly congratulating itself on having frightened me away. When some weeks later I related the occurrence to the Game Warden of Kashmir he expressed great regret at my not having shot the deer, and was very anxious to know the exact locality in which I had seen it, but as my memory for places, and my description of localities, is regrettably faulty, I do not think that particular albino musk-deer is gracing any museum.

It is possible that my assertion that the six deer, as they stood on the knoll, were feeling for sound *and wind direction* with their ears will be questioned. Even so, I maintain that not only deer, but that all other animals—that live above ground—determine wind direction with their ears. My life has often depended on my knowing to a nicety the exact direction in which wind was blowing, and just as I have always relied on my ears to provide me with this information, so also do wild animals rely on their ears to provide them with the same information. Human beings can, and do employ several quite unnecessary methods, as, for instance, a pinch of dust, cigarette smoke, licking a finger, and so on, to find in which direction wind is blowing, but these methods are not available to animals, who rely entirely on the means nature has provided them with, namely, their ears.

Male leopards are very resentful of intrusion of others of their kind in the area they consider to be their own. True, the man-eater's territory extended over an area of five hundred square miles in which there were possibly many other male leopards; still, he had been in this particular area for several weeks, and might very reasonably consider it his own. And again, the mating season was only just over, and the leopard might mistake my call for the call of a female in search of a mate, so waiting until it was quite dark I called and, to my surprise and delight, was immediately answered by a leopard some four hundred yards below and a little to the right.

The ground between us was strewn with great rocks and overgrown with matted thornbushes, and I knew the leopard would not come in a straight line towards me, and that he would probably skirt round the broken ground and come up a subsidiary ridge to the one my tree was on; this I found, when next he called, that he was doing. Five minutes later I located his call as coming from the path that, starting from my tree, ran across the face of the hill, about two hundred yards away. This call I answered, to give the leopard direction. Three, or it may have been four, minutes later, he called again from a distance of a hundred yards.

It was a dark night and I had an electric torch lashed to the side of my rifle, and my thumb on the push button. From the root of the tree the path ran in a straight line for fifty yards, to where there was a sharp bend in it. It would not be possible for me to know when or where to direct the beam of the torch on this part of the path, so I should have to wait until the leopard was on the goat.

Just beyond the bend, and only sixty yards away, the leopard again called and was answered by another leopard far up the mountain-side. A complication as unexpected as it was unfortunate, for my leopard was too close now for me to call, and as he had last heard me from a distance of two hundred yards he would naturally assume that the coy female had removed herself farther up the hill and was calling to him to join her there. There was, however, just a possibility of his continuing along the path to its junction with the path coming down the hill, in which case he would be sure to kill the goat, even if he had no use for it. But the goat's luck was in, and mine out, for the leopard cut across the angle formed by the two paths, and the next time he called he was a hundred yards farther from me, and a hundred yards nearer his prospective coaxing mate. The calling of the two leopards drew nearer and nearer together, and finally stopped. After a long period of silence the caterwauling of these two giant cats came floating down to me from where I judged the grassland ended and the dense forest began.

The leopard's luck too was unfortunately in, in more ways than one, not least of all because it was dark, for leopards when courting are very easy to shoot. The same can be said of tigers, but the sportsman who goes on foot to look for courting tigers should be quite sure that he wants to see them, for a tigress—never a tiger—is very sensitive at these times, and quite understandably so, for males of the cat tribe are rough in their courting, and do not know how sharp their claws are.

The leopard had not died, nor would he die that night but maybe he would die the next day, or the day after, for his sands were running out; and so for a long moment I thought were mine, for without any warning a sudden blast of wind struck the tree, and my heels and my head changed their relative position with the land of Garhwal. For seconds I thought it impossible for the tree to re-gain its upright position, or for me to retain contact with it. When the pressure eased, the tree and I got back to where we were before the wind struck us, and fearing that worse might follow, I hurriedly tied the rifle to a branch, to have the use of both hands. The pine had possibly withstood many wind-storms equally bad, if not worse, but never with a human being on it to add weight and increase wind-pressure. When the rifle was safe, I climbed out on to one branch after another, and broke off all the tassels of pine-needles that I could reach. It may only have been my imagination, but after I had lightened the tree it did not appear to heel over as dangerously as it had at first done. Fortunately the pine was comparatively young and supple, and its roots firm set, for it was tossed about like a blade of grass for an hour and then, as suddenly as it had started, the wind died down. There was no possibility of the leopard returning, so, after I had smoked a cigarette, I followed the goat into the land of dreams.

As the sun was rising a *cooee* brought me back to within fifty feet of earth, and under the tree were my two companions of the previ-ous evening, reinforced by two youths from their village. When they saw that I was awake they asked whether I had heard the leopards during the night, and what had happened to the tree, and were hugely amused when I told them I had had a friendly conversation with the leopards, and that having nothing else to do I had amused myself by breaking the branches of the tree. I then asked them if by chance they had noticed that there had been some little wind during the night, on which one of the youths answered, 'A little wind, sahib! Such a big wind has never been known, and it has blown away my hut!' To which his companion rejoined, 'That is no matter for regret, sahib, for Sher Singh has long been threatening to rebuild his hut, and the wind has saved him the trouble of dismantling the old one.'

22

My Night of Terror

For several days after my experience on the pine-tree I lost touch with the man-eater. He did not return to the broken ground and I found no trace of him, or of the female who had saved his life, in the miles of forest I searched on the high ground above the cultivated land. In these forests I was more at home, and if the leopards had been anywhere in them I should have been able to find them, for there were birds and animals in the forest that would have helped me.

The female, being restless, was quite evidently straying far from her home when she heard me call from the top of the pine-tree, and on being joined by the male had gone back to her own area, accompanied by the mate I had helped her to find. The male would presently return alone, and as the precautions now being taken by the people on the left bank were making it difficult for him to procure a human kill, he would probably try to cross over to the right bank of the Alaknanda, so for the next few nights I mounted guard on the Rudraprayag bridge.

There were three approaches to the bridge on the left bank, the one from the south passing close to the bridge *Chowkidar's* house, and on the fourth night I heard the leopard killing the *Chowkidar's* dog; a friendly nondescript little beast that used to run out and greet me every time I passed that way. The dog seldom barked, but that night it had been barking for five minutes when suddenly the bark ended in a yelp, followed by the shouting of the *Chowkidar* from inside his house, after which there was silence. The thornbushes had been removed from the archway and the bridge was open, yet though I lay with finger on trigger for the rest of the night the leopard did not try to cross.

After killing the dog and leaving it lying on the road, the leopard, as I found from his tracks next morning, came to the tower. Five more steps in the direction in which he was going would have brought him out on the bridge, but those five steps he did not take. Instead he turned to the right, and after going a short distance up the footpath towards the bazaar, he returned and went up the pilgrim road to the north. A mile up the road I lost his tracks.

Two days later I received a report that a cow had been killed the previous evening, seven miles up the pilgrim road. It was suspected that the cow had been killed by the man-eater, for the previous night—the night the dog had been killed—the leopard had tried to break open the door of a house close to where, the next evening, the cow had been killed.

On the road I found a number of men waiting for me who, knowing that the walk up from Rudraprayag would be a hot one, had very thoughtfully provided a dish of tea. While we sat in the shade of a mango-tree and smoked, and I drank the dish of tea, they told me that the cow had not returned with the herd the previous evening, and that it had been found between the road and the river when a search had been made for it that morning. They also told me of the many hairbreadth escapes each of them had had from the man-eater during the past eight years. I was very interested to learn from them that the leopard had only adopted his present habit of trying—and in many cases succeeding—to break open the doors of houses three years previously, and that before he had been content to take people who were outside their houses, or from houses the doors of which had been left open. 'Now,' they said, 'the *Shaitan* has become so bold that sometimes when he has not been able to break down the door of a house, he has dug a hole through the mud wall, and got at his victims in that way.'

To those who do not know our hill-people, or understand their fear of the supernatural, it will seem incredible that a people renowned for their courage, and who have won the highest awards on the field of battle, should permit a leopard to break open a door, or to dig a hole in a wall of a house, in which in many cases there must have been men with axes, *kukris*, or even in some cases firearms at hand. I know of only one case in all those eight long years in which resistance was offered to the man-eater, and in that case the resister was a woman. She was sleeping alone in a house, the door of which she had left unfastened; this door, as in the case of the door of the house occupied by the woman who escaped with a lacerated arm, opened inwards. On entering the room the leopard seized the woman's left leg, and as it dragged her across the room the woman's hand came in contact with a *gandesa*—a tool used for chopping chaff for cattle—and with this the woman dealt the leopard a blow. The leopard did not release his hold, but backed out of the room, and as it did so either the woman pushed the door to, or else this happened accidentally. Whichever it may have been, with the woman on one side of the door and the leopard on the other, the leopard exerted its great strength and tore the limb from the woman's body. Mukandi Lal, at that time Member for Garhwal in the United Provinces Legislative Council, who was on an electioneering tour, arrived in the village the following day and spent a night in the room, but the leopard did not return. In a report to the Council Mukandi Lal stated that seventy-five human beings had been killed by the leopard in the course of that one year, and he asked the Government to launch a vigorous campaign against the man-eater.

Accompanied by one of the villagers to show me the way, and by Madho Singh, I went down to the kill. The cow had been killed in a deep ravine a quarter of a mile from the road and a hundred yards from the river. On one side of the ravine there were big rocks with dense brushwood between, and on the other side of the ravine there were a few small trees, none of which was big enough to sit in. Under the trees, and about thirty yards from the kill, there was a rock with a little hollow at the base of it, so in the hollow I decided to sit.

Both Madho Singh and the villager objected very strongly to my sitting on the ground, but as this was the first animal kill I had got since my arrival at Rudraprayag in a place where it was reasonable to expect the leopard to come at an early hour—about sundown— I overruled their objections, and sent them back to the village.

My seat was dry and comfortable, and with my back to the rock and a small bush to conceal my legs I was confident the leopard would not see me, and that I should be able to kill it before it was aware of my presence. I had provided myself with a torch and a knife, and with my good rifle across my knees I felt that in this secluded spot my chances of killing the leopard were better than any I had yet had.

Without movement and with my eyes on the rocks in front of me I sat through the evening, each second bringing the time nearer when the undisturbed and unsuspecting leopard would to a certainty return to his kill. The time I had been waiting for had come, and was passing. Objects near at hand were beginning to get blurred and indistinct. The leopard was a little later in coming than I had expected him to be, but that was not worrying me, for I had a torch, and the kill was only thirty yards from me, and I would be careful over my shot and make quite sure that I did not have a wounded animal to deal with.

In the deep ravine there was absolute silence. The hot sun of the past few days had made the dead leaves on the bank on which I was sitting as dry as tinder. This was very reassuring, for it was now dark and whereas previously I had depended on my eyes for protection I now had to depend on my ears, and with thumb on the button of the torch and finger on trigger I was prepared to shoot in any direction in which I heard the slightest sound.

The non-appearance of the leopard was beginning to cause me uneasiness. Was it possible that from some concealed place among the rocks he had been watching me all these hours, and was he now licking his lips in anticipation of burying his teeth in my throat?—for he had long been deprived of human flesh. In no other way could I account for his not having come, and if I were to have the good fortune to leave the ravine on my feet, my ears would have to serve me now as they had never served me before.

For what seemed like hours I strained my ears and then, noticing it was getting darker than it should have been, I turned my eyes up to the sky and saw that a heavy bank of clouds was drifting across the sky, obscuring the stars one by one. Shortly thereafter big drops of rain started to fall, and where there had been absolute and complete silence there was now sound and movement all round—the opportunity the leopard had been waiting for had come. Hastily taking off my coat I wound it round my neck, fastening it securely in place with the sleeves. The rifle was now useless but might help to cause a diversion, so transferring it to my left hand I unsheathed my knife and got a good grip of it with my right hand. The knife was what is called an Afridi stabbing knife, and I devoutly hoped it would serve me as well as it had served its late owner, for when buying it from the Government store at Hangu on the North-west Frontier, the Deputy Commissioner had drawn my attention to a label attached to it and to three notches on the handle, and said it had figured in three murders. Admittedly a gruesome relic, but I was glad to have it in my hand, and I clutched it tight while the rain lashed down.

Leopards, that is ordinary forest leopards, do not like rain and invariably seek shelter, but the man-eater was not an ordinary leopard, and there was no knowing what his likes or dislikes were, or what he might or might not do.

When Madho Singh was leaving he asked how long I intended sitting up, and I had answered 'Until I have shot the leopard,' so I could expect no help from him, and of help I was at that time in urgent need. Should I go or should I remain were the questions that were exercising me, and the one was as unattractive as the other. If the leopard up to then had not seen me it would be foolish to give my position away, and possibly fall across him on the difficult ground I should have to negotiate on my way up to the pilgrim road. On the other hand to remain where I was for another six hours—momentarily expecting to have to fight for my life with an unfamiliar weapon—would put a strain on my nerves which they were not capable of standing; so getting to my feet and shouldering the rifle, I set off.

I had not far to go, only about five hundred yards, half of which was over wet clay and the other half over rocks worn smooth with bare feet and the hooves of cattle. Afraid to use the torch for fear of attracting the man-eater, and with one hand occupied with the rifle and the other with the knife, my body made as many contacts with the ground as my rubber-shod feet. When I eventually reached the road I sent a full-throated *cooee* into the night, and a moment later I saw a door in the village far up the hillside open and Madho Singh and his companion emerge, carrying a lantern.

When the two men joined me Madho Singh said he had had no uneasiness about me until the rain started, and that he had then lit the lantern, and sat with his ear against the door listening. Both men were willing to accompany me back to Rudraprayag, so we set out on our seven-mile walk, Bachi Singh leading, Madho Singh carrying the lantern following, and I bringing up the rear. When I returned next day I found the kill had not been touched, and on the road I found the tracks of the man-eater. What time had elapsed between our going down the road and the man-eater following us, it was not possible to say.

When I look back on that night, I look back on it as my night of terror. I have been frightened times without number, but never have I been frightened as I was that night when the unexpected rain came down and robbed me of all my defences, and left me for protection a murder's knife.

23

Leopard Fights Leopard

After following us to Rudraprayag the leopard went down the pilgrim road through Golabrai, past the ravine up which he had gone a few days previously, and then up a rough track which the people living on the hills to the east of Rudraprayag use as a short cut on their way to and from Hardwar.

The pilgrimage to Kedarnath and Badrinath is seasonal, and the commencement of the pilgrimage and its duration depend in the one case on the melting, and in the other on the falling, of snow in the upper reaches of the high mountains in which these two shrines are situated. The High Priest of Badrinath temple had a few days previously sent the telegram that is eagerly awaited by good Hindus throughout the length and breadth of India, announcing that the road was open, and for the past few days pilgrims in small numbers had been passing through Rudraprayag.

During the past few years the man-eater had killed several pilgrims on the road, and it appeared to be his more or less regular habit while the pilgrim season lasted to go down the road to the extent of his beat, and then circle round through the villages on the hills to the east of Rudraprayag, and rejoin the road anything up to fifteen miles above Rudraprayag. The time taken for this round trip varied, but on an average I had seen the leopard's tracks on the stretch of road between Rudraprayag and Golabrai once in every five days, so on my way back to the Inspection Bungalow I selected a place from where I could overlook the road, and for the next two nights sat in great comfort on a hayrick, without however seeing anything of the leopard.

I received no news of the man-eater from outlying villages for two days, and on the third morning I went down the pilgrim road for six miles to try to find out if he had recently visited any of the villages in that direction. From this twelve-mile walk I returned at midday, and while I was having a late breakfast two men arrived and reported that a boy had been killed the previous evening at Bhainswara, a village eighteen miles south-east of Rudraprayag.

The intelligence system introduced by Ibbotson was working splendidly. Under this system cash rewards, on a graduated scale, were paid for information about all kills in the area in which the man-eater was operating. These rewards, starting with two rupees for a goat and working up to twenty rupees for a human being, were keenly contested for, and so ensured our receiving information about all kills in the shortest time possible.

When I put ten rupees into the hands of each of the men who had brought me news about the boy, one of them offered to accompany me back to Bhainswara to show me the way, while the other said he would stay the night at Rudraprayag as he had recently had fever and could not do another eighteen miles that day. I finished breakfast while the men were telling me their tale, and a little before 1 p.m. I set off, taking only my rifle, a few cartridges, and a torch with me. As we crossed the road near the Inspection Bungalow and started up the steep hill on the far side of it, my companion informed me we had a very long way to go, adding that it would not be safe for us to be out after dark, so I told him to walk ahead and set the pace. I never—if I can help it—walk uphill immediately after a meal, but here I had no option, and for the first three miles, in which we climbed four thousand feet, I had great difficulty in keeping up with my guide. A short stretch of comparatively flat ground at the end of the three miles gave me back my wind, and after that I walked ahead and set the pace.

On their way to Rudraprayag the two men had told the people in the villages they had passed through about the kill, and of their intention to try and persuade me to accompany them back to Bhainswara. I do not think that anyone doubted that I would answer to the call, for at every village the entire population were waiting for me, and while some gave me their blessings, others begged me not to leave the district until I had killed their enemy.

My companion had assured me that we had eighteen miles to go, and as we crested hill after hill with deep valleys between I realized I had undertaken to walk against time eighteen of the longest and hardest miles I had ever walked. The sun was near setting when, from the crest of one of these unending hills, I saw a number of men standing on a ridge a few hundred yards ahead of us. On catching sight of us some of the men disappeared over the edge, while others came forward to meet us. The headman of Bhainswara was among the latter, and after he had greeted me, he cheered me by telling me that his village was just over the crest of the hill, and that he had sent his son back to get tea ready.

The 14th of April 1926 is a date that will long be remembered in Garhwal, for it was on that day that the man-eating leopard of Rudraprayag killed his last human victim. On the evening of that day a widow and her two children, a girl aged nine and a boy aged twelve, accompanied by a neighbour's son aged eight, went to a spring a few yards from Bhainswara village to draw water for the preparation of their evening meal.

The widow and her children occupied a house in the middle of a long row of homesteads. These homesteads were double-storied, the low-ceilinged ground floor being used for the storage of grain and fuel, and the first floor for residences. A veranda four feet wide ran the entire length of the building, and short flights of stone steps flanked with walls gave access to the veranda, each flight of steps being used by two families. A flagged courtyard, sixty feet wide and three hundred feet long, bordered by a low wall, extended along the whole length of the building.

The neighbour's son was leading as the party of four approached the steps used by the widow and her children, and as the boy started to mount the steps he saw an animal, which he mistook for a dog, lying in an open room on the ground floor adjoining the steps; he said nothing about the animal at the time, and the others apparently did not see it. The boy was followed by the girl, the widow came next, and her son brought up the rear. When she was half-way up the short flight of stone steps, the mother heard the heavy brass vessel her son was carrying crash on the steps and go rolling down them; reprimanding him for his carelessness, she set her own vessel down on the veranda and turned to see what damage her son had done.

At the bottom of the steps she saw the overturned vessel. She went down and picked it up, and then looked round for her son. As he was nowhere in sight she assumed he had got frightened and had run away, so she started calling to him.

Neighbours in adjoining houses had heard the noise made by the falling vessel and now, hearing the mother calling to her son, they came to their doors and asked what all the trouble was about. It was suggested that the boy might be hiding in one of the ground-floor rooms, so as it was now getting dark in these rooms, a man lit a lantern and came down the steps towards the woman, and as he did so he saw drops of blood on the flagstones where the woman was standing. At the sound of the man's horrified ejaculation other people descended into the courtyard, among whom was an old man who had accompanied his master on many shooting expeditions. Taking the lantern from the owner's hand, this old man followed the blood trail across the courtyard and over the low wall. Beyond the wall was a drop of eight feet into a yam field; here in the soft earth were the splayed-out pug marks of a leopard. Up to that moment no one suspected that the boy had been carried off by a man-eater, for though everyone had heard about the leopard it had never previously been within ten miles of their village. As soon as they realized what had happened the women began screaming and while some men ran to their houses for drums, others ran for guns—of which there were three in the village—and in a few minutes pandemonium broke out. Throughout the night drums were beaten and guns were fired. At daylight the boy's body was recovered, and two men were dispatched to Rudraprayag to inform me.

As I approached the village in company with the headman, I heard the wailing of a woman mourning her dead. It was the mother of the victim, and she was the first to greet me. Even to my unpractised eye it was apparent that the bereaved mother had just weathered one hysterical storm and was heading for another, and as I lack the art of dealing with people in this condition I was anxious to spare the woman a recital of the events of the previous evening; but she appeared to be eager to give me her version of the story, so I let her have her way. As the story unfolded itself it was apparent that her object in telling it was to ventilate her grievance against the men of the village for not having run after the leopard and rescued her son 'as his father would have done had he been alive.' In her accusation against the men I told her she was unjust, and in her belief that her son could have been rescued alive, I told her she was wrong.

For when the leopard clamped his teeth round the boy's throat, the canine teeth dislocated the head from the neck and the boy was already dead before the leopard carried him across the courtyard, and nothing the assembled men—or anyone else—could have done would have been of any use.

Standing in the courtyard drinking the tea that had thoughtfully been provided for me, and noting the hundred or more people who were gathered round, it was difficult to conceive how an animal the size of a leopard had crossed the courtyard in daylight without being seen by any of the people who must have been moving about at that time, or how its presence had gone undetected by the dogs in the village.

I climbed down the eight-foot wall that the leopard carrying the boy had jumped down, and followed the drag across the yam field, down another wall twelve feet high, and across another field. At the edge of this second field there was a thick hedge of rambler roses four feet high. Here the leopard had released his hold on the boy's throat, and after searching for an opening in the hedge and not finding one, he had picked the boy up by the small of the back and, leaping the hedge, gone down a wall ten feet high on the far side. There was a cattle track at the foot of this third wall and the leopard had only gone a short distance along it when the alarm was raised in the village. The leopard had then dropped the boy on the cattle track and gone down the hill. He was prevented from returning to his kill by the beating of drums and the firing of guns which had gone on all night in the village.

The obvious thing for me to have done would have been to carry the body of the boy back to where the leopard had left it, and to have sat over it there. But here I was faced with two difficulties —the absence of a suitable place in which to sit, and my aversion to sitting in an unsuitable place.

The nearest tree, a leafless walnut, was three hundred yards away, and was therefore out of the question, and quite frankly I lacked the courage to sit on the ground. I had arrived at the village at sundown; it had taken a little time to drink the tea, hear the mother's story, and trail the leopard, and there was not sufficient daylight left for me to construct a shelter that would have given me even the semblance of protection; therefore if I sat on the ground I should have to sit just anywhere, not knowing from what direction the leopard would come, and knowing full well that if the leopard attacked me I should get no opportunity of using the one weapon with which I was familiar, my rifle, for when in actual contact with an unwounded leopard or tiger it is not possible to use firearms.

When after my tour of inspection I returned to the courtyard, I asked the headman for a crowbar, a stout wooden peg, a hammer, and a dog chain. With the crowbar I prised up one of the flagstones in the middle of the courtyard, drove the peg firmly into the ground, and fastened one end of the chain to it. Then with the help of the headman I carried the body of the boy to the peg, and chained it there.

The working of the intangible force which sets a period to life, which one man calls Fate and another calls Kismet, is incomprehensible. During the past few days this force had set a period to the life of a breadwinner, leaving his family destitute; had ended in a very painful way the days of an old lady who after a lifetime of toil was looking forward to a few short years of comparative comfort; and now, had cut short the life of this boy who, by the look of him, had been nurtured with care by his widowed mother. Small wonder then that the bereaved mother should, in between her hysterical crying, be repeating over and over and over again, 'What crime, *Parmeshwar*, has my son, who was loved by all, committed, that on the threshold of life he has deserved death in this terrible way?'

Before prising up the flagstone, I had asked for the mother and her daughter to be taken to a room at the very end of the row of buildings. My preparations completed, I washed at the spring and asked for a bundle of straw, which I laid on the veranda in front of the door of the house vacated by the mother.

Darkness had now fallen. Having asked the assembled people to be as silent during the night as it was possible for them to be and sent them to their respective homes, I took up my position on the veranda, where by lying prone on my side and heaping a little straw in front, I could get a clear view of the kill without much chance of being seen myself.

In spite of all the noise that had been made the previous night, I had a feeling that the leopard would return, and that when he failed to find his kill where he had left it, he would come to the village to try to secure another victim.

The ease with which he had got his first victim at Bhainswara would encourage him to try again, and I started my vigil with high hopes.

Heavy clouds had been gathering all the evening, and at 8 p.m., when all the village sounds—except the wailing of the woman— were hushed, a flash of lightning followed by a distant roll of thunder heralded an approaching storm. For an hour the storm raged, the lightning being so continuous and brilliant that had a rat ventured into the courtyard I should have seen and probably been able to shoot it. The rain eventually stopped but, the sky remaining overcast, visibility was reduced to a few inches. The time had now come for the leopard to start from wherever he had been sheltering from the storm, and the time of his arrival would depend on the distance of that place from the village.

The woman had now stopped wailing, and in all the world there appeared to be no sound. This was as I had hoped, for all I had to warn me that the leopard had come were my ears, and to help them I had used the dog chain instead of a rope.

The straw that had been provided for me was as dry as tinder and my ears, straining into the black darkness, first heard the sound

when it was level with my feet—something was creeping, very
stealthily creeping, over the straw on which I was lying. I was wearing an article of clothing called shorts, which left my legs bare in the
region of my knees. Presently, against this bare skin, I felt the hairy
coat of an animal brushing. It could only be the man-eater, creeping up until he could lean over and get a grip of my throat. A little
pressure now on my left shoulder—to get a foothold—and then,
just as I was about to press the trigger of the rifle to cause a diversion, a small animal jumped down between my arms and my chest.
It was a little kitten, soaking wet, that had been caught out in the
storm and, finding every door shut, had come to me for warmth
and protection.

The kitten had hardly made itself comfortable inside my coat,
and I was just beginning to recover from the fright it had given me,
when from beyond the terraced fields there was some low growling
which gradually grew louder, and then merged into the most savage
fight I have ever heard. Quite evidently the man-eater had returned
to the spot where the previous night he had left his kill, and while
he was searching for it, in not too good a temper, another male leopard who looked upon this particular area as his hunting-ground, had
accidentally come across him and set on him. Fights of the nature
of the one that was taking place in hearing of me are very unusual,
for carnivora invariably keep to their own areas, and if by chance
two of a sex happen to meet, they size up each other's capabilities at
a glance, and the weaker gives way to the stronger.

The man-eater, though old, was a big and a very powerful male,
and in the five hundred square miles he ranged over there was possibly no other male capable of disputing his rule, but here at Bhainswara he was a stranger and a trespasser, and to get out of the trouble
he had brought on himself he would have to fight for his life. And
this he was undoubtedly doing.

My chance of getting a shot had now gone, for even if the
man-eater succeeded in defeating his attacker, his injuries would

probably prevent him from taking any interest in kills for some time to come. There was even a possibility of the fight ending fatally for him, and here would indeed be an unexpected end to his career: killed in an accidental encounter by one of his own kind, when the combined efforts of the Government and the public had failed, over a period of eight years, to accomplish this end.

The first round, lasting about five minutes, was fought with un-abating savagery, and was inconclusive, for at the end of it I could still hear both animals. After an interval of ten or fifteen minutes the fight was resumed, but at a distance of two to three hundred yards from where it had originally started; quite evidently the local champion was getting the better of the fight and was gradually driving the intruder out of the ring. The third round was shorter than the two that had preceded it, but was no less savage, and when after another long period of silence the fight was again resumed, the scene had receded to the shoulder of the hill, where after a few minutes it died out of hearing.

There were still six hours of darkness left; even so I knew my mission to Bhainswara had failed, and that my hope that the fight would be fought to a finish and would end in the death of the man-eater had been short-lived. In the running fight into which the contest had now degenerated the man-eater would sustain injuries, but they were not likely to reduce his craving for human flesh or impair his ability to secure it.

The kitten slept peacefully throughout the night, and as the first streak of dawn showed in the east I descended into the courtyard and carried the boy to the shed from where we had removed him, and covered him with the blanket which previously had been used for the purpose. The headman was still asleep when I knocked on his door. I declined the tea, which I knew would take some time to make, and assured him that the man-eater would never again visit his village; and when he had promised to make immediate arrangements to have the boy carried to the burning-*ghat*, I set off on my long walk back to Rudraprayag.

No matter how often we fail in any endeavour, we never get used to the feeling of depression that assails us after each successive failure. Day after day over a period of months I had left the Inspection Bungalow full of hope that on this particular occasion I would meet with success, and day after day I had returned disappointed and depressed. Had my failures only concerned myself they would not have mattered, but in the task I had undertaken those failures concerned others more than they concerned me. Bad luck—for to nothing else could I attribute my failures—was being meted out to me in ever-increasing measure, and the accumulated effect was beginning to depress me and give me the feeling that I was not destined to do what I had set out to do. What but bad luck had made the man-eater drop his kill where there were no trees ? And what but bad luck had made a leopard who possibly had thirty square miles in which to wander, arrive at a particular spot in those thirty miles just as the man-eater, not finding his kill where he had left it, was quite conceivably on his way to the village where I was waiting for him?

The eighteen miles had been long yesterday but they were longer today, and the hills were steeper. In the villages I passed through the people were eagerly awaiting me, and though I only had bad news they did not show their disappointment. Their boundless faith in their philosophy, a faith strong enough to remove mountains, and very soothing to depressed feelings, that no human beings and no animals can die before their appointed time, and that the man-eater's time had not yet come, called for no explanation, and admitted of no argument.

Ashamed of the depression and feeling of frustration that I had permitted to accompany me throughout the morning, I left the last village—where I had been made to halt and drink a cup of tea—greatly cheered, and as I swung down the last four miles to Rudraprayag I became aware that I was treading on the pug marks of the man-eater. Strange how one's mental condition can dull, or sharpen, one's powers of observation. The man-eater had quite possibly joined the track many miles farther back, and now, after my conversation with the simple village-folk—and a drink of tea—I was seeing his pug marks for the first time that morning. The track here ran over red clay which the rain had softened, and the pug marks of the man-eater showed that he was walking at his accustomed pace. Half a mile farther on he started to quicken his pace, and this pace he continued to maintain until he reached the head of the ravine above Golabrai; down this ravine the leopard had gone.

When a leopard or tiger is walking at its normal pace only the imprints of the hind feet are seen, but when the normal pace is for any reason exceeded, the hind feet are placed on the ground in advance of the forefeet, and thus the imprints of all four feet are seen. From the distance between the imprints of the fore and the hind feet it is possible to determine the speed at which an animal of the cat tribe was travelling. The coming of daylight would in this instance have been sufficient reason for the man-eater to have quickened his pace.

I had previously had experience of the man-eater's walking capabilities, but only when ranging his beat in search of food. Here he had a better reason for the long walk he had undertaken, for he was anxious to put as great a distance as possible between himself and the leopard who had given him a lesson in the law of trespass; how severe that lesson had been will be apparent from a description given later.

24

A Shot in the Dark

Mealtimes in India vary according to the season of the year and individual tastes. In most establishments the recognized times for the three principal meals are: breakfast 8 to 9, lunch 1 to 2, and dinner 8 to 9. During all the months I was at Rudraprayag my mealtimes were very erratic, and contrary to the accepted belief that health depends on the composition and regularity of meals, my unorthodox and irregular meals kept me fighting fit. Porridge supped at 8 p.m., soup taken at 8 a.m., one combined meal in the day or no meal at all, appeared to have no injurious effect beyond taking a little flesh off my bones.

I had eaten nothing since my breakfast the previous day, so as I intended spending the night out I had a nondescript meal on my return from Bhainswara, and after an hour's sleep and a bath set off for Golabrai to warn the pundit who owned the pilgrim shelter of the presence in his vicinity of the man-eater.

I had made friends with the pundit on my first arrival at Rudraprayag and I never passed his house without having a few words with him, for in addition to the many interesting tales he had to tell about the man-eater and the pilgrims who passed through Golabrai, he was one of the only two people—the woman who escaped with the lacerated arm being the other—whom I met during my stay in Garhwal who had survived an encounter with the man-eater.

One of his tales concerned a woman who had lived in a village further down the road, and with whom he had been acquainted. After a visit to the Rudraprayag bazaar one day this woman arrived at Golabrai late in the evening, and fearing she would not be able to reach her home before dark she asked the pundit to let her spend the night in his shelter. This he permitted her to do, advising her to sleep in front of the door of the store-room in which he kept the articles of food purchased by the pilgrims, for, he said, she would then be protected by the room on the one side, and by the fifty or more pilgrims who were spending the night in the shelter on the other.

The shelter was a grass shed open on the side nearest the road, and boarded up on the side nearest the hill; the store-room was midway along the shed, but was recessed into the hill and did not obstruct the floor of the shed, so when the woman lay down at the door of the store-room there were rows of pilgrims between her and the road. Some time during the night one of the women pilgrims screamed out and said she had been stung by a scorpion. No lights were available, but with the help of matches the woman's foot was examined and a small scratch from which a little blood was flowing was found on her foot. Grumbling that the woman had made a lot of fuss about nothing, and that in any case blood did not flow from a scorpion sting, the pilgrims soon composed themselves and resumed their sleep.

In the morning, when the pundit arrived from his house on the hill above the mango-tree, he saw a *sari* worn by hill-women lying on the road in front of the shelter, and on the *sari* there was blood. The pundit had given his friend what he considered to be the safest place in the shelter, and with fifty or more pilgrims lying all round her the leopard had walked over the sleeping people, killed the woman, and accidentally scratched the sleeping pilgrim's foot when returning to the road. The explanation given by the pundit as to why the leopard had rejected the pilgrims and carried off the hill-woman was that she was the only person in the shelter that night who was wearing a coloured garment. This explanation is not convincing, and but for the fact that leopards do not hunt by scent, my own explanation would have been that of all the people in the shelter the hill-woman was the only one who had a familiar smell. Was it just bad luck, or fate, or being the only one of all the sleepers who realized the danger of sleeping in an open shed? Had the victim's fear in some inexplicable way conveyed itself to the man-eater, and attracted him to her?

It was not long after this occurrence that the pundit had his own encounter with the man-eater. The exact date—which could if desired be ascertained from the hospital records at Rudraprayag—is immaterial, and for the purpose of my story it will be sufficient to say that it took place during the hottest part of the summer of 1921, that is, four years before I met the pundit. Late one evening of that summer ten pilgrims from Madras arrived weary and footsore at Golabrai, and expressed their intention of spending the night in the pilgrim shelter. Fearing that if any more people were killed at Golabrai his shelter would get a bad reputation, the pundit tried to persuade them to continue on for another two miles to Rudraprayag, where they would be ensured of safe accommodation. Finding that nothing he could say had any effect on the tired pilgrims, he finally consented to give them accommodation in his house, which was fifty yards above the mango-tree to which I have already drawn attention.

The pundit's house was built on the same plan as the homesteads at Bhainswara; a low ground-floor room used for storage of fuel, and a first-floor room used as a residence. A short flight of stone steps gave access to a narrow veranda, the door of the residential room being opposite to the landing at the top of the steps.

After the pundit and the ten guests that had been forced on him had eaten their evening meal, they locked themselves into the room, which was not provided with any means of ventilation. The heat in the room was stifling, and fearing that he would be suffocated the pundit some time during the night opened the door, stepped outside, and stretched his hands to the pillars on either side of the steps supporting the roof of the veranda. As he did so and filled his lungs with the night air, his throat was gripped as in a vice. Retaining his hold on the pillars, he got the soles of his feet against the body of his assailant and with a desperate kick tore the leopard's teeth from his throat, and hurled it down the steps. Then, fearing that he was going to faint, he took a step sideways and supported himself by putting both hands on the railing of the veranda, and the moment he did so the leopard sprang up from below and buried its claws in his left forearm. The downward pull was counteracted by the railing on which the pundit had the palm of his hand, and the weight of the leopard caused its sharp claws to rip through the flesh of his arm until they tore free at his wrist. Before the leopard was able to spring a second time, the pilgrims, hearing the terrifying sounds the pundit was making in his attempts to breathe through the gap torn in his throat, dragged him into the room and bolted the door. For the rest of that long hot night the pundit lay gasping for breath and bleeding profusely, while the leopard growled and clawed at the frail door, and the pilgrims screamed with terror.

At daylight the pilgrims carried the pundit, now mercifully unconscious, to a Kalakamli hospital at Rudraprayag, where for three months he was fed through a silver tube inserted in his throat. After an absence of over six months he returned to his home in Golabrai, broken in health and with his hair turned grey. Photographs were taken five years later, and scarcely show the leopard's teeth-marks on the left side of the pundit's face and in his throat, and its claw-marks on his left arm, though they were still clearly visible.

In his conversations with me the pundit always referred to the man-eater as an evil spirit, and after the first day, when he had asked me what proof I could give him in face of his own experience that evil spirits could not assume material form, I also, to humour him, referred to the man-eater as 'the evil spirit.'

On arrival at Golabrai that evening I told the pundit of my fruit-less visit to Bhainswara, and warned him to take extra precautions for his safety and for the safety of any pilgrims who might be stay-ing in his shelter; for the evil spirit, after its long excursion into the hills, had now returned to the vicinity.

That night, and for the following three nights, I sat on the hay-stack, keeping a watch on the road; and on the fourth day Ibbotson returned from Pauri.

Ibbotson always infused new life into me, for his creed, like that of the locals, was that no one was to blame if the man-eater had not died yesterday, for surely it would die today or maybe tomorrow. I had a lot to tell him, for though I had corresponded with him reg-ularly—extracts from my letters being embodied in his reports to the Government, and by them made available to the press—I had not been able to give him all the details which he was now eager to hear. On his part Ibbotson also had a lot to tell me; this concerned the clamour being made in the press for the destruction of the man-eater, and the suggestion that sportsmen from all parts of India be encouraged to go to Garhwal to assist in killing the leopard. This press campaign had resulted in Ibbotson receiving only one inquiry, and only one suggestion. The inquiry was from a sportsman who said that, if arrangements for his travel, accommodation, food, and so on, were made to his satisfaction he would consider whether it was worth his while to come to Golabrai; and the suggestion was from a sportsman in whose opinion the speediest and easiest way of killing the leopard was to paint a goat over with arsenic, sew up its mouth to prevent it licking itself, and then tie it up in a place where the leopard would find and eat it, and so poison itself.

We talked long that day, reviewing my many failures in minutest detail, and by lunch-time, when I had told Ibbotson of the leopard's habit of going down the road between Rudraprayag and Golabrai on an average once in every five days, I convinced him that the only hope I now had of shooting the leopard was by sitting over the road for ten nights, for, as I pointed out to him, the leopard would be almost certain to use the road at least once during that period. Ibbotson consented to my plan very reluctantly, for I had already sat up many nights and he was afraid that another ten on end would be too much for me. However, I carried my point, and then told Ibbotson that if I did not succeed in killing the leopard within the stipulated time, I would return to Naini Tal and leave the field free for any new-comers who might consider it worth their while to take my place.

That evening Ibbotson accompanied me to Golabrai and helped me to put up a *machan* in the mango-tree a hundred yards from the pilgrim shelter and fifty yards below the pundit's house. Immediately below the tree, and in the middle of the road, we drove a stout wooden peg, and to this peg we tethered a goat with a small bell round its neck. The moon was nearly at its full; even so, the high hill to the east of Golabrai only admitted of the moon lighting up the deep Ganges valley for a few hours, and if the leopard came while it was dark the goat would warn me of his approach.

When all our preparations had been made Ibbotson returned to the bungalow, promising to send two of my men for me early next morning. While I sat on a rock near the foot of the tree and smoked and waited for evening to close down, the pundit came and sat down beside me; he was a *bhakti* and did not smoke. Earlier in the

evening he had seen us building the *machan*, and he now tried to
dissuade me from sitting all night in the tree when I could sleep
comfortably in bed. Nevertheless, I assured him I would sit all that
night in the tree, and for nine nights thereafter, for if I was not able
to kill the evil spirit I could at least guard his house and the pilgrim
shelter from attack from all enemies. Once during the night a kakar
barked on the hill above me, but thereafter the night was silent. At
sunrise next morning two of my men arrived, and I set off for the
Inspection Bungalow, examining the road as I went for pug marks,
and leaving the men to follow with my rug and rifle.

During the following nine days my programme did not vary.
Leaving the bungalow accompanied by two men in the early
evening, I took up my position in the *machan* and sent the men
away in time for them to get back to the bungalow before dusk. The
men had strict orders not to leave the bungalow before it was fully
light, and they arrived each morning as the sun was rising on the
hills on the far side of the river and accompanied me back to the
bungalow.

During all those ten nights the barking of the kakar on the first
night was all that I heard. That the man-eater was still in the vicinity we had ample proof, for twice within those ten nights it had broken into houses and carried off, on the first occasion, a goat and on
the second occasion a sheep. I found both kills with some difficulty
for they had been carried a long distance, but neither had been of
any use to me as they had been eaten out. Once also during those
ten nights the leopard had broken down the door of a house which,
fortunately for the inmates, had two rooms, the door of the inner
room being sufficiently strong to withstand the leopard's onslaught.

On return to the bungalow after my tenth night in the mango-
tree, Ibbotson and I discussed our future plans. No further com-
munications had been received from the sportsman, and no one else
had expressed a desire to accept the Government's invitation, and

no one had responded to the appeals made by the press. Neither Ibbotson nor I could afford to spend more time at Rudraprayag; Ibbotson because he had been away from his headquarters for ten days and it was necessary for him to return to Pauri to attend to urgent work; and I because I had work to do in Africa and had delayed my departure for three months and could not delay it any longer. Both of us were reluctant to leave Garhwal to the tender mercies of the man-eater and yet, situated as we were, it was hard to decide what to do. One solution was for Ibbotson to apply for leave, and for me to cancel my passage to Africa and cut my losses. We finally agreed to leave the decision over for that night, and to decide on our line of action next morning. Having come to this decision I told Ibbotson I would spend my last night in Garhwal in the mango-tree.

Ibbotson accompanied me on that eleventh, and last, evening, and as we approached Golabrai we saw a number of men standing on the side of the road, looking down into a field a little beyond the mango-tree; the men had not seen us and before we got up to them they turned and moved off towards the pilgrim shelter. One of them however looked back, and seeing me beckoning retraced his steps. In answer to our questions he said he and his companions had for an hour been watching a great fight between two big snakes down in the field. No crops appeared to have been grown there for a year or more, and the snakes had last been seen near the big rock in the middle of the field. There were smears of blood on this rock, and the man said they had been made by the snakes, which had bitten each other and were bleeding in several places. Having broken a stick from a nearby bush, I jumped down into the field to see if there were any holes near the rock, and as I did so I caught sight of the snakes in a bush just below the road. Ibbotson had in the meantime armed himself with a stout stick, and as one of the snakes tried to climb up on to the road he killed it. The other one disappeared into a hole in the bank from where we were unable to dislodge it.

The snake Ibbotson had killed was about seven feet long and of a uniform light straw colour, and on its neck it had several bites. It was not a rat snake, and as it had very pronounced poison fangs we concluded it was some variety of hoodless cobra. Cold-blooded creatures are not immune from snake poison, for I have seen a frog bitten by a cobra die in a few minutes, but I do not know if snakes of the same variety can poison each other, and the one that escaped into the hole may have died in a few minutes or it may have lived to die of old age.

After Ibbotson left, the pundit passed under my tree on his way to the pilgrim shelter, carrying a pail of milk. He informed me that a hundred and fifty pilgrims, who had arrived during the day, were determined to spend the night in his shelter and that he was powerless to do anything about it. It was then too late for me to take any action, so I told him to warn the pilgrims to keep close together and not on any account to move about after dark. When he hurried back to his house a few minutes later, he said he had warned the pilgrims accordingly.

In a field adjoining the road, and about a hundred yards from my tree, there was a thorn enclosure in which a packman—not my old friend—earlier in the evening had penned his flock of goats and sheep. With the packman were two dogs who had barked very fiercely at us as we came down the road, and at Ibbotson after he left me to go back to the bungalow.

The moon was a few days past the full, and the valley was in darkness when, a little after 9 p.m., I saw a man carrying a lantern leave the pilgrim shelter and cross the road. A minute or two later, he recrossed the road and on gaining the shelter extinguished the lantern and at the same moment the packman's dogs started barking furiously. The dogs were unmistakably barking at a leopard, which quite possibly had seen the man with the lantern and was now coming down the road on its way to the shelter.

At first the dogs barked in the direction of the road, but after a little while they turned and barked in my direction. The leopard had now quite evidently caught sight of the sleeping goat and lain down out of sight of the dogs—which had stopped barking—to consider his next move. I knew that the leopard had arrived, and I also knew that he was using my tree to stalk the goat, and the question that was tormenting me as the long minutes dragged by was whether he would skirt round the goat and kill one of the pilgrims, or whether he would kill the goat and give me a shot.

During all the nights I had sat in the tree I adopted a position that would enable me to discharge my rifle with the minimum of movement and in the minimum of time. The distance between the goat and my *machan* was about twenty feet, but the night was so dark under the dense foliage of the tree that my straining eyes could not penetrate even this short distance, so I closed them and concentrated on my hearing.

My rifle, to which I had a small electric torch attached, was pointing in the direction of the goat, and I was just beginning to think that the leopard—assuming it was the man-eater—had reached the shelter and was selecting a human victim, when there was a rush from the foot of the tree, and the goat's bell tinkled sharply. Pressing the button of the torch I saw that the sights of the rifle were aligned on the shoulder of a leopard, and without having to move the rifle a fraction of an inch I pressed the trigger, and as I did so the torch went out.

Torches in those days were not in as general use as they are now, and mine was the first I had ever possessed. I had carried it for several months and never had occasion to use it, and I did not know the life of the battery, or that it was necessary to test it. When I pressed the button on this occasion the torch gave only one dim flash and then went out, and I was again in darkness without knowing what the result of my shot had been.

The echo of my shot was dying away in the valley when the pundit opened his door and called out to ask if I needed any help. I was at the time listening with all my ears for any sounds that might come from the leopard, so I did not answer him, and he hurriedly shut his door.

The leopard had been lying across the road with his head away from me when I fired, and I was vaguely aware of his having sprung over the goat and gone down the hillside, and just before the pundit had called I thought I heard what may have been a gurgling sound, but of this I could not be sure. The pilgrims had been aroused by my shot but, after murmuring for a few minutes, they resumed their sleep. The goat appeared to be unhurt, for from the sound of his bell I could tell that he was moving about and apparently eating the grass of which each night he was given a liberal supply.

I had fired my shot at 10 p.m. As the moon was not due to rise for several hours, and as there was nothing I could do in the meantime, I made myself comfortable, and listened and smoked.

Hours later the moon lit up the crest of the hills on the far side of the Ganges and slowly crept down into the valley, and a little later I saw it rise over the top of the hill behind me. As soon as it was overhead I climbed to the top of the tree, but found that the spreading branches impeded my view. Descending again to the *machan*, I climbed out on the branches spreading over the road, but from here also I found it was not possible to see down the hillside in the direction in which I thought the leopard had gone. It was then 3 a.m., and two hours later the moon began to pale. When nearby objects became visible in the light of the day that was being born in the east, I descended from the tree and was greeted by a friendly bleat from the goat.

Beyond the goat, and at the very edge of the road, there was a long low rock, and on this rock there was an inch-wide streak of blood; the leopard from which that blood had come could only have lived a minute or two, so dispensing with the precautions usually taken when following up the blood trail of carnivora, I scrambled down off the road and, taking up the trail on the far side of the rock, followed it for fifty yards, to where the leopard was lying dead. He had slid backwards into a hole in the ground, in which he was now lying crouched up, with his chin resting on the edge of the hole.

No marks by which I could identify the dead animal were visible, even so I never for one moment doubted that the leopard in the hole was the man-eater. But here was no fiend, who while watching me through the long night hours had rocked and rolled with silent fiendish laughter at my vain attempts to outwit him, and licked his lips in anticipation of the time when, finding me off my guard for one brief moment, he would get the opportunity he was waiting for of burying his teeth in my throat. Here was only an old leopard, who differed from others of his kind in that his muzzle was grey and his lips lacked whiskers; the best-hated and the most feared animal in all India, whose only crime—not against the laws of nature, but against the laws of man—was that he had shed human blood, with no object of terrorizing man, but only in order that he might live; and who now, with his chin resting on the rim of the hole and his eyes half-closed, was peacefully sleeping his long last sleep.

While I stood unloading my rifle, one bullet from which had more than cancelled my personal score against the sleeper, I heard a cough, and on looking up saw the pundit peering down at me from the edge of the road. I beckoned to him and he came gingerly down the hill. On catching sight of the leopard's head he stopped, and asked in a whisper whether it was dead, and what it was. When I told him it was dead, and that it was the evil spirit that had torn open his throat five years ago, and for fear of which he had hurriedly closed his door the previous night, he put his hands together and attempted to put his head on my feet. Next minute there was a call from the road above of, 'Sahib, where are you?' It was one of my men calling in great agitation, and when I sent an answering call echoing over the Ganges, four heads appeared, and catching sight of us four men came helter-skelter down the hill, one of them swinging a lighted lantern which he had forgotten to extinguish.

The leopard had got stiff in the hole and was extracted with some little difficulty. While it was being tied to the stout bamboo pole the men had brought with them, they told me they had been unable to sleep that night, and that as soon as Ibbotson's *Jemadar's* watch showed them it was 4.30 a.m., they lit the lantern, and arming themselves with a pole and a length of rope had come to look for me, for they felt that I was in urgent need of them. Not finding me in the *machan* and seeing the goat unhurt, and the streak of blood on the rock, they concluded the man-eater had killed me, and not knowing what to do they had in desperation called to me.

Leaving the pundit to retrieve my rug from the *machan*, and give the pilgrims who were now crowding round his version of the night's happenings, the four men and I, with the goat trotting alongside, set off for the Inspection Bungalow. The goat, who had escaped with very little injury owing to my having fired the moment the leopard caught him, little knew that his night's adventure was to make him a hero for the rest of his life, and that he was to wear a fine brass collar and be a source of income to the man from whom I had purchased him, and to whom I gave him back.

Ibbotson was still asleep when I knocked on the glazed door, and the moment he caught sight of me he jumped out of bed and dashing to the door flung it open, embraced me, and next minute was dancing round the leopard which the men had deposited on the veranda. Shouting for tea, and a hot bath for me, he called for his stenographer and dictated telegrams to the Government, the press, and my sister, and a cable to Jean. Not one question had he asked, for he knew that the leopard which I had brought home at that early hour was the man-eater, so what need was there for questions? On that previous occasion—in spite of all the evidence that had been produced—I had maintained that the leopard killed in the gin-trap was not the man-eater, and on this occasion I had said nothing.

Ibbotson had carried a heavy responsibility since October of the previous year, for to him was left the answering of questions of Councillors anxious to please their constituents, of Government officials who were daily getting more alarmed at the mounting death-roll, and of a press that was clamouring for results. His position had for a long time been like that of the head of a police force who, knowing the identity of a noted criminal, was unable to prevent his committing further crimes, and for this was being badgered on all sides. Little wonder then that Ibbotson on that 2nd of May 1926 was the happiest man I had ever seen, for not only was he now able to inform all concerned that the criminal had been executed, but he was also able to tell the people from the bazaars, and from the surrounding villages, and the pilgrims, all of whom were swarming into the compound of the Inspection Bungalow, that the evil spirit that had tormented them for eight long years was now dead.

After emptying a pot of tea and having a hot bath I tried to get a little sleep, but fear of a repetition of the cramps that twisted my feet, and from which I was only relieved by the vigorous ministrations of Ibbotson, brought me out of bed. Then Ibbotson and I measured the leopard, and carefully examined it. The following are the results of our measurements and of our examination.

MEASUREMENTS

Length, between pegs, 7 feet 6 inches
Length, over curves, 7 feet 10 inches
[*Note.* These measurements were taken after the leopard had been dead twelve hours.]

DESCRIPTION

Colour. Light straw.
Hair. Short and brittle.
Whiskers. None.
Teeth. Worn and discoloured, one canine tooth broken.
Tongue and mouth. Black.
Wounds. One fresh bullet-wound in right shoulder.
   One old bullet-wound in pad of left hind foot, and part of one toe and one claw missing from same foot.
   Several deep and partly healed cuts on head.
   One deep and partly healed cut on right hind leg.
   Several partly healed cuts on tail.
   One partly healed wound on stifle of left hind leg.

I am unable to account for the leopard's tongue and mouth being black. It was suggested that this might have been caused by cyanide, but whether this was so or not I cannot say. Of the partly healed wounds, those on the head, right hind leg, and tail were acquired in his fight at Bhainswara, and the one on the stifle of his left hind leg was the result of his having been caught in the gin-trap, for the piece of skin and tuft of hair we found in the trap fitted into this wound.

The injuries on the left hind foot were the result of the bullet fired on the bridge by the young army officer in 1921. When skinning the leopard later, I found a pellet of buckshot embedded in the skin of his chest which an Indian Christian—years later—claimed he had fired at the leopard the year it became a man-eater.

After Ibbotson and I had measured and examined the leopard it was laid in the shade of a tree, and throughout the day thousands of men, women, and children came to see it.

When the people of our hills visit an individual for any particular purpose, as for instance to show their gratitude or to express their thanks, it is customary for them not to go on their mission empty-handed. A rose, a marigold, or a few petals of either flower, suffices, and the gift is proffered in hands cupped together. When the recipient has touched the gift with the tips of the fingers of his right hand, the person proffering the gift goes through the motion of pouring the gift on to the recipient's feet, in the same manner as if his cupped hands contained water.

I have on other occasions witnessed gratitude, but never as I witnessed it that day at Rudraprayag, first at the Inspection Bungalow and later at a reception in the bazaar.

'He killed our only son, sahib, and we being old, our house is now desolate.'

'He ate the mother of my five children, and the youngest but a few months old, and there is none in the home now to care for the children, or to cook the food.'

'My son was taken ill at night and no one dared go to the hospital for medicine, and so he died.'

Tragedy upon pitiful tragedy, and while I listened the ground round my feet was strewn with flowers.

MAN-EATERS
of
KUMAON

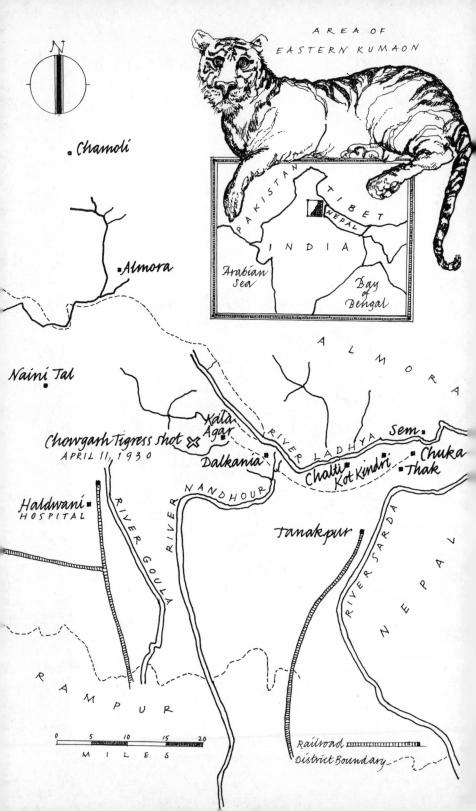

AREA OF
EASTERN KUMAON

N

Chamoli

Almora

PAKISTAN
TIBET
NEPAL
INDIA
Arabian Sea
Bay of Bengal

ALMORA

Naini Tal

Kala Agar

RIVER LADHYA

Sem

Chowgarh Tigress shot
APRIL 11, 1930

Dalkania

Chalti
Kot Kindri

Chuka
Thak

RIVER NANDHOUR

Haldwani
HOSPITAL

RIVER GOULA

Tanakpur

RIVER SARDA

NEPAL

RAMPUR

0   5   10   15   20
MILES

Railroad
District Boundary

The Chowgarh Tigers

1

The map of Eastern Kumaon that hangs on the wall before me is marked with a number of crosses, and below each cross is a date. These crosses indicate the locality, and the date, of the officially recorded human victims of the man-eating tiger of Chowgarh. There are sixty-four crosses on the map. I do not claim this as being a correct tally, for the map was posted up by me for two years, and during this period all kills were not reported to me; further, victims who were only mauled, and who died subsequently, have not been awarded a cross and a date.

The first cross is dated 15 December 1925, and the last, 21 March 1930. The distance between the extreme crosses, north to south, is fifty miles, and east to west, thirty miles, an area of 1,500 square miles of mountain and vale where the snow lies deep during winter and the valleys are scorching hot in summer. Over this area the Chowgarh tiger had established a reign of terror. Villages of varying size, some with a population of a hundred or more, and others with only a small family or two, are scattered throughout the area. Footpaths, beaten hard by bare feet, connect the villages. Some of these paths pass through thick forests, and when a man-eater renders their passage dangerous, inter-village communication is carried on by shouting. Standing on a commanding point, maybe a big rock or the roof of a house, a man cooees to attract the attention of the people in a neighbouring village, and when the cooee is answered the message is shouted across in a high-pitched voice. From village to village the message is tossed, and is broadcast throughout large areas in an incredibly short space of time.

It was at a District Conference in February 1929 that I found myself committed to have a try for this tiger. There were at that time three man-eaters in the Kumaon Division, and as the Chowgarh tiger had done most damage I promised to go in pursuit of it first.

The map with the crosses and dates, furnished to me by Government, showed that the man-eater was most active in the villages on the north and east face of the Kala Agar ridge. This ridge, some forty miles in length, rises to a height of 8,500 feet and is thickly wooded along the crest. A forest road runs along the north face of the ridge, in some places passing for miles through dense forests of oak and rhododendron, and in others forming a boundary between the forest and cultivated land. In one place the road forms a loop, and in this loop is situated the Kala Agar Forest Bungalow. This bungalow was my objective, and after a four days' march, culminating in a stiff climb of 4,000 feet, I arrived at it one evening in April 1929. The last human victim in this area was a young man of twenty-two, who had been killed while out grazing cattle, and while I was having breakfast, the morning after my arrival, the grandmother of the young man came to see me.

She informed me that the man-eater had, without any provocation, killed the only relative she had in the world. After giving me her grandson's history from the day he was born, and extolling his virtues, she pressed me to accept her three milch buffaloes to use as bait for the tiger, saying that if I killed the tiger with the help of her

HUMAN BEINGS KILLED BY THE CHOWGARH MAN-EATER	
Village	*Number*
THALI	1
DEBGURA	1
BARHON .	2
CHAMOLI	6
KAHOR	1
AM	2
DALKANIA	7
LOHAR	8
AHGAURA	2
PAHARPANI	1
PADAMPURI	2
TANDA	1
NESORIYA	1
JHANGARON	1
KABRAGAON	1
KALA AGAR	8
RIKHAKOT	1
MATELA	3
KUNDAL	3
BABYAR	1
GARGARI	1
HAIRAKHAN	2
UKHALDHUNGA	1
PAKHARI	1
DUNGARI	2
GALNI	3
TOTAL	64

ANNUAL TOTALS	
1926	15 KILLED
1927	9 KILLED
1928	14 KILLED
1929	17 KILLED
1930	9 KILLED
TOTAL	64

buffaloes she would have the satisfaction of feeling that she had assisted in avenging her grandson. These full-grown animals were of no use to me, but knowing that refusal to accept them would give offence, I thanked the old lady and assured her I would draw on her for bait as soon as I had used up the four young male buffaloes I had brought with me from Naini Tall. The Headmen of nearby villages had now assembled, and from them I learned that the tiger had last been seen ten days previously in a village twenty miles away, on the eastern slope of the ridge, where it had killed and eaten a man and his wife.

A trail ten days old was not worth following up, and after a long discussion with the Headman I decided to make for Dalkania village on the eastern side of the ridge. Dalkania is ten miles from Kala Agar, and about the same distance from the village where the man and his wife had been killed.

From the number of crosses Dalkania and the villages adjoining it had earned, it appeared that the tiger had its headquarters in the vicinity of these villages.

After breakfast next morning I left Kala Agar and followed the forest road, which I was informed would take me to the end of the ridge, where I should have to leave the road and take a path two miles downhill to Dalkania. This road, running right to the end of the ridge through dense forest, was very little used, and, examining it for tracks as I went along, I arrived at the point where the path took off at about 2 p.m. Here I met a number of men from Dalkania. They had heard—via the cooee method of communication—of my intention of camping at their village and had come up to the ridge to inform me that the tiger had that morning attacked a party of women, while they had been cutting their crops in a village ten miles to the north of Dalkania.

The men carrying my camp equipment had done eight miles and were quite willing to carry on, but on learning from the villagers that the path to this village, ten miles away, was very rough and ran through dense forest, I decided to send my men with the villagers to Dalkania, and visit the scene of the tiger's attack alone. My servant immediately set about preparing a substantial meal for me, and at 3 p.m., having fortified myself, I set out on my ten-mile walk. Ten miles under favourable conditions is a comfortable two-and-a-half hours' walk, but here the conditions were anything but favourable. The track running along the east face of the hill wound in and out through deep ravines and was bordered alternately by rocks, dense undergrowth, and trees; and when every obstruction capable of concealing sudden death, in the form of a hungry man-eater, had to be approached with caution, progress was of necessity slow. I was still several miles from my objective when the declining day warned me it was time to call a halt.

In any other area, sleeping under the stars on a bed of dry leaves would have ensured a restful night, but here, to sleep on the ground would have been to court death in a very unpleasant form. Long practice in selecting a suitable tree, and the ability to dispose myself comfortably in it have made sleeping up aloft a simple matter. On this occasion I selected an oak-tree, and, with the rifle tied securely to a branch, had been asleep for some hours when I was awakened by the rustling of several animals under the tree. The sound moved on, and presently I heard the scraping of claws on bark and realized that a family of bears were climbing some *karphal*[1] trees I had noticed growing a little way down the hill-side. Bears are very quarrelsome when feeding, and sleep was impossible until they had eaten their fill and moved on.

The sun had been up a couple of hours when I arrived at the village, which consisted of two huts and a cattle-shed in a clearing of five acres surrounded by forest. The small community were in a state of terror and were overjoyed to see me. The wheatfield, a few yards from the huts, where the tiger, belly to ground, had been

[1] *Karphal* is found on our hills at an elevation of 6,000 feet. The tree grows to a height of about forty feet and produces a small red and very sweet berry, which is greatly fancied by both human beings and bears.

detected only just in time, stalking the three women cutting the crop, was eagerly pointed out to me. The man who had seen the tiger, and given the alarm, told me the tiger had retreated into the jungle, where it had been joined by a second tiger, and that the two animals had gone down the hill-side into the valley below. The occupants of the two huts had had no sleep, for the tigers, balked of their prey, had called at short intervals throughout the night, and had only ceased calling a little before my arrival. This statement, that there were two tigers, confirmed the reports I had already received that the man-eater was accompanied by a full-grown cub.

Our hill folk are very hospitable, and when the villagers learned that I had spent the night in the jungle, and that my camp was at Dalkania, they offered to prepare a meal for me. This I knew would strain the resources of the small community, so I asked for a dish of tea, but as there was no tea in the village I was given a drink of fresh milk sweetened to excess with jaggery, a very satisfying and not unpleasant drink—when one gets used to it. At the request of my hosts I mounted guard while the remaining portion of the wheat crop was cut; and at midday, taking the good wishes of the people with me, I went down into the valley in the direction in which the tigers had been heard calling.

The valley, starting from the watershed of the three rivers Ladhya, Nandhour, and Eastern Goula, runs south-west for twenty miles and is densely wooded. Tracking was impossible, and my only hope of seeing the tigers was to attract them to myself, or helped by the jungle folk to stalk them.

To those of you who may be inclined to indulge in the sport of man-eater hunting on foot, it will be of interest to know that the birds and animals of the jungle, and the four winds of heaven, play a very important part in this form of sport. This is not the place to give the names of the jungle folk on whose alarm-calls the sportsman depends, to a great extent, for his safety and knowledge of his quarry's movements; for in a country in which a walk up or down hill of three or four miles might mean a difference in altitude of as many thousand feet, the variation in fauna, in a well-stocked area, is considerable. The wind, however, at all altitudes, remains a constant factor, and a few words relevant to its importance in connexion with man-eater hunting on foot will not be out of place.

Tigers do not know that human beings have no sense of smell, and when a tiger becomes a man-eater it treats human beings exactly as it treats wild animals, that is, it approaches its intended victims up-wind, or lies up in wait for them down-wind.

The significance of this will be apparent when it is realized that, while the sportsman is trying to get a sight of the tiger, the tiger in all probability is trying to stalk the sportsman, or is lying up in wait for him. The contest, owing to the tiger's height, colouring, and ability to move without making a sound, would be very unequal were it not for the wind-factor operating in favour of the sportsman.

In all cases where killing is done by stalking or stealth, the victim is approached from behind. This being so, it would be suicidal for the sportsman to enter dense jungle, in which he had every reason to believe a man-eater was lurking, unless he was capable of making full use of the currents of air. For example, assuming that the sportsman has to proceed, owing to the nature of the ground, in the direction from which the wind is blowing, the danger would lie behind him, where he would be least able to deal with it, but by frequently tacking across the wind he could keep the danger alternately to right and left of him. In print this scheme may not appear very attractive, but in practice it works, and, short of walking backwards, I do not know of a better or safer method of going up-wind through dense cover in which a hungry man-eater is lurking.

By evening I had reached the upper end of the valley, without having seen the tigers and without having received any indication from birds or animal of their presence in the jungle. The only

habitation then in sight was a cattle-shed, high up on the north side
of the valley.

I was careful in the selection of a tree on this second night, and
was rewarded by an undisturbed night's rest. Not long after dark the
tigers called, and a few minutes later two shots from a muzzle-loader
came echoing down the valley, followed by a lot of shouting from
the graziers at the cattle-station. Thereafter the night was silent.

By the afternoon of the following day I had explored every bit
of the valley, and I was making my way up a grassy slope intent
on rejoining my men at Dalkania when I heard a long-drawn-out
cooee from the direction of the cattle-shed. The cooee was repeated
once and again, and on my sending back an answering call I saw a
man climb on a projecting rock, and from this vantage point he
shouted across the valley to ask if I was the sahib who had come
from Naini Tal to shoot the man-eater. On my telling him I was that
sahib, he informed me that his cattle had stampeded out of a ravine
on my side of the valley at about midday, and that when he counted
them on arrival at the cattle-station he found that one—a white
cow—was missing.

He suspected that the cow had been killed by the tigers he had
heard calling the previous night, half a mile to the west of where
I was standing. Thanking him for his information, I set off to investigate the ravine. I had gone but a short distance along the edge
of the ravine when I came on the tracks of the stampeding cattle,
and following these tracks back I had no difficulty in finding the
spot where the cow had been killed. After killing the cow the tigers
had taken it down the steep hill-side into the ravine. An approach
along the drag was not advisable, so going down into the valley
I made a wide detour, and approached the spot where I expected the
kill to be from the other side of the ravine. This side of the ravine
was less steep than the side down which the kill had been taken, and
was deep in young bracken—ideal ground for stalking over. Step

by step, and as silently as a shadow, I made my way through the bracken, which reached above my waist, and when I was some thirty yards from the bed of the ravine a movement in front of me caught my eye. A white leg was suddenly thrust up into the air and violently agitated, and next moment there was a deep-throated growl—the tigers were on the kill and were having a difference of opinion over some toothful morsel.

For several minutes I stood perfectly still; the leg continued to be agitated, but the growl was not repeated. A nearer approach was not advisable, for even if I succeeded in covering the thirty yards without being seen, and managed to kill one of the tigers, the other, as likely as not, would blunder into me, and the ground I was on would give me no chance of defending myself. Twenty yards to my left front, and about the same distance from the tigers, there was an outcrop of rock, some ten to fifteen feet high. If I could reach this rock without being seen, I should in all probability get an easy shot at the tigers. Dropping on hands and knees, and pushing the rifle before me, I crawled through the bracken to the shelter of the rock, paused a minute to regain my breath and make quite sure the rifle was loaded, and then climbed the rock. When my eyes were level with the top, I looked over, and saw the two tigers.

One was eating at the hind quarters of the cow, while the other was lying near by licking its paws. Both tigers appeared to be about the same size, but the one that was licking its paws was several shades lighter than the other; and concluding that her light colouring was due to age and that she was the old man-eater, I aligned the sights very carefully on her, and fired. At my shot she reared up and fell backwards, while the other bounded down the ravine and was out of sight before I could press the second trigger. The tiger I had shot did not move again, and after pelting it with stones to make sure it was dead, I approached and met with a great disappointment; for a glance at close quarters showed me I had made a mistake and shot the cub—a mistake that during the ensuing twelve months cost the district fifteen lives and incidentally nearly cost me my own life.

Disappointment was to a certain extent mitigated by the thought that this young tigress, even if she had not actually killed any human beings herself, had probably assisted her old mother to kill (this assumption I later found to be correct), and in any case, having been nurtured on human flesh, she could—to salve my feelings—be classed as a potential man-eater.

Skinning a tiger with assistance on open ground and with the requisite appliances is an easy job, but here the job was anything but easy, for I was alone, surrounded by thick cover, and my only appliance was a penknife; and though there was no actual danger to be apprehended from the man-eater, for tigers never kill in excess of their requirements, there was the uneasy feeling in the back of my mind that the tigress had returned and was watching my every movement.

The sun was near setting before the arduous task was completed, and as I should have to spend yet another night in the jungle I decided to remain where I was. The tigress was a very old animal, as I could see from her pug-marks, and having lived all her life in a district in which there are nearly as many fire-arms as men to use them, had nothing to learn about men and their ways. Even so, there was just a chance that she might return to the kill some time during the night, and remain in the vicinity until light came in the morning.

My selection of a tree was of necessity limited, and the one I spent that night in proved, by morning, to be the most uncomfortable tree I have ever spent twelve hours in. The tigress called at intervals throughout the night, and as morning drew near the calling became fainter and fainter, and eventually died away on the ridge above me.

Cramped, and stiff, and hungry—I had been without food for sixty-four hours—and with my clothes clinging to me—it had rained for an hour during the night—I descended from the tree when objects were clearly visible, and, after tying the tiger's skin up in my coat, set off for Dalkania.

I have never weighed a tiger's skin when green, and if the skin, plus the head and paws, which I carried for fifteen miles that day weighed forty pounds at the start, I would have taken my oath it weighed two hundred pounds before I reached my destination.

In a courtyard flagged with great slabs of blue slate and common to a dozen houses, I found my men in conference with a hundred or more villagers. My approach, along a yard-wide lane between two houses, had not been observed, and the welcome I received when, bedraggled and covered with blood, I staggered into the circle of squatting men will live in my memory as long as memory lasts.

My forty-pound tent had been pitched in a field of stubble a hundred yards from the village, and I had hardly reached it before tea was laid out for me on a table improvised out of a couple of suit-cases and planks borrowed from the village. I was told later by the villagers that my men, who had been with me for years and had accompanied me on several similar expeditions, refusing to believe that the man-eater had claimed me as a victim, had kept a kettle on the boil night and day in anticipation of my return, and, further, had stoutly opposed the Headmen of Dalkania and the adjoining villages sending a report to Almora and Naini Tal that I was missing.

A hot bath, taken of necessity in the open and in full view of the village—I was too dirty and too tired to care who saw me—was followed by an ample dinner, and I was thinking of turning in for the night when a flash of lightning succeeded by a loud peal of thunder heralded the approach of a storm. Tent-pegs are of little use in a field, so long stakes were hurriedly procured and securely driven into the ground, and to these stakes the tent-ropes were tied.

For further safety all the available ropes in camp were cries-crossed over the tent and lashed to the stakes. The storm of wind and rain lasted an hour and was one of the worst the little tent had ever weathered. Several of the guy-ropes were torn from the canvas, but the stakes and cries-cross ropes held. Most of my things were soaked through, and a little stream several inches deep was running from end to end of the tent; my bed, however, was comparatively dry, and by ten o'clock my men were safely lodged behind locked doors in the house the villagers had placed at their disposal, while I, with a loaded rifle for company, settled down to a sleep which lasted for twelve hours.

The following day was occupied in drying my kit and in cleaning and pegging out the tiger's skin. While these operations were in progress the villagers, who had taken a holiday from their field work, crowded round to hear my experiences and to tell me theirs. Every man present had lost one or more relatives, and several bore teeth and claw marks, inflicted by the man-eater, which they will carry to their graves. My regret at having lost an opportunity of killing the man-eater was not endorsed by the assembled men. True, there had originally been only one man-eater; but, of recent months, rescue parties who had gone out to recover the remains of human victims had found two tigers on the kills, and only a fortnight previously a man and his wife had been killed simultaneously, which was proof sufficient for them that both tigers were established man-eaters.

My tent was on a spur of the hill and commanded an extensive view. Immediately below me was the valley of the Nandhour River, with a hill, devoid of any cultivation, rising to a height of 9,000 feet on the far side. As I sat on the edge of the terraced fields that evening with a pair of good binoculars in my hand and the Government map spread out beside me, the villagers pointed out the exact positions where twenty human beings had been killed during the past three years. These kills were more or less evenly distributed over an area of forty square miles.

The forests in this area were open to grazing, and on the cattle-paths leading to them I decided to tie up my four young buffaloes.

During the following ten days no news was received of the tigress, and I spent the time in visiting the buffaloes in the morning, searching the forests in the day, and tying out the buffaloes in the evening. On the eleventh day my hopes were raised by the report that a cow had been killed in a ravine on the hill above my tent. A visit to the kill, however, satisfied me the cow had been killed by an old leopard, whose pug-marks I had repeatedly seen. The villagers complained that the leopard had for several years been taking heavy toll of their cattle and goats, so I decided to sit up for him. A shallow cave close to the dead cow gave me the cover I needed. I had not been long in the cave when I caught sight of the leopard coming down the opposite side of the ravine, and I was raising my rifle for a shot when I heard a very agitated voice from the direction of the village calling to me.

There could be but one reason for this urgent call, and grabbing up my hat I dashed out of the cave, much to the consternation of the leopard, who first flattened himself out on the ground, and then with an angry woof went bounding back the way he had come, while I scrambled up my side of the ravine; and, arriving at the top, shouted to the man that I was coming, and set off at top speed to join him.

The man had run all the way uphill from the village and when he regained his breath he informed me that a woman had just been killed by the man-eater, about half a mile on the far side of the village. As we ran down the hill-side I saw a crowd of people collected in the courtyard already alluded to. Once again my approach through the narrow lane was not observed, and looking over the heads of the assembled men, I saw a girl sitting on the ground.

The upper part of her clothing had been torn off her young body, and with head thrown back and hands resting on the ground behind to support her, she sat without sound or movement, other than the heaving up and down of her breast, in the hollow of which the blood that was flowing down her face and neck was collecting in a sticky congealed mass.

My presence was soon detected and a way made for me to approach the girl. While I was examining her wounds, a score of people, all talking at the same time, informed me that the attack on the girl had been made on comparatively open ground in full view of a number of people, including the girl's husband; that alarmed at their combined shouts the tiger had left the girl and gone off in the direction of the forest; that leaving the girl for dead where she had fallen her companions had run back to the village to inform me; that subsequently the girl had regained consciousness and returned to the village; that she would without doubt die of her injuries in a few minutes; and that they would then carry her back to the scene of the attack, and I could sit up over her corpse and shoot the tiger.

While this information was being imparted to me the girl's eyes never left my face and followed my every movement with the liquid pleading gaze of a wounded and frightened animal. Room to move unhampered, quiet to collect my wits, and clean air for the girl to breathe were necessary, and I am afraid the methods I employed to gain them were not as gentle as they might have been. When the last of the men had left in a hurry, I set the women, who up to now had remained in the background, to warming water and to tearing my shirt, which was comparatively clean and dry, into bandages, while one girl, who appeared to be on the point of getting hysterics, was bundled off to scour the village for a pair of scissors. The water and bandages were ready before the girl I had sent for the scissors returned with the only pair, she said, the village could produce. They had been found in the house of a tailor, long since dead, and had been used by the widow for digging up potatoes. The rusty blades, some eight inches long, could not be made to meet at any point, and after a vain attempt I decided to leave the thick coils of blood-caked hair alone.

The major wounds consisted of two claw cuts, one starting between the eyes and extending right over the head and down to the nape of the neck, leaving the scalp hanging in two halves, and the other, starting near the first, running across the forehead up to the right ear. In addition to these ugly gaping wounds there were a number of deep scratches on the right breast, right shoulder and neck, and one deep cut on the back of the right hand, evidently inflicted when the girl had put up her hand in a vain attempt to shield her head.

A doctor friend whom I had once taken out tiger-shooting on foot had, on our return after an exciting morning, presented me with a two-ounce bottle of yellow fluid which he advised me to carry whenever I went out shooting. I had carried the bottle in the inner pocket of my shooting-jacket for over a year and a portion of the fluid had evaporated; but the bottle was still three-parts full, and after I had washed the girl's head and body I knocked the neck off the bottle and poured the contents, to the last drop, into the wounds. This done I bandaged the head, to try to keep the scalp in position, and then picked up the girl and carried her to her home—a single room combining living-quarters, kitchen, and nursery—with the women following behind.

Dependent from a rafter near the door was an open basket, the occupant of which was now clamouring to be fed. This was a complication with which I could not deal, so I left the solution of it to the assembled women. Ten days later, when on the eve of my departure I visited the girl for the last time, I found her sitting on the doorstep of her home with the baby asleep in her lap.

Her wounds, except for a sore at the nape of her neck where the tiger's claws had sunk deepest into the flesh, were all healed, and when parting her great wealth of raven-black hair to show me where the scalp had made a perfect join, she said, with a smile, that she was very glad her young sister had—quite by mistake—borrowed the wrong pair of scissors from the tailor's widow (for a shorn head here is the sign of widowhood). If these lines should ever be read by my friend the doctor I should like him to know that the little bottle of yellow fluid he so thoughtfully provided for me saved the life of a very brave young mother.

While I had been attending to the girl my men had procured a goat. Following back the blood trail made by the girl I found the spot where the attack had taken place, and tying the goat to a bush I climbed into a stunted oak, the only tree in the vicinity, and prepared for an all-night vigil. Sleep, even in snatches, was not possible, for my seat was only a few feet from the ground, and the tigress was still without her dinner. However, I neither saw nor heard anything thoughout the night.

On examining the ground in the morning—I had not had time to do this the previous evening—I found that the tigress, after attacking the girl, had gone up the valley for half a mile to where a cattle-track crossed the Nandhour River. This track it had followed for two miles, to its junction with the forest road on the ridge above Dalkania. Here on the hard ground I lost the tracks.

For two days the people in all the surrounding villages kept as close to their habitations as the want of sanitary conveniences permitted, and then on the third day news was brought to me by four runners that the man-eater had claimed a victim at Lohali, a village five miles to the south of Dalkania. The runners stated that the distance by the forest road was ten miles, but only five by a short cut by which they proposed taking me back. My preparations were soon made, and a little after midday I set off with my four guides.

A very stiff climb of two miles brought us to the crest of the long ridge south of Dalkania and in view of the valley three miles below, where the 'kill' was reported to have taken place. My guides could give me no particulars. They lived in a small village a mile on the near side of Lohali, and at 10 a.m. a message had come to them —in the manner already described—that a woman of Lohali had been killed by the man-eater, and they were instructed to convey this information to me at Dalkania.

The top of the hill on which we were standing was bare of trees, and, while I regained my breath and had a smoke, my companions pointed out the landmarks. Close to where we were resting, and under the shelter of a great rock, there was a small ruined hut, with a circular thorn enclosure near by. Questioned about this hut, the men told me the following story. Four years previously a Bhutia (a man from across the border), who had all the winter been sending packages of *gur*, salt, and other commodities from the bazaars at the foot-hills into the interior of the district, had built the hut with the object of resting and fattening his flock of goats through the summer and rains, and getting them fit for the next winter's work. After a few weeks the goats wandered down hill and damaged my informants' crops, and when they came up to lodge a protest, they found the hut empty, and the fierce sheep-dog these men invariably keep with them, to guard their camps at night, chained to an iron stake and dead. Foul play was suspected, and next day men were collected from adjoining villages and a search organized. Pointing to an oak-tree scored by lightning and distant some four hundred yards, my informants said that under it the remains of the man—his skull and a few splinters of bone— and his clothes had been found. This was the Chowgarh man-eater's first human victim.

There was no way of descending the precipitous hill from where we were sitting, and the men informed me we should have to proceed half a mile along the ridge to where we should find a very steep and rough track which would take us straight down, past their village, to Lohali, which we could see in the valley below. We had covered about half the distance we had to go along the ridge, when all at once, and without being able to ascribe any reason for it, I felt we were being followed. Arguing with myself against this feeling was of no avail; there was only one man-eater in all this area and she had procured a kill three miles away which she was not likely to leave. However, the uneasy feeling persisted, and as we were now at the widest part of the grassy ridge, I made the men sit down, instructing them not to move until I returned, and myself set out on a tour of investigation. Retracing my steps to where we had first come out on the ridge, I entered the jungle, and carefully worked round the open ground and back to where the men were sitting. No alarm-call of animal or bird indicated that a tiger was anywhere in the vicinity, but from there on I made the four men walk in front of me, while I brought up the rear, with thumb on safety-catch and a constant look-out behind.

When we arrived at the little village my companions had started from, they asked for permission to leave me. I was very glad of this

request, for I had a mile of dense scrub jungle to go through, and though the feeling that I was being followed had long since left me, I felt safer and more comfortable with only my own life to guard. A little below the outlying terraced fields, and where the dense scrub started, there was a crystal-clear spring of water, from which the village drew its water-supply. Here in the soft wet ground I found the fresh pug-marks of the man-eater.

These pug-marks, coming from the direction of the village I was making for, coupled with the uneasy feeling I had experienced on the ridge above, convinced me that something had gone wrong with the 'kill' and that my quest would be fruitless. As I emerged from the scrub jungle I came in view of Lohali, which consisted of five or six small houses. Near the door of one of these houses a group of people were collected.

My approach over the steep open ground and narrow terraced fields was observed, and a few men detached themselves from the group near the door and advanced to meet me. One of the number, an old man, bent down to touch my feet, and with tears streaming down his cheeks implored me to save the life of his daughter. His story was as short as it was tragic. His daughter, who was a widow and the only relative he had in the world, had gone out at about ten o'clock to collect dry sticks with which to cook their midday meal. A small stream flows through the valley, and on the far side of the stream from the village the hill goes steeply up. On the lower slope of this hill there are a few terraced fields. At the edge of the lowest field, and distant about a hundred and fifty yards from the home, the woman had started to collect sticks. A little later, some women who were washing their clothes in the stream heard a scream, and on looking up saw the woman and a tiger disappearing together into the dense thorn bushes, which extended from the edge of the field right down to the stream. Dashing back to the village, the women raised an alarm. The frightened villagers made no attempt at a res-cue, and a message for help was shouted to a village higher up the valley, from where it was tossed back to the village from which the four men had set out to find me. Half an hour after the message had been sent, the wounded woman crawled home. Her story was that she had seen the tiger just as it was about to spring on her, and as there was no time to run, she had jumped down the almost perpendicular hill-side and while she was in the air the tiger had caught her and they had gone down the hill together. She remembered nothing further until she regained consciousness and found herself near the stream; and being unable to call for help, she had crawled back to the village on her hands and knees.

We had reached the door of the house while this tale was being told. Making the people stand back from the door —the only opening in the four walls of the room—I drew the blood-stained sheet off the woman, whose pitiful condition I am not going to attempt to describe. Had I been a qualified doctor, armed with modern appliances, instead of just a mere man with a little permanganate of potash in his pocket, I do not think it would have been possible to have saved the woman's life; for the deep tooth and claw wounds in her face, neck, and other parts of her body had, in that hot, unventilated room, already turned septic. Mercifully she was only semi-conscious. The old father had followed me into the room, and, more for his satisfaction than for any good I thought it would do, I washed the caked blood from the woman's head and body, and cleaned out the wounds as best I could with my handkerchief and a strong solution of permanganate.

It was now too late to think of returning to my camp, and a place would have to be found in which to pass the night. A little way up the stream, and not far from where the women had been washing their clothes, there was a giant pipal-tree, with a foot-high masonry platform round it used by the villagers for religious ceremonies.

I undressed on the platform and bathed in the stream; and when the wind had carried out the functions of a towel, dressed again, put my back to the tree and, laying the loaded rifle by my side, prepared to see the night out. Admittedly it was an unsuitable place in which to spend the night, but any place was preferable to the village and that dark room, with its hot fetid atmosphere and swarm of buzzing flies, where a woman in torment fought desperately for breath.

During the night the wailing of women announced that the sufferer's troubles were over, and when I passed through the village at daybreak preparations for the funeral were well advanced.

From the experience of this unfortunate woman, and that of the girl at Dalkania, it was now evident that the old tigress had depended, to a very great extent, on her cub to kill the human beings she attacked. Usually only one out of every hundred people attacked by man-eating tigers escapes, but in the case of this man-eater it was apparent that more people would be mauled than killed outright, and as the nearest hospital was fifty miles away, when I returned to Naini Tal I appealed to Government to send a supply of disinfectants and dressings to all the Headmen of villages in the area in which the man-eater was operating. On my subsequent visit I was glad to learn that the request had been complied with, and that the disinfectants had saved the lives of a number of people.

I stayed at Dalkania for another week and announced on a Saturday that I would leave for home the following Monday. I had now been in the man-eater's domain for close on a month, and the constant strain of sleeping in an open tent, and of walking endless miles during the day with the prospect of every step being the last, was beginning to tell on my nerves. The villagers received my announcement with consternation, and only desisted from trying to make me change my decision when I promised them I would return at the first opportunity.

After breakfast on Sunday morning the Headman of Dalkania paid me a visit and requested me to shoot them some game before I left. The request was gladly acceded to, and half an hour later, accompanied by four villagers and one of my own men, and armed with a .275 rifle and a clip of cartridges, I set off for the hill on the far side of the Nandhour River, on the upper slopes of which I had, from my camp, frequently seen ghooral feeding.

One of the villagers accompanying me was a tall gaunt man with a terribly disfigured face. He had been a constant visitor to my camp, and finding in me a good listener had told and re-told his encounter with the man-eater so often that I could, without effort, repeat the whole story in my sleep. The encounter had taken place four years previously, and is best told in his own words.

'Do you see that pine-tree, sahib, at the bottom of the grassy slope on the shoulder of the hill? Yes, the pine-tree with a big white rock to the east of it. Well, it was at the upper edge of the grassy slope that the man-eater attacked me. The grassy slope is as perpendicular as the wall of a house, and none but a hillman could find foothold on it. My son, who was eight years of age at the time, and I had cut grass on that slope on the day of my misfortune, carrying the grass up in armfuls to the belt of trees where the ground is level.

'I was stooping down at the very edge of the slope, tying the grass into a big bundle, when the tiger sprang at me and buried its teeth, one under my right eye, one in my chin, and the other two here at the back of my neck. The tiger's mouth struck me with a great blow and I fell over on my back, while the tiger lay on top of me chest to chest, with its stomach between my legs. When falling backwards I had flung out my arms and my right hand had come in contact with an oak-sapling. As my fingers grasped the sapling, an idea came to me. My legs were free, and if I could draw them up and insert my feet under and against the tiger's belly, I might be able to push the tiger off, and run away. The pain, as the tiger crushed all the bones on the right side of my face, was terrible; but I did not lose consciousness, but you see, sahib, at that time I was a young man, and in all the hills there was no one to compare with me in strength. Very slowly, so as not to anger the tiger, I drew my legs up on either side of it, and gently, very gently, inserted my bare feet against its belly. Then placing my left hand against its chest and pushing and kicking upwards with all my might, I lifted the tiger right off the ground and, we being on the very edge of the perpendicular hill-side, the tiger went crashing down and belike would have taken me with him, had my hold on the sapling not been a good one.

'My son had been too frightened to run away, and when the tiger had gone, I took his loincloth from him and wrapped it round my head, and holding his hand I walked back to the village. Arrived at my home I told my wife to call all my friends together, for I wished to see their faces before I died. When my friends were assembled and saw my condition, they wanted to put me on a charpoy and carry me fifty miles to the Almora hospital, but this I would not consent to; for my suffering was great, and being assured that my time had come, I wanted to die where I had been born, and where I had lived all my life. Water was brought, for I was thirsty and my head was on fire, but when it was poured into my mouth, it all flowed out through the holes in my neck. Thereafter, for a period beyond measure, there was great confusion in my mind, and much pain in my head and in my neck, and while I waited and longed for death to end my sufferings my wounds healed of themselves, and I became well.

'And now, sahib, I am as you see me, old and thin, and with white hair, and a face that no man can look on without repulsion. My enemy lives and continues to claim victims; but do not be deceived into thinking it is a tiger, for it is no tiger but an evil spirit, who, when it craves for human flesh and blood, takes on for a little while the semblance of a tiger. But they say you are a *sadhu*, sahib, and the spirits that guard sadhus are more powerful than this evil spirit, as is proved by the fact that you spent three days and three nights alone in the jungle, and came out—as your men said you would—alive and unhurt.'

Looking at the great frame of the man, it was easy to picture him as having been a veritable giant. And a giant in strength he must have been, for no man, unless he had been endowed with strength far above the average, could have lifted the tigress into the air, torn its hold from the side of his head, carrying away, as it did, half his face with it, and hurled it down the precipitous hill.

My gaunt friend constituted himself our guide, and with a beautifully polished axe, with long tapering handle, over his shoulder, led us by devious steep paths to the valley below. Fording the Nandhour River, we crossed several wide terraced fields, now gone out of cultivation for fear of the man-eater, and on reaching the foot of the hill started what proved to be a very stiff climb, through forest, to the grass slopes above. Gaunt my friend may have been, but he lacked nothing in wind, and tough as I was, it was only by calling frequent halts—to admire the view—that I was able to keep up with him.

Emerging from the tree forest, we went diagonally across the grassy slope, in the direction of a rock cliff that extended upwards for a thousand feet or more. It was on this cliff, sprinkled over with tufts of short grass, that I had seen ghooral feeding from my tent. We had covered a few hundred yards when one of these small mountain-goats started up out of a ravine, and at my shot crumpled up and slipped back out of sight. Alarmed by the report of the rifle, another ghooral, that had evidently been lying asleep at the foot of the cliff, sprang to his feet and went up the rock face, as only he or his big brother the tahr could have done. As he climbed upwards, I lay down and, putting the sight to two hundred yards, waited for him to stop. This he presently did, coming out on a projecting rock to look down on us. At my shot he staggered, regained his footing, and very slowly continued his climb. At the second shot he fell, hung for a second or two on a narrow ledge, and then fell through space to the grassy slope whence he had started. Striking the ground he rolled over and over, passing within a hundred yards of us, and eventually came to rest on a cattle-track a hundred and fifty yards below.

I have only once, in all the years I have been shooting, witnessed a similar sight to the one we saw during the next few minutes, and on that occasion the marauder was a leopard.

The ghooral had hardly come to rest when a big Himalayan bear came lumbering out of a ravine on the far side of the grassy slope and, with never a pause or backward look, came at a fast trot along the cattle-track. On reaching the dead goat he sat down and took it into his lap, and as he started nosing the goat, I fired. Maybe I hurried over my shot, or allowed too much for refraction; anyway the bullet went low and struck the bear in the stomach instead of in the chest. To the six of us who were intently watching, it appeared that the bear took the smack of the bullet as an assault from the ghooral, for, rearing up, he flung the animal from him and came galloping along the track, emitting angry grunts. As he passed a hundred yards below us I fired my fifth and last cartridge, the bullet, as I found later, going through the fleshy part of his hind quarters.

While the men retrieved the two ghooral, I descended to examine the blood trail. The blood on the track showed the bear to be hard hit, but even so there was danger in following it up with an empty rifle, for bears are bad-tempered at the best of times, and are very ugly customers to deal with when wounded.

When the men rejoined me a short council of war was held. Camp was three and a half miles away, and as it was now 2 p.m. it would not be possible to fetch more ammunition, track down and kill the bear, and get back home by dark; so it was unanimously decided that we should follow up the wounded animal and try to finish it off with stones and the axe.

The hill was steep and fairly free of undergrowth, and by keeping above the bear there was a sporting chance of our being able to accomplish our task without serious mishap. We accordingly set off, I leading the way, followed by three men, the rear being brought up by two men each with a ghooral strapped to his back. Arrived at the spot where I had fired my last shot, additional blood on the track greatly encouraged us. Two hundred yards farther on, the blood trail led down into a deep ravine. Here we divided up our force, two men crossing to the far side, the owner of the axe and I remaining on the near side, with the men carrying the ghooral following in our rear. On the word being given we started to advance down the hill. In the bed of the ravine, and fifty feet below us, was a dense patch of stunted bamboo, and when a stone was thrown into this thicket, the bear got up with a scream of rage; and six men, putting their best foot foremost, went straight up the hill. I was not trained to this form of exercise, and on looking back to see if the bear was gaining on us, I saw, much to my relief, that he was going as hard downhill as we were going uphill. A shout to my companions, a rapid change of direction, and we were off in full cry and rapidly gaining on our quarry. A few well-aimed shots had been registered, followed by de-lighted shouts from the marksmen and angry grunts from the bear, when at a sharp bend in the ravine, which necessitated a cautious advance, we lost touch with the bear. To have followed the blood trail would have been easy, but here the ravine was full of big rocks, behind any of which the bear might have been lurking, so while the encumbered men sat down for a rest, a cast was made on either side of the ravine. While my companion went forward to look down into the ravine, I went to the right to prospect a rocky cliff that went sheer down for some two hundred feet. Holding to a tree for sup-port, I leaned over and saw the bear lying on a narrow ledge forty feet immediately below me. I picked up a stone, about thirty pounds in weight, and, again advancing to the edge and in immi-nent danger of going over myself, I raised the stone above my head with both hands and hurled it.

The stone struck the ledge a few inches from the bear's head, and scrambling to his feet he disappeared from sight, to reappear a minute later on the side of the hill. Once again the hunt was on. The ground was here more open and less encumbered with rocks, and the four of us who were running light had no difficulty in keeping up with him. For a mile or more we ran him at top speed, until we eventually cleared the forest and emerged on to the terraced fields. Rain-water had cut several deep and narrow channels across the fields, and in one of these channels the bear took cover.

The man with the distorted face was the only armed member of the party and he was unanimously elected executioner. Nothing loath, he cautiously approached the bear and, swinging his beautifully polished axe aloft, brought the square head down on the bear's skull. The result was as alarming as it was unexpected. The axehead rebounded off the bear's skull as though it had been struck on a block of rubber, and with a scream of rage the animal reared up on his hind legs. Fortunately he did not follow up his advantage, for we were bunched together, and in trying to run got in each other's way.

The bear did not appear to like this open ground, and after going a short way down the channel again took cover. It was now my turn for the axe. The bear, however, having once been struck, resented my approach, and it was only after a great deal of maneuvering that I eventually got within striking distance. It had been my ambition when a boy to be a lumberman in Canada, and I had attained sufficient proficiency with an axe to split a matchstick. I had no fear, therefore, as the owner had, of the axe glancing off and getting damaged on the stones, and the moment I got within reach I buried the entire blade in the bear's skull.

Himalayan bearskins are very greatly prized by our hill folk, and the owner of the axe was a very proud and envied man when I told him he could have the skin in addition to a double share of the ghooral meat. Leaving the men, whose numbers were being rapidly

augmented by new arrivals from the village, to skin and divide up the bag, I climbed up to the village and paid, as already related, a last visit to the injured girl. The day had been a strenuous one, and if the man-eater had paid me a visit that night she would have 'caught me napping.'

On the road I had taken when coming to Dalkania there were several long, stiff climbs up treeless hills, and when I mentioned the discomforts of this road to the villagers they had suggested that I should go back via Haira Khan. This route would necessitate only one climb to the ridge above the village, from where it was down-hill all the way to Ranibagh, whence I could complete the journey to Naini Tal by car.

I had warned my men overnight to prepare for an early start, and a little before sunrise, leaving them to pack up and follow me, I said good-bye to my friends at Dalkania and started on the two-mile climb to the forest road on the ridge above. The footpath I took was not the one by which my men, and later I, had arrived at Dalkania, but was one the villagers used when going to, and returning from, the bazaars in the foot-hills.

The path wound in and out of deep ravines, through thick oak and pine forests and dense undergrowth. There had been no news of the tigress for a week. This absence of news made me all the more careful, and an hour after leaving camp I arrived without mishap at an open glade near the top of the hill, within a hundred yards of the forest road.

The glade was pear-shaped, roughly a hundred yards long and fifty yards wide, with a stagnant pool of rain-water in the centre of it. Sambur and other game used this pool as a drinking-place and wallow and, curious to see the tracks round it, I left the path, which skirted the left-hand side of the glade and passed close under a cliff of rock which extended up to the road. As I approached the pool I saw the pug-marks of the tigress in the soft earth at the edge of the water. She had approached the pool from the same direction as I had, and, evidently disturbed by me, had crossed the water and gone into the dense tree and scrub jungle on the right-hand side of the glade. A great chance lost, for had I kept as careful a look-out in front as I had behind I should have seen her before she saw me. However, though I had missed a chance, the advantages were now all on my side and distinctly in my favour.

The tigress had seen me, or she would not have crossed the pool and hurried for shelter, as her tracks showed she had done. Having seen me, she had also seen that I was alone, and watching me from cover as she undoubtedly was, she would assume I was going to the pool to drink as she had done. My movements up to this had been quite natural, and if I could continue to make her think I was un-aware of her presence, she would possibly give me a second chance. Stooping down and keeping a very sharp look-out from under my hat, I coughed several times, splashed the water about, and then, moving very slowly and gathering dry sticks on the way, I went to the foot of the steep rock. Here I built a small fire, and putting my back to the rock lit a cigarette. By the time the cigarette had been smoked the fire had burnt out. I then lay down, and pillowing my head on my left arm placed the rifle on the ground with my finger on the trigger.

The rock above me was too steep for any animal to find foot-hold on. I had therefore only my front to guard, and as the heavy cover nowhere approached to within less than twenty yards of my position I was quite safe. I had all this time neither seen nor heard anything; nevertheless, I was convinced that the tigress was watching me. The rim of my hat, while effectually shading my eyes, did not obstruct my vision, and inch by inch I scanned every bit of the jungle within my range of view. There was not a breath of wind blowing, and not a leaf or blade of grass stirred. My men, whom I had instructed to keep close together and sing from the time they left camp until they joined me on the forest road, were not due for an hour and a half, and during this time it was more than likely that the tigress would break cover and try to stalk or rush me.

There are occasions when time drags, and others when it flies. My left arm, on which my head was pillowed, had long since ceased to prick and had gone dead, but even so the singing of the men in the valley below reached me all too soon. The voices grew louder, and presently I caught sight of the men as they rounded a sharp bend. It was possibly at this bend that the tigress had seen me as she turned round to re-trace her steps after having her drink. Another failure, and the last chance on this trip gone.

After my men had rested we climbed up to the road, and set off on what proved to be a very long twenty-mile march to the Forest Rest House at Haira Khan. After going a couple of hundred yards over open ground, the road entered very thick forest, and here I made the men walk in front while I brought up the rear. We had gone about two miles in this order, when on turning a corner I saw a man sitting on the road, herding buffaloes. It was now time to call a halt for breakfast, so I asked the man where we could get water.

He pointed down the hill straight in front of him, and said there was a spring down there from which his village, which was just round the shoulder of the hill, drew its water-supply. There was, however, no necessity for us to go down the hill for water, for if we continued a little farther we should find a good spring on the road.

His village was at the upper end of the valley in which the woman of Lohali had been killed the previous week, and he told me that nothing had been heard of the man-eater since, and added that the animal was possibly now at the other end of the district. I disabused his mind on this point by telling him about the fresh pug-marks I had seen at the pool, and advised him very strongly to collect his buffaloes and return to the village. His buffaloes, some ten in number, were straggling up towards the road, and he said he would leave as soon as they had grazed up to where he was sitting. Handing him a cigarette, I left him with a final warning. What occurred after I left was related to me by the men of the village, when I paid the district a second visit some months later.

When the man eventually got home that day he told the assembled villagers of our meeting, and my warning, and said that after he had watched me go round a bend in the road a hundred yards away he started to light the cigarette I had given him. A wind was blowing, and to protect the flame of the match he bent forward, and while in this position he was seized from behind by the right shoulder and pulled backwards. His first thought was of the party who had just left him, but unfortunately his cry for help was not heard by them. Help, however, was near at hand, for as soon as the buffaloes heard his cry, mingled with the growl of the tigress, they charged on to the road and drove the tigress off. His shoulder and arm were broken, and with great difficulty he managed to climb on the back of one of his brave rescuers, and, followed by the rest of the herd, reached his home. The villagers tied up his wounds as best they could and carried him thirty miles, non-stop, to the Haldwani hospital, where he died shortly after admission.

When Atropos, who snips the threads of life, misses one thread she cuts another, and we who do not know why one thread is missed and another cut call it Fate, Kismet, or what we will.

For a month I had lived in an open tent, a hundred yards from the nearest human being, and from dawn to dusk had wandered through the jungles, and on several occasions had disguised myself as a woman and cut grass in places where no local inhabitant dared to go. During this period the man-eater had, quite possibly, missed many opportunities of adding me to her bag and now, when making a final effort, she had quite by chance encountered this unfortunate man and claimed him as a victim.

2

The following February I returned to Dalkania. A number of human beings had been killed, and many more wounded, over a wide area since my departure from the district the previous summer, and as the whereabouts of the tigress was not known and the chances in one place were as good as in another, I decided to return and camp on the ground with which I was now familiar.

On my arrival at Dalkania I was told that a cow had been killed the previous evening, on the hill on which the bear hunt had taken place. The men who had been herding the cattle at the time were positive that the animal they had seen killing the cow was a tiger. The kill was lying near some bushes at the edge of a deserted field, and was clearly visible from the spot where my tent was being put up. Vultures were circling over the kill, and looking through my field-glasses I saw several of these birds perched on a tree, to the left of the kill. From the fact the kill was lying out in the open and the

vultures had not descended on it, I concluded: *(a)* that the cow had been killed by a leopard, and *(b)* that the leopard was lying up close to the kill.

The ground below the field on which the cow was lying was very steep and overgrown with dense brushwood. The man-eater was still at large, and an approach over this ground was therefore inadvisable.

To the right was a grassy slope, but the ground here was too open to admit of my approaching the hill without being seen. A deep, heavily wooded ravine, starting from near the crest of the hill, ran right down to the Nandhour River, passing within a short distance of the kill. The tree on which the vultures were perched was growing on the edge of this ravine. I decided on this ravine as my line of approach. While I had been planning out the stalk with the assistance of the villagers, who knew every foot of the ground, my men had prepared tea for me. The day was now on the decline, but by going hard I should just have time to visit the kill and return to camp before nightfall.

Before setting off I instructed my men to be on the lookout. If, after hearing a shot, they saw me on the open ground near the kill, three or four of them were immediately to leave camp and, keeping to the open ground, to join me. On the other hand, if I did not fire, and failed to return by morning, a search party was to be organized.

The ravine was overgrown with raspberry bushes and strewn with great rocks, and as the wind was blowing downhill, my progress was slow. After a stiff-climb I eventually reached the tree on which the vultures were perched, only to find that the kill was not visible from this spot. The deserted field, which through my field-glasses had appeared to be quite straight, I found to be crescent-shaped, ten yards across at its widest part and tapering to a point at both ends. The outer edge was bordered with dense undergrowth, and the hill fell steeply away from the inner edge. Only two-thirds of the field was visible from where I was standing, and in order to see the remaining one-third, on which the kill was lying, it would be necessary either to make a wide detour and approach from the far side or climb the tree on which the vultures were perched.

I decided on the latter course. The cow, as far as I could judge, was about twenty yards from the tree, and it was quite possible that the animal that had killed her was even less than that distance from me. To climb the tree without disturbing the killer would have been an impossible feat, and would not have been attempted had it not been for the vultures. There were by now some twenty of these birds on the tree, and their number was being added to by new arrivals, and as the accommodation on the upper branches was limited there was much flapping of wings and quarrelling. The tree was leaning outwards away from the hill, and about ten feet from the ground a great limb projected out over the steep hill-side. Hampered with the rifle, I had great difficulty in reaching this limb. Waiting until a fresh quarrel had broken out among the vultures, I stepped out along the branch—a difficult balancing feat where a slip or false step would have resulted in a fall of a hundred or more feet on to the rocks below—reached a fork, and sat down.

The kill, from which only a few pounds of flesh had been eaten, was now in full view. I had been in position about ten minutes, and was finding my perch none too comfortable, when two vultures, who had been circling round and were uncertain of their reception on the tree, alighted on the field a short distance from the cow. They had hardly come to rest when they were on the wing again, and at the same moment the bushes on my side of the kill were gently agitated and out into the open stepped a fine male leopard.

Those who have never seen a leopard under favourable conditions in his natural surroundings can have no conception of the grace of movement, and beauty of colouring, of this the most graceful and the most beautiful of all animals in our Indian jungles. Nor are his attractions limited to outward appearances, for, pound for pound, his strength is second to none, and in courage he lacks nothing. To class such an animal as vermin, as is done in some parts of India, is a crime which only those could perpetrate whose knowledge of the leopard is limited to the miserable, underfed, and mangy specimens seen in captivity.

But beautiful as the specimen was that stood before me, his life was forfeit, for he had taken to cattle killing, and I had promised the people of Dalkania and other villages on my last visit that I would rid them of this their minor enemy, if opportunity offered. The opportunity had now come, and I do not think the leopard heard the shot that killed him.

Of the many incomprehensible things one meets with in life, the hardest to assign any reason for is the way in which misfortune dogs an individual, or a family. Take as an example the case of the owner of the cow over which I had shot the leopard. He was a boy, eight years of age, and an only child. Two years previously his mother, while out cutting grass for the cow, had been killed and eaten by the man-eater, and twelve months later his father had suffered a like fate. The few pots and pans the family possessed had been sold to pay off the small debt left by the father, and the son started life as the owner of one cow; and this particular cow the leopard had selected, out of a herd of two or three hundred head of village cattle, and killed. (I am afraid my attempt to repair a heartbreak was not very successful in this case, for though the new cow, a red one, was an animal of parts, it did not make up to the boy for the loss of his lifelong white companion.)

My young buffaloes had been well cared for by the man in whose charge I had left them, and the day after my arrival I started tying them out, though I had little hope of the tigress's accepting them as bait.

Five miles down the Nandhour valley nestles a little village at the foot of a great cliff of rock, some thousand or more feet high. The man-eater had, during the past few months, killed four people on the outskirts of this village. Shortly after I shot the leopard, a deputation came from this village to request me to move my camp from Dalkania to a site that had been selected for me near their village. I was told that the tiger had frequently been seen on the cliff above the village and that it appeared to have its home in one of the many caves in the cliff face. That very morning, I was informed, some women out cutting grass had seen the tiger, and the villagers were now in a state of terror, and too frightened to leave their homes. Promising the deputation I would do all I could to help them, I made a very early start next morning, climbed the hill opposite the village, and scanned the cliff for an hour or more through my field-glasses. I then crossed the valley, and by way of a very deep ravine climbed the cliff above the village. Here the going was very difficult and not at all to my liking, for added to the danger of a fall, which would have resulted in a broken neck, was the danger of an attack on ground on which it would be impossible to defend oneself.

By 2 p.m. I had seen as much of the rock cliff as I shall ever want to see again, and was making my way up the valley towards my camp and breakfast, when on looking back before starting the stiff climb to Dalkania I saw two men running towards me from the direction in which I had just come. On joining me the men informed me that a tiger had just killed a bullock in the deep ravine up which I had gone earlier in the day. Telling one of the men to go on up to my camp and instruct my servant to send tea and some food, I turned round and, accompanied by the other man, re-traced my steps down the valley.

The ravine where the bullock had been killed was about two hundred feet deep and one hundred feet wide. As we approached it I saw a number of vultures rising, and when we arrived at the kill I found the vultures had cleaned it out, leaving only the skin and bones. The spot where the remains of the bullock were lying was only a hundred yards from the village, but there was no way up the steep bank, so my guide took me a quarter of a mile down the ravine, to where a cattle-track crossed it. This track, after gaining the high ground, wound in and out through dense scrub jungle before it finally fetched up at the village. On arrival at the village I told the Headman that the vultures had ruined the kill, and asked him to provide me with a young buffalo and a short length of stout rope; while these were being procured, two of my men arrived from Dalkania with the food I had sent for.

The sun was near setting when I re-entered the ravine, followed by several men leading a vigorous young male buffalo which the Headman had purchased for me from an adjoining village. Fifty yards from where the bullock had been killed, one end of a pine-tree washed down from the hill above had been buried deep in the bed of the ravine. After tying the buffalo very securely to the exposed end of the pine, the men returned to the village. There were no trees in the vicinity, and the only possible place for a sit-up was a narrow ledge on the village side of the ravine. With great difficulty I climbed to this ledge, which was about two feet wide by five feet long, and twenty feet above the bed of the ravine. From a little below the ledge, the rock shelved inwards, forming a deep recess that was not visible from the ledge. The ledge canted downwards at an uncomfortable angle, and when I had taken my seat on it, I had my back towards the direction from which I expected the tiger to come, while the tethered buffalo was to my left front, and distant about thirty yards from me.

The sun had set when the buffalo, who had been lying down, scrambled to his feet and faced up the ravine, and a moment later a stone came rolling down. It would not have been possible for me to have fired in the direction from which the sound had come, so to avoid detection I sat perfectly still. After some time the buffalo gradually turned to the left until he was facing in my direction. This showed that whatever he was frightened of—and I could see he was frightened—was in the recess below me.

Presently the head of a tiger appeared directly under me. A head-shot at a tiger is only justified in an emergency, and any movement on my part might have betrayed my presence. For a long minute or two the head remained perfectly still, and then, with a quick dash forward, and one great bound, the tiger was on the buffalo. The buffalo, as I have stated, was facing the tiger, and to avoid a frontal attack with the possibility of injury from the buffalo's horns, the tiger's dash carried him to the left of the buffalo, and he made his attack at right angles. There was no fumbling for tooth-hold, no struggle, and no sound beyond the impact of the two heavy bodies, after which the buffalo lay quite still with the tiger lying partly over it and holding it by the throat. It is generally believed that tigers kill by delivering a smashing blow on the neck. This is incorrect. Tigers kill with their teeth.

The right side of the tiger was towards me and, taking careful aim with the .275 I had armed myself with when leaving camp that morning, I fired. Relinquishing its hold on the buffalo, the tiger, without making a sound, turned and bounded off up the ravine and out of sight. Clearly a miss, for which I was unable to assign any reason. If the tiger had not seen me or the flash of the rifle there was a possibility that it would return; so recharging the rifle I sat on.

The buffalo, after the tiger left him, lay without movement, and the conviction grew on me that I had shot him instead of the tiger. Ten, fifteen minutes had dragged by, when the tiger's head for a second time appeared from the recess below me. Again there was a long pause, and then, very slowly, the tiger emerged, walked up to the buffalo and stood looking down at it. With the whole length of the back as a target I was going to make no mistake the second time. Very carefully the sights were aligned, and the trigger slowly pressed; but instead of the tiger's falling dead as I expected it to, it sprang to the left and went tearing up a little side ravine, dislodging stones as it went up the steep hill-side.

Two shots fired in comparatively good light at a range of thirty yards, and heard by anxious villagers for miles round: and all I should have to show for them would be, certainly one, and quite possibly two, bullet holes in a dead buffalo. Clearly my eyesight was failing, or in climbing the rock I had knocked the foresight out of alignment. But on focussing my eyes on small objects I found there was nothing wrong with my eyesight, and a glance along the barrel showed that the sights were all right, so the only reason I could assign for having missed the tiger twice was bad shooting.

There was no chance of the tiger's returning a third time; and even if it did return, there was nothing to be gained by risking the possibility of only wounding it in bad light when I had not been able to kill it while the light had been comparatively good. Under these circumstances there was no object in my remaining any longer on the ledge.

My clothes were still damp from my exertions earlier in the day, a cold wind was blowing and promised to get colder, my shorts were of thin khaki and the rock was hard and cold, and a hot cup of tea awaited me in the village. Good as these reasons were, there was a better and a more convincing reason for my remaining where I was—the man-eater. It was now quite dark. A quarter-of-a-mile walk along a boulder-strewn ravine and a winding path through dense undergrowth lay between me and the village. Beyond the suspicions of the villagers that the tiger they had seen the previous day—and that I had quite evidently just fired at—was the man-eater, I had no definite knowledge of the man-eater's whereabouts; and though at that moment she might have been fifty miles away, she might also have been watching me from a distance of fifty yards; so, uncomfortable as my perch was, prudence dictated that I should remain where I was. As the long hours dragged by, the conviction grew on me that man-eater shooting, by night, was not a pastime that appealed to me, and that if this animal could not be shot during daylight hours she would have to be left to die of old age. This conviction was strengthened when, cold and stiff, I started to climb down as soon as there was sufficient light to shoot by, and slipping on the dew-drenched rock completed the descent with my feet in the air. Fortunately I landed on a bed of sand, without doing myself or the rifle any injury.

Early as it was I found the village astir, and I was quickly the middle of a small crowd. In reply to the eager questions from all sides, I was only able to say that I had been firing at an imaginary tiger with blank ammunition.

A pot of tea drunk while sitting near a roaring fire did much to restore warmth to my inner and outer man, and then, accompanied.

by most of the men and all the boys of the village, I went to where
a rock jutted out over the ravine and directly above my overnight
exploit. To the assembled throng I explained how the tiger had
appeared from the recess under me and had bounded on to the
buffalo, and how, after I had fired, it had dashed off in that direction; and as I pointed up the ravine there was an excited shout
of 'Look, sahib, there's the tiger lying dead!' My eyes were strained
with an all-night vigil, but even after looking away and back again
there was no denying the fact that the tiger was lying there, dead.
To the very natural question of why I had fired a second shot
after a period of twenty or thirty minutes, I said that the tiger had
appeared a second time from exactly the same place, and that I
had fired at it while it was standing near the buffalo, and that it had
gone up that side ravine—and there were renewed shouts, in which
the women and girls who had now come up joined, of 'Look, sahib,
there is another tiger lying dead!' Both tigers appeared to be about
the same size, and both were lying sixty yards from where I had
fired.

Questioned on the subject of this second tiger, the villagers said
that when the four human beings had been killed, and also on the
previous day when the bullock had been killed, only one tiger had
been seen. The mating season for tigers is an elastic one extending
from November to April, and the man-eater—if either of the two
tigers lying within view was the man-eater—had evidently provided
herself with a mate.

A way into the ravine, down the steep rock face, was found some
two hundred yards below where I had sat up, and, followed by the
entire population of the village, I went past the dead buffalo to
where the first tiger was lying. As I approached it hopes rose high,
for she was an old tigress. Handing the rifle to the nearest man I got
down on my knees to examine her feet. On that day when the tigress had tried to stalk the women cutting wheat she had left some

beautiful pug-marks on the edge of the field. They were the first pug-marks I had seen of the man-eater, and I had examined them very carefully. They showed the tigress to be a very old animal, whose feet had splayed out with age. The pads of the forefeet were heavily rutted, one deep rut running right across the pad of the right forefoot, and the toes were elongated to a length I had never before seen in a tiger. With these distinctive feet it would have been easy to pick the man-eater out of a hundred dead tigers. The animal before me was, I found to my great regret, not the man-eater. When I conveyed this information to the assembled throng of people there was a murmur of strong dissent from all sides. It was asserted that I myself, on my previous visit, had declared the man-eater to be an old tigress, and such an animal I had now shot a few yards from where, only a short time previously, four of their number had been killed. Against this convincing evidence, of what value was the evidence of the feet, for the feet of all tigers were alike!

The second tiger could, under the circumstances, only be a male, and while I made preparations to skin the tigress I sent a party of men to fetch him. The side ravine was steep and narrow, and after a great deal of shouting and laughter the second tiger—a fine male—was laid down alongside the tigress.

The skinning of those two tigers, that had been dead fourteen hours, with the sun beating down on my back and an ever-growing crowd pressing round, was one of the most unpleasant tasks I have ever undertaken. By early afternoon the job was completed, and with the skins neatly tied up for my men to carry I was ready to start on my five-mile walk back to camp.

During the morning, Headmen and others had come in from adjoining villages, and before leaving I assured them that the Chowgarh man-eater was not dead and warned them that the slackening of precautions would give the tigress the opportunity she was waiting for. Had my warning been heeded, the man-eater would not have claimed as many victims as she did during the succeeding months.

There was no further news of the man-eater, and after a stay of a few weeks at Dalkania, I left to keep an appointment with the district officials in the terai.

3

In March 1930 Vivian, our District Commissioner, was touring through the man-eater's domain, and on the 22nd of the month I received an urgent request from him to go to Kala Agar, where he said he would await my arrival. It is roughly fifty miles from Naini Tal to Kala Agar, and two days after receipt of Vivian's letter I arrived in time for breakfast at the Kala Agar Forest Bungalow, where he and Mrs Vivian were staying.

Over breakfast the Vivians told me they had arrived at the bungalow on the afternoon of the 21st, and while they were having tea on the veranda, one of six women who were cutting grass in the compound of the bungalow had been killed and carried off by the man-eater. Rifles were hurriedly seized and, accompanied by some of his staff, Vivian followed up the 'drag' and found the dead woman tucked away under a bush at the foot of an oak-tree. On examining the ground later, I found that on the approach of Vivian's party the tigress had gone off down the hill, and throughout the subsequent proceedings had remained in a thicket of raspberry bushes, fifty yards from the kill. A *machan* was put up in the oak-tree for Vivian, and two others in trees near the forest road which passed thirty yards above the kill, for members of his staff. The machans were occupied as soon as they were ready, and the party sat up the whole night, without, however, seeing anything of the tigress.

Next morning the body of the woman was removed for cremation, and a young buffalo was tied up on the forest road about half a mile from the bungalow, and killed by the tigress the same night. The following evening the Vivians sat up over the buffalo. There was no moon, and just as daylight was fading out and nearby objects were becoming indistinct, they first heard and then saw an animal coming up to the kill, which in the uncertain light they mistook for a bear; but for this unfortunate mistake their very sporting effort would have resulted in their bagging the man-eater, for both the Vivians are good rifle shots.

On the 25th the Vivians left Kala Agar, and during the course of the day my four buffaloes arrived from Dalkania. As the tigress now appeared to be inclined to accept this form of bait I tied them up at intervals of a few hundred yards along the forest road. For three nights in succession the tigress passed within a few feet of the buffaloes without touching them, but on the fourth night the buffalo nearest the bungalow was killed. On examining the kill in the morning I was disappointed to find that the buffalo had been killed by a pair of leopards I had heard calling the previous night above the bungalow. I did not like the idea of firing in this locality, for fear of driving away the tigress, but it was quite evident that if I did not shoot the leopards they would kill my three remaining buffaloes, so I stalked them while they were sunning themselves on some big rocks above the kill, and shot both of them.

The forest road from the Kala Agar bungalow runs for several miles due west through very beautiful forests of pine, oak, and rhododendron, and in these forests there is, compared with the rest of Kumaon, quite a lot of game in the way of sambur, kakar, and pig, in addition to a great wealth of bird life. On two occasions I suspected the tigress of having killed sambur in this forest, and though on both occasions I found the blood-stained spot where the animal had been killed, I failed to find either of the kills.

For the next fourteen days I spent all the daylight hours either on the forest road, on which no one but myself ever set foot, or in the jungle, and only twice during that period did I get near the tigress. On the first occasion I had been down to visit an isolated village, on the south face of Kala Agar ridge, that had been abandoned the previous year owing to the depredations of the man-eater, and on the way back had taken a cattle-track that went over the ridge and down the far side to the forest road, when, approaching a pile of rocks, I suddenly felt there was danger ahead. The distance from the ridge to the forest road was roughly three hundred yards. The track, after leaving the ridge, went steeply down for a few yards and then turned to the right and ran diagonally across the hill for a hundred yards; the pile of rocks was about midway on the right-hand side of this length of the track. Beyond the rocks a hairpin bend carried the track to the left, and a hundred yards farther on another sharp bend took it down to its junction with the forest road.

I had been along this track many times, and this was the first occasion on which I hesitated to pass the rocks. To avoid them I
should either have had to go several hundred yards through dense
undergrowth or make a wide detour round and above them; the former would have subjected me to very great danger, and there was no
time for the latter, for the sun was near setting and I had still two
miles to go. So, whether I liked it or not, there was nothing for it
but to face the rocks. The wind was blowing up the hill, so I was
able to ignore the thick cover on the left of the track and concen-
trate all my attention on the rocks to my right. A hundred feet
would see me clear of the danger zone, and this distance I covered
foot by foot, walking sideways with my face to the rocks and the
rifle to my shoulder; a strange mode of progression, had there been
any to see it.

Thirty yards beyond the rocks was an open glade, starting from
the right-hand side of the track and extending up the hill for fifty or
sixty yards, and screened from the rocks by a fringe of bushes. In
this glade a kakar was grazing. I saw her before she saw me, and
watched her out of the corner of my eye. On catching sight of me
she threw up her head, and as I was not looking in her direction and
was moving slowly on she stood stock still, as these animals have a
habit of doing when they are under the impression that they have
not been seen. On arrival at the hairpin bend I looked over my
shoulder and saw that the kakar had lowered her head, and was once
more cropping the grass.

I had walked a short distance along the track after passing the
bend when the kakar went dashing up the hill, barking hysterically.
In a few quick strides I was back at the bend, and was just in time
to see a movement in the bushes on the lower side of the track. That
the kakar had seen the tigress was quite evident, and the only place
where she could have seen her was on the track. The movement I
had seen might have been caused by the passage of a bird; on the

other hand, it might have been caused by the tigress; anyway, a little investigation was necessary before proceeding farther on my way.

A trickle of water seeping out from under the rocks had damped the red clay of which the track was composed, making an ideal surface for the impression of tracks. In this damp clay I had left footprints, and over these footprints I now found the splayed-out pug-marks of the tigress where she had jumped down from the rocks and followed me, until the kakar had seen her and given its alarm-call, whereon the tigress had left the track and entered the bushes where I had seen the movement. The tigress was undoubtedly familiar with every foot of the ground, and not having had an opportunity of killing me at the rocks—and her chance of bagging me at the first hairpin bend having been spoilt by the kakar—she was probably now making her way through the dense undergrowth to try to intercept me at the second bend.

Further progress along the track was now not advisable, so I followed the kakar up the glade, and turning to the left, worked my way down, over open ground, to the forest road below. Had there been sufficient daylight I believe I could, that evening, have turned the tables on the tigress, for the conditions, after she left the shelter of the rocks, were all in my favour. I knew the ground as well as she did, and while she had no reason to suspect my intentions towards her, I had the advantage of knowing, very clearly, her intentions towards me. However, though the conditions were in my favour, I was unable to take advantage of them owing to the lateness of the evening.

I have made mention elsewhere of the sense that warns us of impending danger, and will not labour the subject further beyond stating that this sense is a very real one and that I do not know, and therefore cannot explain, what brings it into operation. On this occasion I had neither heard nor seen the tigress, nor had I received any indication from bird or beast of her presence, and yet I knew, without any shadow of doubt, that she was lying up for me among the rocks. I had been out for many hours that day and had covered many miles of jungle with unflagging caution, but without one moment's unease, and then, on cresting the ridge and coming in sight of the rocks, I knew they held danger for me, and this knowledge was confirmed a few minutes later by the kakar's warning call to the jungle folk, and by my finding the man-eater's pug-marks superimposed on my footprints.

4

To those of my readers who have had the patience to accompany me so far in my narrative, I should like to give a clear and a detailed account of my first—and last—meeting with the tigress.

The meeting took place in the early afternoon of 11 April 1930, nineteen days after my arrival at Kala Agar.

I had gone out that day at 2 p.m. with the intention of tying up my three buffaloes at selected places along the forest road, when at a point a mile from the bungalow, where the road crosses a ridge and goes from the north to the west face of the Kala Agar range, I came on a large party of men who had been out collecting firewood. In the party was an old man who, pointing down the hill to a thicket of young oak-trees some five hundred yards from where we were standing, said it was in that thicket where the man-eater, a month previously, had killed his only son, a lad eighteen years of age. I had not heard the father's version of the killing of his son, so, while we sat on the edge of the road smoking, he told his story, pointing out the spot where the lad had been killed, and where all that was left of him had been found the following day. The old man blamed the twenty-five men who had been out collecting firewood on that day for the death of his son, saying, very bitterly, that they had run away and left him to be killed by the tiger. Some of the men sitting near me had been in that party of twenty-five, and they hotly repudiated responsibility for the lad's death, accusing him of having been responsible for the stampede by screaming out that he had heard the tiger growling and telling everyone to run for their lives. This did not satisfy the old man. He shook his head and said, 'You are grown men and he was only a boy, and you ran away and left him to be killed.' I was sorry for having asked the questions that had led to this heated discussion, and more to placate the old man than for any good it would do, I said I would tie up one of my buffaloes near the spot where he said his son had been killed. So, handing two of the buffaloes over to the party to take back to the bungalow, I set off followed by two of my men leading the remaining buffalo.

A footpath, taking off close to where we had been sitting, went down the hill to the valley below and zigzagged up the opposite pine-clad slope to join the forest road two mild farther on. The path passed close to an open patch of ground which bordered the oak-thicket in which the lad had been killed. On this patch of ground, which was about thirty yards square, there was a solitary pine-sapling. This I cut down. I tied the buffalo to the stump, set one man to cutting a supply of grass for it, and sent the other man, Madho Singh, who served in the Garhwalis during the Great War and is now serving in the United Provinces Civil Pioneer Force, up an oak-tree with instructions to strike a dry branch with the head of his axe and call at the top of his voice as hill people do when cutting leaves for their cattle. I then took up a position on a rock, about four feet high, on the lower edge of the open ground. Beyond the rock the hill fell steeply away to the valley below and was densely clothed with tree and scrub jungle.

The man on the ground had made several trips with the grass he had cut, and Madho Singh on the tree was alternately shouting and singing lustily, while I stood on the rock smoking, with the rifle in the hollow of my left arm, when, all at once, I became aware that the man-eater had arrived. Beckoning urgently to the man on the ground to come to me, I whistled to attract Madho Singh's attention and signalled to him to remain quiet. The ground on three sides was comparatively open. Madho Singh on the tree was to my left front, the man cutting grass had been in front of me, while the buffalo—now showing signs of uneasiness—was to my right front. In this area the tigress could not have approached without my seeing her; and as she had approached, there was only one place where she could now be, and that was behind and immediately below me.

When taking up my position I had noticed that the farther side of the rock was steep and smooth, that it extended down the hill for eight or ten feet, and that the lower portion of it was masked by thick undergrowth and young pine-saplings. It would have been a little difficult, but quite possible, for the tigress to have climbed the rock, and I relied for my safety on hearing her in the undergrowth should she make the attempt.

I have no doubt that the tigress, attracted, as I had intended she should be, by the noise Madho Singh was making, had come to the rock, and that it was while she was looking up at me and planning her next move that I had become aware of her presence. My change of front, coupled with the silence of the men, may have made her suspicious; anyway, after a lapse of a few minutes, I heard a dry twig snap a little way down the hill; thereafter the feeling of unease left me, and the tension relaxed. An opportunity lost; but there was still a very good chance of my getting a shot, for she would undoubtedly return before long, and when she found us gone would probably content herself with killing the buffalo. There were still four or five hours of daylight, and by crossing the valley and going up the opposite slope I should be able to overlook the whole of the hill-side on which the buffalo was tethered. The shot, if I did get one, would be a long one of from two to three hundred yards, but the .275 rifle I was carrying was accurate, and even if I only wounded the tigress

I should have a blood trail to follow, which would be better than feeling about for her in hundreds of square miles of jungle, as I had been doing these many months.

The men were a difficulty. To have sent them back to the bunga-low alone would have been nothing short of murder, so of necessity I kept them with me.

Tying the buffalo to the stump in such a manner as to make it impossible for the tigress to carry it away, I left the open ground and rejoined the path to carry out the plan I have outlined, of trying to get a shot from the opposite hill.

About a hundred yards along the path I came to a ravine. On the far side of this, the path entered very heavy undergrowth, and as it was inadvisable to go into thick cover with two men following me, I decided to take to the ravine, follow it down to its junction with the valley, work up the valley, and pick up the path on the far side of the undergrowth.

The ravine was about ten yards wide and four or five feet deep, and as I stepped down into it a nightjar fluttered off a rock on which I had put my hand. On looking at the spot from which the bird had risen, I saw two eggs. These eggs, straw-coloured, with rich brown markings, were of a most unusual shape, one being long and very pointed, while the other was as round as a marble; and as my col-lection lacked nightjar eggs I decided to add this odd clutch to it. I had no receptacle of any kind in which to carry the eggs, so cupping my left hand I placed the eggs in it and packed them round with a little moss.

As I went down the ravine the banks became higher, and sixty yards from where I had entered it I came on a deep drop of some twelve to fourteen feet. The water that rushes down all these hill ravines in the rains had worn the rock as smooth as glass, and as it was too steep to offer a foot-hold I handed the rifle to the men and, sitting on the edge, proceeded to slide down. My feet had hardly touched the sandy bottom when the two men, with a flying leap, landed one on either side of me, and thrusting the rifle into my hand asked in a very agitated manner if I had heard the tiger. As a matter of fact I had heard nothing, possibly due to the scraping of my clothes on the rocks, and when questioned, the men said that what they had heard was a deep-throated growl from somewhere close at hand, but exactly from which direction the sound had come, they were unable to say. Tigers do not betray their presence by growling when looking for their dinner, and the only, and very unsatisfactory, explanation I can offer is that the tigress followed us after we left the open ground, and on seeing that we were going down the ravine had gone ahead and taken up a position where the ravine narrowed to half its width; and that when she was on the point of springing out on me, I had disappeared out of sight down the slide and she had involuntarily given vent to her disappointment with a low growl. Not a satisfactory reason, unless one assumes— without any reason—that she had selected me for her dinner, and therefore had no interest in the two men.

Where the three of us now stood in a bunch we had the smooth steep rock behind us, to our right a wall of rock slightly leaning over the ravine and fifteen feet high, and to our left a tumbled bank of big rocks thirty or forty feet high. The sandy bed of the ravine, on which we were standing, was roughly forty feet long and ten feet wide. At the lower end of this sandy bed a great pine-tree had fallen across, damming the ravine, and the collection of sand was due to this dam. The wall of overhanging rock came to an end twelve or fifteen feet from the fallen tree, and as I approached the end of the rock, my feet making no sound on the sand, I very fortunately noticed that the sandy bed continued round to the back of the rock.

This rock about which I have said so much I can best describe as a giant school slate, two feet thick at its lower end, and standing up—not quite perpendicularly—on one of its long sides.

As I stepped clear of this giant slate, I looked behind me over my right shoulder and—looked straight into the tigress's face.

I would like you to have a clear picture of the situation.

The sandy bed behind the rock was quite flat. To the right of it was the smooth slate fifteen feet high and leaning slightly outwards, to the left of it was a scoured-out steep bank also some fifteen feet high overhung by a dense tangle of thorn bushes, while at the far end was a slide similar to, but a little higher than, the one I had glissaded down. The sandy bed, enclosed by these three natural walls, was about twenty feet long and half as wide, and lying on it, with her fore-paws stretched out and her hind legs well tucked under her, was the tigress. Her head, which was raised a few inches off her paws, was eight feet (measured later) from me, and on her face was a smile, similar to that one sees on the face of a dog welcoming his master home after a long absence.

Two thoughts flashed through my mind: one, that it was up to me to make the first move, and the other, that the move would have to be made in such a manner as not to alarm the tigress or make her nervous.

The rifle was in my right hand held diagonally across my chest, with the safety-catch off, and in order to get it to bear on the tigress the muzzle would have to be swung round three-quarters of a circle.

The movement of swinging round the rifle, with one hand, was begun very slowly, and hardly perceptibly, and when a quarter of a circle had been made, the stock came in contact with my right side. It was now necessary to extend my arm, and as the stock cleared my side, the swing was very slowly continued. My arm was now at full stretch and the weight of the rifle was beginning to tell. Only a little farther now for the muzzle to go, and the tigress—who had not once taken her eyes off mine—was still looking up at me, with the pleased expression still on her face.

How long it took the rifle to make the three-quarter circle, I am not in a position to say. To me, looking into the tigress's eyes and unable therefore to follow the movement of the barrel, it appeared that my arm was paralysed, and that the swing would never be completed. However, the movement was completed at last, and as soon as the rifle was pointing at the tiger's body, I pressed the trigger.

I heard the report, exaggerated in that restricted space, and felt the jar of the recoil, and but for these tangible proofs that the rifle had gone off, I might, for all the immediate result the shot produced, have been in the grip of one of those awful nightmares in which triggers are vainly pulled of rifles that refuse to be discharged at the critical moment.

For a perceptible fraction of time the tigress remained perfectly still, and then, very slowly, her head sank on to her outstretched paws, while at the same time a jet of blood issued from the bullet-hole. The bullet had injured her spine and shattered the upper portion of her heart.

The two men who were following a few yards behind me, and who were separated from the tigress by the thickness of the rock, came to a halt when they saw me stop and turn my head. They knew instinctively that I had seen the tigress and judged from my behaviour that she was close at hand, and Madho Singh said afterwards that he wanted to call out and tell me to drop the eggs and get both hands on the rifle. When I had fired my shot and lowered the point of the rifle on to my toes, Madho Singh, at a sign, came forward to relieve me of it, for very suddenly my legs appeared to be unable to support me, so I made for the fallen tree and sat down. Even before looking at the pads of her feet I knew it was the Chowgarh tigress I had sent to the Happy Hunting Grounds, and that the shears that had assisted her to cut the threads of sixty-four human lives—the people of the district put the number at twice that figure—had, while the game was in her hands, turned, and cut the thread of her own life.

Three things, each of which would appear to you to have been to my disadvantage, were actually in my favour. These were: *(a)* the eggs in my left hand, *(b)* the light rifle I was carrying, and *(c)* the tiger being a man-eater. If I had not had the eggs in my hand I should have had both hands on the rifle, and when I looked back and saw the tiger at such close quarters I should instinctively have tried to swing round to face her, and the spring that was arrested by my lack of movement would inevitably have been launched. Again, if the rifle had not been a light one it would not have been possible for me to have moved it in the way it was imperative I should move it, and then discharge it at the full extent of my arm. And lastly, if the tiger had been just an ordinary tiger, and not a man-eater, it would, on finding itself cornered, have made for the opening and wiped me out of the way; and to be wiped out of the way by a tiger usually has fatal results.

While the men made a detour and went up the hill to free the buffalo and secure the rope, which was needed for another and more pleasant purpose, I climbed over the rocks and went up the ravine

to restore the eggs to their rightful owner. I plead guilty to being as superstitious as my brother sportsmen. For three long periods, extending over a whole year, I had tried—and tried hard—to get a shot at the tigress, and had failed; and now within a few minutes of having picked up the eggs my luck had changed.

The eggs, which all this time had remained safely in the hollow of my left hand, were still warm when I replaced them in the little depression in the rock that did duty as a nest, and when I again passed that way half an hour later, they had vanished under the brooding mother, whose colouring so exactly matched the mottled rock that it was difficult for me, who knew the exact spot where the nest was situated, to distinguish her from her surroundings.

The buffalo, who, after months of care was now so tame that it followed like a dog, came scrambling down the hill in the wake of the men, nosed the tigress, and lay down on the sand to chew the cud of contentment, while we lashed the tigress to the stout pole the men had cut.

I had tried to get Madho Singh to return to the bungalow for help, but this he would not hear of doing. With no one would he and his companion share the honour of carrying in the man-eater, and if I would lend a hand the task, he said, with frequent halts for rest, would not be too difficult. We were three hefty men—two accustomed from childhood to carrying heavy loads—and all three hardened by a life of exposure; but even so, the task we set ourselves was a Herculean one.

The path down which we had come was too narrow and too winding for the long pole to which the tigress was lashed, so, with frequent halts to regain breath and re-adjust pads to prevent the pole biting too deep into shoulder muscles, we went straight up the hill through a tangle of raspberry and briar bushes, on the thorns of which we left a portion of our clothing and an amount of skin which made bathing for many days a painful operation.

The sun was still shining on the surrounding hills when three dishevelled and very happy men, followed by a buffalo, carried the tigress to the Kala Agar Forest Bungalow, and from that evening to this day no human being has been killed—or wounded—over the hundreds of square miles of mountain and vale over which the Chowgarh tigress, for a period of five years, held sway.

I have added one more cross and date to the map of Eastern Kumaon that hangs on the wall before me—the cross and the date the man-eater earned. The cross is two miles west of Kala Agar, and the date under it is 11 April 1930.

The tigress's claws were broken and bushed out, and one of her canine teeth was broken, and her front teeth were worn down to the bone. It was these defects that had made her a man-eater and were the cause of her not being able to kill outright—and by her own efforts—a large proportion of the human beings she had attacked since the day she had been deprived of the assistance of the cub I had, on my first visit, shot by mistake.

The Thak Man-eater

1

Peace had reigned in the Ladhya valley for many months when in September '38 a report was received in Naini Tal that a girl, twelve years of age, had been killed by a tiger at Kot Kindri village. The report, which reached me through Donald Stewart, of the Forest Department, gave no details, and it was not until I visited the village some weeks later that I was able to get particulars of the tragedy. It appeared that, about noon one day, this girl was picking up windfalls from a mango-tree close to and in full view of the village, when a tiger suddenly appeared. Before the men working near by were able to render any assistance, it carried her off. No attempt was made to follow up the tiger, and as all signs of drag and blood trail had been obliterated and washed away long before I arrived on the scene, I was unable to find the place where the tiger had taken the body to.

Kot Kindri is about four miles south-west of Chuka, and three miles due west of Thak. It was in the valley between Kot Kindri and Thak that the Chuka man-eater had been shot the previous April.

During the summer of '38 the Forest Department had marked all the trees in this area for felling, and it was feared that if the man-eater was not accounted for before November—when the felling of the forest was due to start—the contractors would not be able to secure labour, and would repudiate their contracts. It was in this connexion that Donald Stewart had written to me shortly after the girl had been killed, and when in compliance with his request I promised to go to Kot Kindri, I must confess that it was more in the interests of the local inhabitants than in the interests of the contractors that I gave my promise.

My most direct route to Kot Kindri was to go by rail to Tanakpur, and from there by foot via Kaldhunga and Chuka. This route, how-ever, though it would save me a hundred miles of walking, would necessitate my passing through the most deadly malaria belt in northern India, and to avoid it I decided to go through the hills to Mornaula, and from there along the abandoned Sherring road to its termination on the ridge above Kot Kindri.

While my preparations for this long trek were still under way a second report reached Naini Tal of a kill at Sem, a small village on the left bank of the Ladhya and distant about half a mile from Chuka.

The victim on this occasion was an elderly woman, the mother of the Headman of Sem. This unfortunate woman had been killed while cutting brushwood on a steep bank between two terraced fields. She had started work at the farther end of the fifty-yard-long bank, and had cut the brushwood to within a yard of her hut when the tiger sprang on her from the field above. So sudden and unexpected was the attack that the woman only had time to scream once before the tiger killed her, and taking her up the twelve-foot-high bank crossed the upper field and disappeared with her into the dense jungle beyond. Her son, a lad some twenty years of age, was at the time working in a paddy field a few yards away and witnessed the whole occurrence, but was too frightened to try to render any assistance. In response to the lad's urgent summons the *Patwari* arrived at Sem two days later, accompanied by eighty men he had collected. Following up in the direction the tiger had gone, he found the woman's clothes and a few small bits of bone. This kill had taken place at 2 p.m. on a bright sunny day, and the tiger had eaten its victim only sixty yards from the hut where it had killed her.

On receipt of this second report, Ibbotson, Deputy Commissioner of the three Districts of Almora, Naini Tal, and Garhwal, and I held a council of war, the upshot of which was that Ibbotson, who was on the point of setting out to settle a land dispute at Askot on the border of Tibet, changed his tour programme and, instead of going via Bagashwar, decided to accompany me to Sem, and from there go on to Askot.

The route I had selected entailed a considerable amount of hill-climbing, so we eventually decided to go up the Nandhour valley, cross the watershed between the Nandhour and Ladhya, and follow the latter river down to Sem. The Ibbotsons accordingly left Naini Tal on 12 October, and the following day I joined them at Chaurgallia.

Going up the Nandhour and fishing as we went—our best day's catch on light trout rods was a hundred and twenty fish—we arrived on the fifth day at Durga Pepal. Here we left the river, and after a very stiff climb camped for the night on the watershed. Making an early start next morning, we pitched our tents that night on the left bank of the Ladhya, twelve miles from Chalti.

The monsoon had given over early, which was very fortunate for us, for owing to the rock cliffs that run sheer down into the valley, the river has to be crossed every quarter of a mile or so. At one of these fords my cook, who stands five feet in his boots, was washed away and only saved from a watery grave by the prompt assistance of the man who was carrying our lunch basket.

On the tenth day after leaving Chaurgallia we made camp on a deserted field at Sem, two hundred yards from the hut where the woman had been killed, and a hundred yards from the junction of the Ladhya and Sarda Rivers.

Gill Waddell, of the Police, whom we met on our way down the Ladhya, had camped for several days at Sem and had tied out a buffalo that MacDonald of the Forest Department had very kindly placed at our disposal; and though the tiger had visited Sem several times during Waddell's stay, it had not killed the buffalo.

The day following our arrival at Sem, while Ibbotson was interviewing Patwaris, Forest Guards, and Headmen of the surrounding villages, I went out to look for pug-marks. Between our camp and the junction, and also on both banks of the Ladhya, there were long stretches of sand. On this sand I found the tracks of a tigress and of a young male tiger—possibly one of the cubs I had seen in April. The tigress had crossed and re-crossed the Ladhya a number of times during the last few days, and the previous night had walked along the strip of sand in front of our tents. It was this tigress the villagers suspected of being the man-eater, and as she had visited Sem repeatedly since the day the Headman's mother had been killed they were probably correct.

An examination of the pug-marks of the tigress showed her as being an average-sized animal, in the prime of life. Why she had become a man-eater would have to be determined later, but one of the reasons might have been that she had assisted to eat the victims of the Chuka tiger when they were together the previous mating season, and having acquired a taste for human flesh and no longer having a mate to provide her with it, had now turned a man-eater herself. This was only a surmise, and proved later to be incorrect.

Before leaving Naini Tal I had written to the Tahsildar of Tanakpur and asked him to purchase four young male buffaloes for me, and to send them to Sem. One of these buffaloes died on the road, the other three arrived on the 24th, and we tied them out the same evening, together with the one MacDonald had given us. On going out to visit these animals next morning I found the people of Chuka in a great state of excitement. The fields round the village had been recently ploughed, and the previous night the tigress had passed close to three families who were sleeping out on the fields with their cattle; fortunately in each case the cattle had seen the tigress and warned the sleepers of her approach. After leaving the cultivated land the tigress had gone up the track in the direction of Kot Kindri, and had passed close to two of our buffaloes without touching either of them.

The *Patwari*, Forest Guards, and villagers had told us on our arrival at Sem that it would be a waste of time tying out our young buffaloes, as they were convinced the man-eater would not kill them. The reason they gave was that this method of trying to shoot the man-eater had been tried by others without success, and that in any case if the tigress wanted to eat buffaloes there were many grazing in the jungles for her to choose from. In spite of this advice, however, we continued to tie out our buffaloes, and for the next two nights the tigress passed close to one or more of them, without touching them.

On the morning of the 27th, just as we were finishing breakfast, a party of men led by Tewari, the brother of the Headman of Thak, arrived in camp and reported that a man of their village was missing. They stated that this man had left the village at about noon the previous day, telling his wife before leaving that he was going to see that his cattle did not stray beyond the village boundary, and as he had not returned they feared he had been killed by the man-eater.

Our preparations were soon made, and at ten o'clock the Ibbotsons and I set off for Thak, accompanied by Tewari and the men he had brought with him. The distance was only about two miles, but the climb was considerable, and as we did not want to lose more time than we could possibly help, we arrived at the outskirts of the village out of breath and in a lather of sweat.

As we approached the village over the scrub-covered flat bit of ground which I have reason to refer to later, we heard a woman crying. The wailing of an Indian woman mourning her dead is unmistakable, and on emerging from the jungle we came on the mourner—the wife of the missing man—and some ten or fifteen men, who were waiting for us on the edge of the cultivated land. These people informed us that from their houses above they had seen some white object, which looked like part of the missing man's clothing, in a field over-grown with scrub thirty yards from where we were now standing. Ibbotson, Tewari, and I set off to investigate the white object, while Mrs Ibbotson took the woman and the rest of the men up to the village.

The field, which had been out of cultivation for some years, was covered with a dense growth of scrub not unlike chrysanthemum, and it was not until we were standing right over the white object that Tewari recognized it as the loincloth of the missing man. Near it was the man's cap. A struggle had taken place at this spot, but there was no blood. The absence of blood where the attack had taken place and for some considerable distance along the drag could be accounted for by the tigress's having retained her first hold, for no blood would flow in such a case until the hold had been changed.

Thirty yards on the hill above us there was a clump of bushes roofed over with creepers. This spot would have to be looked at before following up the drag, for it was not advisable to have the tigress behind us. In the soft earth under the bushes we found the pug-marks of the tigress, and where she had lain before going forward to attack the man.

Returning to our starting point, we agreed on the following plan of action. Our primary object was to try to stalk the tigress and shoot her on her kill: to achieve this end I was to follow the trail and at the same time keep a look-out in front, with Tewari—who was unarmed—a yard behind me keeping a sharp look-out to right and left, and Ibbotson a yard behind Tewari to safeguard us against an attack from the rear. In the event of either Ibbotson or I seeing so much as a hair of the tigress, we were to risk a shot.

Cattle had grazed over this area the previous day, disturbing the ground, and as there was no blood and the only indication of the tigress's passage was an occasional turned-up leaf or crushed blade of grass, progress was slow. After carrying the man for two hundred yards the tigress had killed and left him, and had returned and carried him off several hours later, when the people of Thak had heard several sambur calling in this direction. The reason for the tigress's not having carried the man away after she had killed him was possibly because his cattle may have witnessed the attack on him, and driven her away.

A big pool of blood had formed where the man had been lying, and as the blood from the wound in his throat had stopped flowing by the time the tigress had picked him up again, and further, as she was now holding him by the small of the back, whereas she had previously held him by the neck, tracking became even more difficult. The tigress kept to the contour of the hill, and as the undergrowth here was very dense and visibility only extended to a few yards, our advance was slowed down. In two hours we covered half a mile, and reached a ridge beyond which lay the valley in which, six months previously, we had tracked down and killed the Chuka man-eater. On this ridge was a great slab of rock, which sloped upwards and away from the direction in which we had come. The tigress's tracks went down to the right of the rock, and I felt sure she was lying up under the overhanging portion of it, or in the close vicinity.

Both Ibbotson and I had on light rubber-soled shoes—Tewari was bare-footed—and we had reached the rock without making a

sound. Signing to my two companions to stand still and keep a careful watch all round, I got a foot-hold on the rock, and inch by inch
went forward. Beyond the rock was a short stretch of flat ground,
and as more of this ground came into view, I felt certain my suspicion that the tigress was lying under the projection was correct. I
had still a foot or two to go before I could look over, when I saw a
movement to my left front. A golden-rod that had been pressed
down had sprung erect, and a second later there was a slight movement in the bushes beyond, and a monkey in a tree on the far side
of the bushes started calling.

The tigress had chosen the spot for her after-dinner sleep with
great care, but unfortunately for us she was not asleep; and when she
saw the top of my head—I had removed my hat—appearing over
the rock, she had risen and, taking a step sideways, had disappeared
under a tangle of blackberry bushes. Had she been lying anywhere
but where she was she could not have got away, no matter how
quickly she had moved, without my getting a shot at her. Our
so-carefully-carried-out stalk had failed at the very last moment, and
there was nothing to be done now but find the kill, and see if there
was sufficient of it left for us to sit up over. To have followed her
into the blackberry thicket would have been useless, and would also
have reduced our chance of getting a shot at her later.

The tigress had eaten her meal close to where she had been lying,
and as this spot was open to the sky and to the keen eyes of vultures
she had removed the kill to a place of safety where it would not be
visible from the air. Tracking now was easy, for there was a blood
trail to follow. The trail led over a ridge of great rocks, and fifty
yards beyond these rocks we found the kill.

I am not going to harrow your feelings by attempting to describe
that poor torn and mangled thing; stripped of every stitch of clothing and atom of dignity, which only a few hours previously had

been a man, the father of two children and the breadwinner of that wailing woman who was facing—without any illusions—the fate of a widow of India. I have seen many similar sights, each more terrible than the one preceding it, in the thirty-two years I have been hunting man-eaters, and on each occasion I have felt that it would have been better to have left the victim to the slayer than recover a mangled mass of flesh to be a nightmare ever after to those who saw it. And yet the cry of blood for blood, and the burning desire to rid a countryside of a menace than which there is none more terrible, is irresistible; and then there is always the hope, no matter how absurd one knows it to be, that the victim by some miracle may still be alive and in need of succour.

The chance of shooting—over a kill—an animal that has in all probability become a man-eater through a wound received over a kill is very remote, and each succeeding failure, no matter what its cause, tends to make the animal more cautious, until it reaches a state when it either abandons its kill after one meal or approaches it as silently and as slowly as a shadow, scanning every leaf and twig with the certainty of discovering its would-be slayer, no matter how carefully he may be concealed or how silent and motionless he may be; a one in a million chance of getting a shot, and yet, who is there among us who would not take it?

The thicket into which the tigress had retired was roughly forty yards square, and she could not leave it without the monkey's seeing her and warning us, so we sat down back to back, to have a smoke and listen if the jungle had anything further to tell us while we considered our next move.

To make a *machan* it was necessary to return to the village, and during our absence the tigress was almost certain to carry away the kill. It had been difficult to track her when she was carrying a whole human being, but now, when her burden was considerably lighter and she had been disturbed, she would probably go for miles and we might never find her kill again, so it was necessary for one of us to remain on the spot, while the other two went back to the village for ropes.

Ibbotson, with his usual disregard for danger, elected to go back, and while he and Tewari went down the hill to avoid the difficult ground we had recently come over, I stepped up on to a small tree close to the kill. Four feet above ground the tree divided in two, and by leaning on one half and putting my feet against the other, I was able to maintain a precarious seat which was high enough off the ground to enable me to see the tigress if she approached the kill, and also high enough, if she had any designs on me, to see her before she got to within striking distance.

Ibbotson had been gone fifteen or twenty minutes when I heard a rock tilt forward, and then back. The rock was evidently very delicately poised, and when the tigress had put her weight on it and felt it tilt forward she had removed her foot and let the rock fall back into place. The sound had come from about twenty yards to my left front, the only direction in which it would have been possible for me to have fired without being knocked out of the tree.

Minutes passed, each pulling my hopes down a little lower from the heights to which they had soared, and then, when tension on my nerves and the weight of the heavy rifle were becoming unbearable, I heard a stick snap at the upper end of the thicket. Here was an example of how a tiger can move through the jungle. From the sound she had made I knew her exact position, had kept my eyes fixed on the spot, and yet she had come, seen me, stayed some time watching me, and then gone away without my having seen a leaf or a blade of grass move.

When tension on nerves is suddenly relaxed, cramped and aching muscles call loudly for ease, and though in this case it only meant the lowering of the rifle on to my knees to take the strain off my shoulders and arms, the movement, small though it was, sent a comforting feeling through the whole of my body. No further sound came from the tigress, and an hour or two later I heard Ibbotson returning.

Of all the men I have been on shikar with, Ibbotson is by far and away the best, for not only has he the heart of a lion, but he thinks of everything, and with it all is the most unselfish man that carries a gun. He had gone to fetch a rope, and he returned with rugs, cushions, more hot tea than ever I could drink, and an ample lunch; and while I sat—on the windward side of the kill—to refresh myself, Ibbotson put a man in a tree forty yards away to distract the tigress's attention, and climbed into a tree overlooking the kill to make a rope *machan*.

When the *machan* was ready Ibbotson moved the kill a few feet—a very unpleasant job—and tied it securely to the foot of a sapling to prevent the tigress's carrying it away, for the moon was on the wane and the first two hours of the night at this heavily wooded spot would be pitch dark. After a final smoke I climbed on to the *machan*, and when I had made myself comfortable Ibbotson recovered the man who was making a diversion and set off in the direction of Thak to pick up Mrs Ibbotson and return to camp at Sem.

The retreating party were out of sight, but were not yet out of sound when I heard a heavy body brushing against leaves, and at the same moment the monkey, which had been silent all this time and which I could now see sitting in a tree on the far side of the blackberry thicket, started calling. Here was more luck than I had hoped for, and our ruse of putting a man up a tree to cause a diversion appeared to be working as successfully as it had done on a previous occasion. A tense minute passed, a second, and a third, and then from the ridge where I had climbed on to the big slab of rock a kakar came dashing down towards me, barking hysterically. The tigress was not coming to the kill but had gone off after Ibbotson. I was

now in a fever of anxiety, for it was quite evident that she had abandoned her kill and gone to try to secure another victim.

Before leaving, Ibbotson had promised to take every precaution,
but on hearing the kakar barking on my side of the ridge he would
naturally assume the tigress was moving in the vicinity of the kill,
and if he relaxed his precautions the tigress would get her chance.
Ten very uneasy minutes for me passed, and then I heard a second
kakar barking in the direction of Thak; the tigress was still following, but the ground there was more open, and there was less fear of
her attacking the party. The danger to the Ibbotsons was, however,
not over by any means, for they had to go through two miles of very
heavy jungle to reach camp; and if they stayed at Thak until sundown listening for my shot, which I feared they would do and
which as a matter of fact they did do, they would run a very grave
risk on the way down. Ibbotson fortunately realized the danger and
kept his party close together, and though the tigress followed them

the whole way—as her pug-marks the following morning showed—they got back to camp safely.

The calling of kakar and sambur enabled me to follow the movements of the tigress. An hour after sunset she was down at the bottom of the valley two miles away. She had the whole night before her, and though there was only one chance in a million of her returning to the kill, I determined not to lose that chance. Wrapping a rug round me, for it was a bitterly cold night, I made myself comfortable in a position in which I could remain for hours without movement.

I had taken my seat on the *machan* at 4 p.m., and at 10 p.m. I heard two animals coming down the hill towards me. It was too dark under the trees to see them, but when they got to the lee of the kill I knew they were porcupines. Rattling their quills, and making the peculiar booming noise that only a porcupine can make, they approached the kill and, after walking round it several times, continued on their way. An hour later, and when the moon had been up some time, I heard an animal in the valley below. It was moving from east to west, and when it came into the wind blowing downhill from the kill it made a long pause, and then came cautiously up the hill. While it was still some distance away I heard it snuffing the air, and knew it to be a bear. The smell of blood was attracting him, but mingled with it was the less welcome smell of a human being, and taking no chances, he was very carefully stalking the kill. His nose, the keenest of any animal's in the jungle, had apprised him while he was still in the valley that the kill was the property of a tiger. This to a Himalayan bear who fears nothing, and who will, as I have on several occasions seen, drive a tiger away from its kill, was no deterrent, but what was, and what was causing him uneasiness, was the smell of a human being mingled with the smell of blood and tiger.

On reaching the flat ground the bear sat down on his haunches a few yards from the kill, and when he had satisfied himself that the hated human smell held no danger for him he stood erect and turning his head sent a long-drawn-out cry, which I interpreted as a call to a mate, echoing down into the valley. Then without any further hesitation he walked boldly up to the kill, and as he nosed it I aligned the sights of my rifle on him. I know of only one instance of a Himalayan bear eating a human being; on that occasion a woman cutting grass had fallen down a cliff and been killed, and a bear finding the mangled body had carried it away and had eaten it. This bear, however, on whose shoulder my sights were aligned, appeared to draw the line at human flesh, and after looking at and smelling the kill continued his interrupted course to the west. When the sounds of his retreat died away in the distance the jungle settled down to silence until interrupted, a little after sunrise, by Ibbotson's very welcome arrival.

With Ibbotson came the brother and other relatives of the dead man, who very reverently wrapped the remains in a clean white cloth and, laying it on a cradle made of two saplings and rope which Ibbotson provided, set off for the burning ghat on the banks of the Sarda, repeating under their breath as they went the Hindu hymn of praise *'Ram nam sat hai'* with its refrain, *'Satya bol gat hai.'*

Fourteen hours in the cold had not been without its effect on me, but after partaking of the hot drink and food Ibbotson had brought, I felt none the worse for my long vigil.

2

After following the Ibbotsons down to Chuka on the evening of the 27th, the tigress, some time during the night, crossed the Ladhya into the scrub jungle at the back of our camp. Through this scrub ran a path that had been regularly used by the villagers of the Ladhya valley until the advent of the man-eater had rendered its passage unsafe. On the 28th the two mail-runners who carried Ibbotson's dak on its first stage to Tanakpur got delayed in camp, and to save time took, or more correctly started to take, a short cut through this scrub. Very fortunately the leading man was on the alert and saw the tigress as she crept through the scrub and lay down near the path ahead of them.

Ibbotson and I had just got back from Thak when these two men dashed into camp, and taking our rifles we hurried off to investigate. We found the pug-marks of the tigress where she had come out on the path and followed the men for a short distance, but we did not see her, though in one place where the scrub was very dense we saw a movement and heard an animal moving off.

On the morning of the 29th a party of men came down from Thak to report that one of their bullocks had not returned to the cattle-shed the previous night, and on a search being made where it had last been seen a little blood had been found. At 2 p.m. the Ibbotsons and I were at this spot, and a glance at the ground satisfied us that the bullock had been killed and carried away by a tiger. After a hasty lunch Ibbotson and I, with two men following carrying ropes for a *machan*, set out along the drag. It went diagonally across the face of the hill for a hundred yards and then straight down into the ravine in which I had fired at and missed the big tiger in April. A few hundred yards down this ravine the bullock, which was an enormous animal, had got fixed between two rocks and, not being able to move it, the tiger had eaten a meal off its hind quarters and left it.

The pug-marks of the tiger, owing to the great weight she was carrying, were splayed out, and it was not possible to say whether she was the man-eater or not; but as every tiger in this area was suspect I decided to sit up over the kill. There was only one tree within reasonable distance of the kill, and as the men climbed into it to make a *machan* the tiger started calling in the valley below. Very hurriedly a few strands of rope were tied between two branches, and while Ibbotson stood on guard with his rifle I climbed the tree and took my seat on what, during the next fourteen hours, proved to be the most uncomfortable as well as the most dangerous *machan* I have ever sat on. The tree was leaning away from the hill, and from the three uneven strands of rope I was sitting on there was a drop of over a hundred feet into the rocky ravine below.

The tiger called several times as I was getting into the tree and continued to call at longer intervals late into the evening, the last call coming from a ridge half a mile away. It was now quite evident that the tiger had been lying up close to the kill and had seen the men climbing into the tree. Knowing from past experience what this meant, she had duly expressed resentment at being disturbed and then gone away, for though I sat on the three strands of rope until Ibbotson returned next morning, I did not see or hear anything throughout the night.

Vultures were not likely to find the kill, for the ravine was deep and overshadowed by trees, and as the bullock was large enough to provide the tiger with several meals we decided not to sit up over it again where it was now lying, hoping the tiger would remove it to some more convenient place where we should have a better chance of getting a shot. In this, however, we were disappointed, for the tiger did not again return to the kill.

Two nights later the buffalo we had tied out behind our camp at Sem was killed, and through a little want of observation on my part a great opportunity of bagging the man-eater was lost.

The men who brought in the news of this kill reported that the rope securing the animal had been broken, and that the kill had been carried away up the ravine at the lower end of which it had been tied. This was the same ravine in which MacDonald and I had chased a tigress in April, and as on that occasion she had taken her kill some distance up the ravine I now very foolishly concluded she had done the same with this kill.

After breakfast Ibbotson and I went to out find the kill and see what prospect there was for an evening sit-up.

The ravine in which the buffalo had been killed was about fifty yards wide and ran deep into the foot-hills. For two hundred yards the ravine was straight, and then bent round to the left. Just beyond the bend, and on the left-hand side of it, there was a dense patch of young saplings backed by a hundred-foot ridge on which thick grass was growing. In the ravine, and close to the saplings, there was a small pool of water. I had been up the ravine several times in April and had failed to mark the patch of saplings as being a likely place for a tiger to lie up in, and did not take the precautions I should have taken when rounding the bend, with the result that the tigress, who was drinking at the pool, saw us first. There was only one safe line of retreat for her, and she took it. This was straight up the steep hill, over the ridge, and into sal forest beyond.

The hill was too steep for us to climb, so we continued on up the ravine to where a sambur track crossed it, and following this track we gained the ridge. The tigress was now in a triangular patch of jungle bounded by the ridge, the Ladhya, and a cliff down which no animal could go. The area was not large, and there were several deer in it which from time to time advised us of the position of the tigress, but unfortunately the ground was cut up by a number of deep and narrow rain-water channels in which we eventually lost touch with her.

We had not yet seen the kill, so we re-entered the ravine by the sambur track and found the kill hidden among the saplings. These saplings were from six inches to a foot in girth, and were not strong enough to support a platform, so we had to abandon the idea of a *machan.* With the help of a crowbar, a rock could possibly have been pried from the face of the hill and a place made in which to sit, but this was not advisable when dealing with a man-eater.

Reluctant to give up the chance of a shot, we considered the possibility of concealing ourselves in the grass near the kill, in the hope that the tigress would return before dark and that we should see her before she saw us. There were two objections to this plan: (*a*) if we did not get a shot and the tigress saw us near her kill she might abandon it, as she had done her other two kills; and (*b*) between the kill and camp there was very heavy scrub jungle, and if we tried to go through this jungle in the dark the tigress would have us at her mercy. So very reluctantly we decided to leave the kill to the tigress for that night, and hope for the best on the morrow.

On our return next morning we found that the tigress had carried away the kill. For three hundred yards she had gone up the bed of the ravine, stepping from rock to rock, and leaving no drag marks. At this spot—three hundreds yards from where she had picked up the kill—we were at fault, for though there were a number of tracks on a wet patch of ground, none of them had been made while she was carrying the kill. Eventually, after casting round in circles, we found where she had left the ravine and gone up the hill on the left.

This hill up which the tigress had taken her kill was overgrown with ferns and golden-rod and tracking was not difficult, but the going was, for the hill was very steep, and in places a detour had to be made and the track picked up farther on. After a stiff climb of a thousand feet we came to a small plateau, bordered on the left by a cliff a mile wide. On the side of the plateau nearest the cliff the ground was seamed and cracked, and in these cracks a dense growth of sal, two to six feet in height, had sprung up. The tigress had taken her kill into this dense cover, and it was not until we actually trod on it that we were aware of its position.

As we stopped to look at all that remained of the buffalo there was a low growl to our right. With rifles raised we waited for a minute and then, hearing a movement in the undergrowth a little beyond where the growl had come from, we pushed our way through the young sal for ten yards and came on a small clearing, where the tigress had made herself a bed on some soft grass. On the far side of this grass the hill sloped upwards for twenty yards to another plateau, and it was from this slope that the sound we had heard had come. Proceeding up the slope as silently as possible, we had just reached the flat ground, which was about fifty yards wide, when the tigress left the far side and went down into the ravine, disturbing some kaleege pheasants and a kakar as she did so. To have followed her would have been useless, so we went back to the kill and, as there was still a good meal on it, we selected two trees to sit in, and returned to camp.

After an early lunch we went back to the kill and, hampered with our rifles, climbed with some difficulty into the trees we had selected. We sat up for five hours without seeing or hearing anything. At dusk we climbed down from our trees, and stumbling over the cracked and uneven ground eventually reached the ravine when it was quite dark. Both of us had an uneasy feeling that we were being followed, but by keeping close together we reached camp without incident at 9 p.m.

The Ibbotsons had now stayed at Sem as long as it was possible for them to do so, and early next morning they set out on their twelve days' walk to keep their appointment at Askot. Before leaving, Ibbotson extracted a promise from me that I would not follow up any kills alone, or further endanger my life by prolonging my stay at Sem for more than a day or two.

After the departure of the Ibbotsons and their fifty men, the camp, which was surrounded by dense scrub, was reduced to my two servants and myself—my coolies were living in a room in the

Headman's house—so throughout the day I set all hands to collecting driftwood, of which there was an inexhaustible supply at the junction, to keep a fire going all night. The fire would not scare away the tigress, but it would enable us to see her if she prowled round our tents at night, and anyway the nights were setting in cold and there was ample excuse, if one were needed, for keeping a big fire going all night.

Towards evening, when my men were safely back in camp, I took a rifle and went up the Ladhya to see if the tigress had crossed the river. I found several tracks in the sand, but no fresh ones, and at dusk I returned, convinced that the tigress was still on our side of the river. An hour later, when it was quite dark, a kakar started barking close to our tents and barked persistently for half an hour.

My men had taken over the job of tying out the buffaloes, a task which Ibbotson's men had hitherto performed, and next morning I accompanied them when they went out to bring in the buffaloes. Though we covered several miles, I did not find any trace of the tigress. After breakfast I took a rod and went down to the junction, and had one of the best day's fishing I have ever had. The junction was full of big fish, and though my light tackle was broken frequently, I killed sufficient mahseer to feed the camp.

Again, as on the previous evening, I crossed the Ladhya, with the intention of taking up a position on a rock overlooking the open ground on the right bank of the river and watching for the tigress to cross. As I got away from the roar of the water at the junction I heard a sambur and a monkey calling on the hill to my left, and as I neared the rock I came on the fresh tracks of the tigress. Following them back, I found the stones still wet where she had forded the river. A few minutes' delay in camp to dry my fishing-line and have a cup of tea cost a man his life, several thousand men weeks of anxiety, and myself many days of strain, for though I stayed at Sem for another three days I did not get another chance of shooting the tigress.

On the morning of the 7th, as I was breaking camp and preparing to start on my twenty-mile walk to Tanakpur, a big contingent of men from all the surrounding villages arrived and begged me not to leave them to the tender mercies of the man-eater. Giving them what advice it was possible to give people situated as they were, I promised to return as soon as it was possible for me to do so.

I caught the train at Tanakpur next morning and arrived back in Naini Tal on 9 November, having been away nearly a month.

3

I left Sem on 7 November, and on the 12th the tigress killed a man at Thak. I received news of this kill through the Divisional Forest Officer, Haldwani, shortly after we had moved down to our winter home at the foot of the hills, and by doing forced marches I arrived at Chuka a little after sunrise on the 24th.

It had been my intention to breakfast at Chuka and then go on to Thak and make that village my headquarters, but the Headman of Thak, whom I found installed at Chuka, informed me that every man, woman, and child had left Thak immediately after the man had been killed on the 12th, and added that if I carried out my intention of camping at Thak I might be able to safeguard my own life, but it would not be possible to safeguard the lives of my men. This was quite reasonable, and while waiting for my men to arrive, the Headman helped me to select a site for my camp at Chuka, where my men would be reasonably safe and I should have some privacy from the thousands of men who were now arriving to fell the forest.

On receipt of the Divisional Forest Officer's telegram acquainting me of the kill, I had telegraphed to the Tahsildar at Tanakpur to send three young male buffaloes to Chuka. My request had been promptly complied with, and the three animals had arrived the previous evening.

After breakfast I took one of the buffaloes and set out for Thak, intending to tie it up on the spot where the man had been killed on the 12th. The Headman had given me a very graphic account of the events of that date, for he himself had nearly fallen a victim to the tigress. It appeared that towards the afternoon, accompanied by his grand-daughter, a girl ten years of age, he had gone to dig up ginger tubers in a field some sixty yards from his house. This field is about half an acre in extent and is surrounded on three sides by jungle, and being on the slope of a fairly steep hill it is visible from the Headman's house. After the old man and his grand-daughter had been at work for some time, his wife, who was husking rice in the courtyard of the house, called out in a very agitated voice and asked him if he was deaf that he could not hear the pheasants and other birds that were chattering in the jungle above him. Fortunately for him, he acted promptly. Dropping his hoe, he grabbed the child's hand and together they ran back to the house, urged on by the woman who said she could now see a red animal in the bushes at the upper end of the field. Half an hour later the tigress killed a man who was lopping branches off a tree in a field three hundred yards from the Headman's house.

From the description I had received from the Headman I had no difficulty in locating the tree. It was a small gnarled tree growing out of a three-foot-high bank between two terraced fields, and had been lopped year after year for cattle-fodder. The man who had been killed was standing on the trunk holding one branch and cutting another, when the tigress came up from behind, tore his hold from the branch and, after killing him, carried him away into the dense brushwood bordering the fields.

Thak village was a gift from the Chand Rajahs, who ruled Kumaon for many hundreds of years before the Gurkha occupation, to the forefathers of the present owners in return for their services at

the Punagiri temples. (The promise made by the Chand Rajas that the lands of Thak and two other villages would remain rent-free for all time has been honoured by the British Government for a hundred years.) From a collection of grass huts the village has in the course of time grown into a very prosperous settlement with masonry houses roofed with slate tiles, for not only is the land very fertile, but the revenue from the temples is considerable.

Like all other villages in Kumaon, Thak during its hundreds of years of existence has passed through many vicissitudes, but never before in its long history had it been deserted as it now was. On my previous visits I had found it a hive of industry, but when I went up to it on this afternoon, taking the young buffalo with me, silence reigned over it. Every one of the hundred or more inhabitants had fled, taking their livestock with them—the only animal I saw in the

village was a cat, which gave me a warm welcome; so hurried had
the evacuation been that many of the doors of the houses had been
left wide open. On every path in the village, in the courtyard of the
houses, and in the dust before all the doors I found the tigress's
pug-marks. The open doorways were a menace, for the path as it
wound through the village passed close to them, and in any of the
houses the tigress may have been lurking.

On the hill thirty yards above the village were several cattle-shelters, and in the vicinity of these shelters I saw more kaleege pheasants, red jungle fowl, and white-capped babblers than I have ever
before seen, and from the confiding way in which they permitted
me to walk among them it is quite evident that the people of Thak
have a religious prejudice against the taking of life.

From the terraced fields above the cattle-shelters a bird's-eye view
of the village is obtained, and it was not difficult, from the description the Headman had given me, to locate the tree where the tigress
had secured her last victim. In the soft earth under the tree there
were signs of a struggle and a few clots of dried blood. From here
the tigress had carried her kill a hundred yards over a ploughed field,
through a stout hedge, and into the dense brushwood beyond. The
foot-prints from the village and back the way they had come showed
that the entire population of the village had visited the scene of the
kill, but from the tree to the hedge there was only one track, the
track the tigress had made when carrying away her victim. No attempt had been made to follow her up and recover the body.

Scraping away a little earth from under the tree I exposed a root,
and to this root I tied my buffalo, bedding it down with a liberal
supply of straw taken from a nearby haystack.

The village, which is on the north face of the hill, was now in
shadow, and if I was to get back to camp before dark it was time for
me to make a start. Skirting round the village to avoid the menace
of the open doorways, I joined the path below the houses.

This path after it leaves the village passes under a giant mango-tree from the roots of which issues a cold spring of clear water. After running along a groove cut in a massive slab of rock, this water falls into a rough masonry trough, from where it spreads on to the surrounding ground, rendering it soft and slushy. I had drunk at the spring on my way up, leaving my footprints in this slushy ground, and on approaching the spring now for a second drink, I found the tigress's pug-marks superimposed on my footprints. After quenching her thirst the tigress had avoided the path and had gained the village by climbing a steep bank overgrown with strobilanthes and nettles, and taking up a position in the shelter of one of the houses had possibly watched me while I was tying up the buffalo, expecting me to return the way I had gone; it was fortunate for me that I had noted the danger of passing those open doorways a second time, and had taken the longer way round.

When coming up from Chuka I had taken every precaution to guard against a sudden attack, and it was well that I had done so, for I now found from her pug-marks that the tigress had followed me all the way up from my camp, and next morning when I went back to Thak I found she had followed me from where I had joined the path below the houses, right down to the cultivated land at Chuka.

Reading with the illumination I had brought with me was not possible, so after dinner that night, while sitting near a fire which was as welcome for its warmth as it was for the feeling of security it gave me, I reviewed the whole situation and tried to think out some plan by which it would be possible to circumvent the tigress.

When leaving home on the 22nd I had promised that I would return in ten days, and that this would be my last expedition after man-eaters. Years of exposure and strain and long absences from home—extending as in the case of the Chowgarh tigress and the Rudraprayag leopard to several months on end—were beginning to tell as much on my constitution as on the nerves of those at home, and if by 30 November I had not succeeded in killing this man-eater, others would have to be found who were willing to take on the task.

It was now the night of the 24th, so I had six clear days before me. Judging from the behaviour of the tigress that evening, she appeared to be anxious to secure another human victim, and it should not therefore be difficult for me, in the time at my disposal, to get in touch with her. There were several methods by which this could be accomplished, and each would be tried in turn. The method that offers the greatest chance of success of shooting a tiger in the hills is to sit up in a tree over a kill, and if during that night the tigress did not kill the buffalo I had tied up at Thak, I would the following night, and every night thereafter, tie up the other two buffaloes in places I had already selected, and failing to secure a human kill it was just possible that the tigress might kill one of my buffaloes, as she had done on a previous occasion when the Ibbotsons and I were camped at Sem in April. After making up the fire with logs that would burn all night, I turned in, and went to sleep listening to a kakar barking in the scrub jungle behind my tent.

While breakfast was being prepared the following morning I picked up a rifle and went out to look for tracks on the stretch of sand on the right bank of the river, between Chuka and Sem. The path, after leaving the cultivated land, runs for a short distance through scrub jungle, and here I found the tracks of a big male leopard, possibly the same animal that had alarmed the kakar the previous night. A small male tiger had crossed and re-crossed the Ladhya many times during the past week, and in the same period the man-eater had crossed only once, coming from the direction of Sem. A big bear had traversed the sand a little before my arrival, and when I got back to camp the timber contractors complained that while distributing work that morning they had run into a bear which had taken up a very threatening attitude, in consequence of which their labour had refused to work in the area in which the bear had been seen.

Several thousand men—the contractors put the figure at five thousand—had now concentrated at Chuka and Kumaya Chak to fell and saw up the timber and carry it down to the motor road that was being constructed, and all the time this considerable labour force was working they shouted at the tops of their voices to keep up their courage. The noise in the valley resulting from axe and saw, the crashing of giant trees down the steep hill-side, the breaking of rocks with sledge hammers, and combined with it all the shouting of thousands of men, can better be imagined than described. That there were many and frequent alarms in this nervous community was only natural, and during the next few days I covered much ground and lost much valuable time in investigating false rumours of attacks and kills by the man-eater, for the dread of the tigress was not confined to the Ladhya valley, but extended right down the Sarda through Kaldhunga to the gorge, an area of roughly fifty square miles in which an additional ten thousand men were working.

That a single animal should terrorize a labour force of these dimensions in addition to the residents of the surrounding villages and the hundreds of men who were bringing foodstuffs for the labourers or passing through the valley with hill produce in the way of oranges (purchasable at twelve annas a hundred), walnuts, and chillies to the market at Tanakpur is incredible, and would be unbelievable were it not for the historical, and nearly parallel, case of the man-eaters of Tsavo, where a pair of lions, operating only at night, held up work for long periods on the Uganda Railway.

To return to my story. Breakfast disposed of on the morning of the 25th, I took a second buffalo and set out for Thak. The path, after leaving the cultivated land at Chuka, skirts along the foot of the hill for about half a mile before it divides. One arm goes straight up a ridge to Thak and the other, after continuing along the foot of the hill for another half-mile, zigzags up through Kumaya Chak to Kot Kindri.

At the divide I found the pug-marks of the tigress and followed them all the way back to Thak. The fact that she had come down the hill after me the previous evening was proof that she had not killed the buffalo. This, though very disappointing, was not at all unusual; for tigers will on occasions visit an animal that is tied up for several nights in succession before they finally kill it, for tigers do not kill unless they are hungry.

Leaving the second buffalo at the mango-tree, where there was an abundance of green grass, I skirted round the houses and found No. 1 buffalo sleeping peacefully after a big feed and a disturbed night. The tigress, coming from the direction of the village, as her pug-marks showed, had approached to within a few feet of the buffalo, and had then gone back the way she had come. Taking the buffalo down to the spring, I let it graze for an hour or two, and then took it back and tied it up at the same spot where it had been the previous night.

The second buffalo I tied up fifty yards from the mango-tree and at the spot where the wailing woman and villagers had met us the day the Ibbotsons and I had gone up to investigate the human kill. Here a ravine a few feet deep crossed the path, on one side of which there was a dry stump, and on the other an almond-tree in which a *machan* could be made. I tied No. 2 buffalo to the stump, and bedded it down with sufficient hay to keep it going for several days. There was nothing more to be done at Thak, so I returned to camp and, taking the third buffalo, crossed the Ladhya and tied it up behind Sem, in the ravine where the tigress had killed one of our buffaloes in April.

At my request the Tahsildar of Tanakpur had selected three of the fattest young male buffaloes he could find. All three were now tied up in places frequented by the tigress, and as I set out to visit them on the morning of the 26th I had great hopes that one of them had been killed and that I should get an opportunity of shooting the tigress over it. Starting with the one across the Ladhya, I visited all in turn and found that the tigress had not touched any of them. Again, as on the previous morning, I found her tracks on the path leading to Thak, but on this occasion there was a double set of pug-marks, one coming down and the other going back. On both her journeys the tigress had kept to the path and had passed within a few feet of the buffalo that was tied to the stump, fifty yards from the mango-tree.

On my return to Chuka a deputation of Thak villagers led by the Headman came to my tent and requested me to accompany them to the village to enable them to replenish their supply of foodstuffs, so at midday, followed by the Headman his tenants, and by four of my own men carrying ropes for a *machan* and food for me, I returned to Thak and mounted guard while the men hurriedly collected the provisions they needed.

After watering and feeding the two buffaloes I re-tied No. 2 to the stump and took No. 1 half a mile down the hill and tied it to a sapling on the side of the path. I then took the villagers back to Chuka and returned a few hundred yards up the hill for a scratch meal while my men were making the *machan*.

It was now quite evident that the tigress had no fancy for my fat buffaloes, and as in three days I had seen her tracks five times on the path leading to Thak, I decided to sit up over the path and try to get a shot at her that way. To give me warning of the tigress's approach I tied a goat with a bell round its neck on the path, and at 4 p.m. I climbed into the tree. I told my men to return at 8 a.m. the following morning, and began my watch.

At sunset a cold wind started blowing, and while I was attempting to pull a coat over my shoulders the ropes on one side of the *machan* slipped, rendering my seat very uncomfortable. An hour later a storm came on, and though it did not rain for long it wet me to the skin, greatly adding to my discomfort. During the sixteen hours I sat in the tree I did not see or hear anything. The men turned up at 8 a.m. I returned to camp for a hot bath and a good meal, and then, accompanied by six of my men, set out for Thak.

The overnight rain had washed all the old tracks off the path, and two hundred yards above the tree I had sat in I found the fresh pug-marks of the tigress, where she had come out of the jungle and gone up the path in the direction of Thak. Very cautiously I stalked the first buffalo, only to find it lying asleep on the path; the tigress had skirted round it, rejoined the path a few yards farther on, and continued up the hill. Following on her tracks, I approached the second buffalo, and as I got near the place where it had been tied two blue Himalayan magpies rose off the ground and went screaming down the hill.

The presence of these birds indicated: (*a*) that the buffalo was dead, (*b*) that it had been partly eaten and not carried away, and (*c*) that the tigress was not in the close vicinity.

On arrival at the stump to which it had been tied I saw that the buffalo had been dragged off the path and partly eaten, and on examining the animal I found it had not been killed by the tigress, but that it had in all probability died of snake-bite (there were many hamadryads in the surrounding jungles), and that, finding it lying dead on the path, the tigress had eaten a meal off it and had then tried to drag it away. When she found she could not break the rope, she had partly covered it over with dry leaves and brushwood and continued on her way up to Thak.

Tigers as a rule are not carrion eaters, but they do on occasions eat animals they themselves have not killed. For instance, on one occasion I left the carcass of a leopard on a fire-track and, when I returned next morning to recover a knife I had forgotten, I found that a tiger had removed the carcass to a distance of a hundred yards and eaten two-thirds of it.

On my way up from Chuka I had dismantled the *machan* I had sat on the previous night, and while two of my men climbed into the almond-tree to make a seat for me—the tree was not big enough for a *machan*—the other four went to the spring to fill a kettle and boil some water for tea. By 4 p.m. I had partaken of a light meal of biscuits and tea, which would have to keep me going until next day, and refusing the men's request to be permitted to stay the night in one of the houses in Thak I sent them back to camp. There was a certain amount of risk in doing this, but it was nothing compared to the risk they would run if they spent the night in Thak.

My seat on the tree consisted of several strands of rope tied between two upright branches, with a couple of strands lower down for my feet to rest on. When I had settled down comfortably I pulled the branches round me and secured them in position with a thin cord, leaving a small opening to see and fire through. My 'hide' was soon tested, for shortly after the men had gone the two magpies returned, and attracted others, and nine of them fed on the kill until dusk. The presence of the birds enabled me to get some sleep, for they would have given me warning of the tigress's approach, and with their departure my all-night vigil started.

There was still sufficient daylight to shoot by when the moon, a day off the full, rose over the Nepal hills behind me and flooded the hill-side with brilliant light. The rain of the previous night had cleared the atmosphere of dust and smoke and, after the moon had been up a few minutes, the light was so good that I was able to see a sambur and her young one feeding in a field of wheat a hundred and fifty yards away.

The dead buffalo was directly in front and about twenty yards away, and the path along which I expected the tigress to come was two or three yards nearer, so I should have an easy shot at a range at which it would be impossible to miss the tigress—provided she came; and there was no reason why she should not do so.

The moon had been up two hours, and the sambur had approached to within fifty yards of my tree, when a kakar started barking on the hill just above the village. The kakar had been barking for some minutes when suddenly a scream, which I can only, very inadequately, describe as 'Ar-Ar-Arr' dying away on a long-drawn-out note, came from the direction of the village. So sudden and so unexpected had the scream been that I involuntarily stood up with the intention of slipping down from the tree and dashing up to the village, for the thought flashed through my mind that the man-eater was killing one of my men. Then in a second flash of thought I remembered I had counted them one by one as they had passed my tree, and that I had watched them out of sight on their way back to camp to see if they were obeying my instructions to keep close together.

The scream had been the despairing cry of a human being in mortal agony, and reason questioned how such a sound could have come from a deserted village. It was not a thing of my imagination, for the kakar had heard it and had abruptly stopped barking, and the sambur had dashed away across the fields closely followed by her young one. Two days previously, when I had escorted the men to the village, I had remarked that they appeared to be very confiding to leave their property behind doors that were not even shut or latched, and the Headman had answered that even if their village remained untenanted for years their property would be quite safe, for they were priests of Punagiri and no one would dream of robbing them; he added that as long as the tigress lived she was a better guard of their property—if guard were needed—than any hundred men could be, for no one in all that countryside would dare to approach the village, for any purpose, through the dense forests that surrounded it, unless escorted by me as they had been.

The screams were not repeated, and as there appeared to be nothing that I could do I settled down again on my rope seat. At 10 p.m. a kakar that was feeding on the young wheat crop at the lower end of the fields dashed away barking, and a minute later the tigress called twice. She had now left the village and was on the move, and even if she did not fancy having another meal off the buffalo there was every hope of her coming along the path which she had used twice every day for the past few days. With finger on trigger and eyes straining on the path I sat hour after hour until daylight succeeded moonlight, and when the sun had been up an hour, my men returned. Very thoughtfully they had brought a bundle of dry wood with them, and in a surprisingly short time I was sitting down to a hot cup of tea. The tigress may have been lurking in the bushes close to us, or she may have been miles away, for after she had called at 10 p.m. the jungles had been silent.

When I got back to camp I found a number of men sitting near my tent. Some of these men had come to inquire what luck I had had the previous night, and others had come to tell me that the tigress had called from midnight to a little before sunrise at the foot of the hill, and that all the labourers engaged in the forests and on the new export road were too frightened to go to work. I had already heard about the tigress from my men, who had informed me that, together with the thousands of men who were camped round Chuka, they had sat up all night to keep big fires going.

Among the men collected near my tent was the Headman of Thak, and when the others had gone I questioned him about the kill at Thak on the 12th of the month, when he so narrowly escaped falling a victim to the man-eater.

Once again the Headman told me in great detail how he had gone to his fields to dig ginger, taking his grandchild with him, and how on hearing his wife calling he had caught the child's hand and run back to the house—where his wife had said a word or two to him about not keeping his ears open and thereby endangering his own and the child's life—and how a few minutes later the tigress had killed a man while he was cutting leaves off a tree in a field above his house.

All this part of the story I had heard before, and I now asked him if he had actually seen the tigress killing the man. His answer was no; and he added that the tree was not visible from where he had been standing. I then asked him how he knew that the man had been killed, and he said, because he had heard him. In reply to further questions he said the man had not called for help but had cried out; and when asked if he had cried out once he said, 'No, three times', and then at my request he gave an imitation of the man's cry. It was the same—but a very modified rendering—as the screams I had heard the previous night.

I then told him what I had heard and asked him if it was possible for anyone to have arrived at the village accidentally, and his answer was an emphatic negative. There were only two paths leading to Thak, and every man, woman, and child in the villages through which these two paths passed knew that Thak was deserted and the reason for its being so. It was known throughout the district that it was dangerous to go near Thak in daylight, and it was therefore quite impossible for anyone to have been in the village at eight o'clock the previous night.

When asked if he could give any explanation for screams having come from a village in which there could not—according to him

—have been any human beings, his answer was that he could not. And as I can do no better than the Headman, it were best to assume that neither the kakar, the sambur, nor I heard those very real screams—the screams of a human being in mortal agony.

4

When all my visitors, including the Headman, had gone, and I was having breakfast, my servant informed me that the Headman of Sem had come to the camp the previous evening and had left word for me that his wife, while cutting grass near the hut where his mother had been killed, had come on a blood trail, and that he would wait for me near the ford over the Ladhya in the morning. So after breakfast I set out to investigate this trail.

While I was fording the river I saw four men hurrying towards me, and as soon as I was on dry land they told me that when they were coming down the hill above Sem they had heard a tiger calling across the valley on the hill between Chuka and Thak. The noise of the water had prevented my hearing the call. I told the men that I was on my way to Sem and would return to Chuka shortly, and left them.

The Headman was waiting for me near his house, and his wife took me to where she had seen the blood trail the previous day. The trail, after continuing along a field for a short distance, crossed some big rocks, on one of which I found the hairs of a kakar. A little farther on I found the pug-marks of a big male leopard, and while I was looking at them I heard a tiger call. Telling my companions to sit down and remain quiet, I listened, in order to locate the tiger. Presently I heard the call again, and thereafter it was repeated at intervals of about two minutes.

It was the tigress calling, and I located her as being five hundred yards below Thak and in the deep ravine which, starting from the spring under the mango-tree, runs parallel to the path and crosses it at its junction with the Kumaya Chak path.

Telling the Headman that the leopard would have to wait to be shot at a more convenient time, I set off as hard as I could go for camp, picking up at the ford the four men who were waiting for my company to Chuka.

On reaching camp I found a crowd of men round my tent, most of them sawyers from Delhi, but including the petty contractors, agents, clerks, timekeepers, and gangmen of the financier who had taken up the timber and road construction contracts in the Ladhya valley. These men had come to see me in connexion with my stay at Chuka. They informed me that many of the hillmen carrying timber and working on the road had left for their homes that morning and that if I left Chuka on 1 December, as they had heard I intended doing, the entire labour force, including themselves, would leave on the same day; for already they were too frightened to eat or sleep, and no one would dare to remain in the valley after I had gone. It was then the morning of 29 November, and I told the men that I still had two days and two nights and that much could happen in that time, but that in any case it would not be possible for me to prolong my stay beyond the morning of the first.

The tigress had by now stopped calling, and when my servant had put up something for me to eat I set out for Thak, intending, if the tigress called again and I could locate her position, to try to stalk her; and if she did not call again, to sit up over the buffalo. I found her tracks on the path and saw where she had entered the ravine, and though I stopped repeatedly on my way up to Thak and listened I did not hear her again. So a little before sunset I ate the biscuits and drank the bottle of tea I had brought with me, and then climbed into the almond-tree and took my seat on the few strands of rope that had to serve me as a *machan*. On this occasion the magpies were absent, so I was unable to get the hour or two's sleep the birds had enabled me to get the previous evening.

If a tiger fails to return to its kill the first night it does not necessarily mean that the kill has been abandoned. I have on occasions seen a tiger return on the tenth night and eat what could no longer be described as flesh. On the present occasion, however, I was not sitting over a kill, but over an animal that the tigress had found dead and off which she had made a small meal, and had she not been a man-eater I would not have considered the chance of her returning the second night good enough to justify spending a whole night in a tree when she had not taken sufficient interest in the dead buffalo to return to it the first night. It was therefore with very little hope of getting a shot that I sat on the tree from sunset to sunrise, and though the time I spent was not as long as it had been the previous night, my discomfort was very much greater for the ropes I was sitting on cut into me, and a cold wind that started blowing shortly after moonrise and continued throughout the night chilled me to the bone. On this second night I heard no jungle or other sounds, nor did the sambur and her young one come out to feed on the fields. As daylight was succeeding moonlight I thought I heard a tiger call in the distance, but could not be sure of the sound or of its direction.

When I got back to camp my servant had a cup of tea and a hot bath ready for me, but before I could indulge in the latter—my forty-pound tent was not big enough for me to bathe in—I had to get rid of the excited throng of people who were clamouring to tell me their experiences of the night before. It appeared that shortly after moonrise the tigress had started calling close to Chuka, and after calling at intervals for a couple of hours had gone off in the direction of the labour camps at Kumaya Chak. The men in these camps hearing her coming started shouting to try to drive her away, but so far from having this effect the shouting only infuriated her the more, and she demonstrated in front of the camps until she had cowed the men into silence. Having accomplished this, she spent the rest of the night between the labour camps and Chuka, daring all and sundry to shout at her. Towards morning she had gone away in the direction of Thak, and my informants were surprised and very disappointed that I had not met her.

This was my last day of man-eater hunting, and though I was badly in need of rest and sleep, I decided to spend what was left of it in one last attempt to get in touch with the tigress.

The people not only of Chuka and Sem but of all the surrounding villages, and especially the men from Talla Des where some years previously I had shot three man-eaters, were very anxious that I should try sitting up over a live goat, for, said they, 'All hill tigers eat goats, and as you have had no luck with buffaloes, why not try a goat?' More to humour them than with any hope of getting a shot, I consented to spend this last day in sitting up over the two goats I had already purchased for this purpose.

I was convinced that no matter where the tigress wandered to at night, her headquarters were at Thak, so at midday, taking the two goats, and accompanied by four of my men, I set out for Thak.

The path from Chuka to Thak, as I have already mentioned, runs up a very steep ridge. A quarter of a mile on this side of Thak the path leaves the ridge, and crosses a more or less flat bit of ground which extends right up to the mango-tree. For its whole length across this flat ground the path passes through dense brushwood, and is crossed by two narrow ravines which run east and join the main ravine. Midway between these two ravines, and a hundred yards from the tree I had sat in the previous two nights, there is a giant almond-tree; this tree had been my objective when I left camp. The path passes right under the tree, and I thought that if I climbed half-way up not only should I be able to see the two goats, one of which I intended tying at the edge of the main ravine and the other at the foot of the hill to the right, but I should also be able to see the dead buffalo. As all three of these points were at some distance from the tree, I armed myself with an accurate .275 rifle, in addition to the 450/400 rifle which I took for an emergency.

I found the climb up from Chuka on this last day very trying, and I had just reached the spot where the path leaves the ridge for the flat ground, when the tigress called about a hundred and fifty yards to my left. The ground here was covered with dense undergrowth and trees interlaced with creepers, and was cut up by narrow and deep ravines, and strewn over with enormous boulders—a very unsuitable place in which to stalk a man-eater. However, before deciding on what action I should take, it was necessary to know whether the tigress was lying down, as she very well might be, for it was then 1 p.m., or whether she was on the move and if so in what direction. So making the men sit down behind me I listened, and

presently the call was repeated; she had moved some fifty yards, and appeared to be going up the main ravine in the direction of Thak.

This was very encouraging, for the tree I had selected to sit in was only fifty yards from the ravine. After enjoining silence on the men and telling them to keep close behind me, we hurried along the path. We had about two hundred yards to go to reach the tree and had covered half the distance when, as we approached a spot where the path was bordered on both sides by dense brushwood, a covey of kaleege pheasants rose out of the brushwood and went screaming away. I knelt down and covered the path for a few minutes, but as nothing happened we went cautiously forward and reached the tree without further incident. As quickly and as silently as possible one goat was tied at the edge of the ravine, while the other was tied at the foot of the hill to the right; then I took the men to the edge of the cultivated land and told them to stay in the upper veranda of the Headman's house until I fetched them, and ran back to the tree. I climbed to a height of forty feet, and pulled the rifle up after me with a cord I had brought for the purpose. Not only were the two goats visible from my seat, one at a range of seventy and the other at a range of sixty yards, but I could also see part of the buffalo, and as the .275 rifle was very accurate I felt sure I could kill the tigress if she showed up anywhere on the ground I was overlooking.

The two goats had lived together ever since I had purchased them on my previous visit, and, being separated now, were calling lustily to each other. Under normal conditions a goat can be heard at a distance of four hundred yards, but here the conditions were not normal, for the goats were tied on the side of a hill down which a strong wind was blowing, and even if the tigress had moved after I had heard her, it was impossible for her not to hear them. If she was hungry, as I had every reason to believe she was, there was a very good chance of my getting a shot.

After I had been on the tree for ten minutes a kakar barked near the spot the pheasants had risen from. For a minute or two my hopes rose sky-high and then dropped back to earth, for the kakar barked only three times and ended on a note of inquiry; evidently there was a snake in the scrub which neither he nor the pheasants liked the look of.

My seat was not uncomfortable and the sun was pleasingly warm, so for the next three hours I remained in the tree without any discomfort. At 4 p.m. the sun went down behind the high hill above Thak, and thereafter the wind became unbearably cold. For an hour I stood the discomfort, and then decided to give up, for the cold had brought on an attack of ague, and if the tigress came now it would not be possible for me to hit her. I re-tied the cord to the rifle and let it down, climbed down myself and walked to the edge of the cultivated land to call up my men.

5

There are few people, I imagine, who have not experienced that feeling of depression that follows failure to accomplish anything they have set out to do. The road back to camp after a strenuous day when the chukor bag is full is only a step compared with the same road which one plods over, mile after weary mile, when the bag is empty, and if this feeling of depression has ever assailed you at the end of a single day, and when the quarry has only been chukor, you will have some idea of the depth of my depression that evening when, after calling up my men and untying the goats, I set off on my two-mile walk to camp, for my effort had been not of a single day or my quarry a few birds, nor did my failure concern only myself.

Excluding the time spent on the journeys from and to home, I had been on the heels of the man-eater from 23 October to 7

November, and again from 24 to 30 November, and it is only those of you who have walked in fear of having the teeth of a tiger meet in your throat who will have any idea of the effect on one's nerves of days and weeks of such anticipation.

Then again my quarry was a man-eater, and my failure to shoot it would very gravely affect everyone who was working in, or whose homes were in, that area. Already work in the forests had been stopped, and the entire population of the largest village in the district had abandoned their homes. Bad as the conditions were they would undoubtedly get worse if the man-eater was not killed, for the entire labour force could not afford to stop work indefinitely, nor could the population of the surrounding villages afford to abandon their homes and their cultivation as the more prosperous people of Thak had been able to do.

The tigress had long since lost her natural fear of human beings, as was abundantly evident from her having carried away a girl picking up mangoes in a field close to where several men were working, killing a woman near the door of her house, dragging a man off a tree in the heart of a village, and, the previous night, cowing a few thousand men into silence. And here was I, who knew full well what the presence of a man-eater meant to the permanent and to the temporary inhabitants and to all the people who passed through the district on their way to the markets at the foot-hills or the temples at Punagiri, plodding down to camp on what I had promised others would be my last day of man-eater hunting; reason enough for a depression of soul which I felt would remain with me for the rest of my days. Gladly at that moment would I have bartered the success that had attended thirty-two years of man-eater hunting for one unhurried shot at the tigress.

I have told you of some of the attempts I made during this period of seven days and seven nights to get a shot at the tigress, but these were by no means the only attempts I made. I knew that I was being watched and followed, and every time I went through the two miles of jungle between my camp and Thak I tried every trick I have learnt in a lifetime spent in the jungles to outwit the tigress. Bitter though my disappointment was, I felt that my failure was not in any way due to anything I had done or left undone.

6

My men when they rejoined me said that, an hour after the kakar had barked, they had heard the tigress calling a long way off, but were not sure of the direction. Quite evidently the tigress had as little interest in goats as she had in buffaloes, but even so it was unusual for her to have moved at that time of day from a locality in which she was thoroughly at home, unless she had been attracted away by some sound which neither I nor my men had heard; however that may have been, it was quite evident that she had gone, and as there was nothing further that I could do I set off on my weary tramp to camp.

The path, as I have already mentioned, joins the ridge that runs down to Chuka a quarter of a mile from Thak, and when I now got to this spot where the ridge is only a few feet wide and from where a view is obtained of the two great ravines that run down to the Ladhya River, I heard the tigress call once and again across the valley on my left. She was a little above and to the left of Kumaya Chak, and a few hundred yards below the Kot Kindri ridge on which the men working in that area had built themselves grass shelters.

Here was an opportunity, admittedly forlorn and unquestionably desperate, of getting a shot; still it was an opportunity and the last I should ever have, and the question was, whether or not I was justified in taking it.

When I got down from the tree I had one hour in which to get back to camp before dark. Calling up the men, hearing what they had to say, collecting the goats, and walking to the ridge had taken about thirty minutes, and judging from the position of the sun, which was now casting a red glow on the peaks of the Nepal hills, I calculated I had roughly half an hour's daylight in hand. This time factor, or perhaps it would be more correct to say light factor, was all-important, for if I took the opportunity that offered, on it would depend the lives of five men.

The tigress was a mile away, and the intervening ground was densely wooded, strewn over with great rocks and cut up by a number of deep nullahs, but she could cover the distance well within the half-hour—if she wanted to. The question I had to decide was, whether or not I should try to call her up. If I called and she heard me, and came while it was still daylight and gave me a shot, all would be well; on the other hand, if she came and did not give me a shot some of us would not reach camp, for we had nearly two miles to go, and the path the whole way ran through heavy jungle, and was bordered in some places by big rocks, and in others by dense brushwood. It was useless to consult the men, for none of them had ever been in a jungle before coming on this trip, so the decision would have to be mine. I decided to try to call up the tigress.

Handing my rifle over to one of the men, I waited until the tigress called again and, cupping my hands round my mouth and filling my lungs to their utmost limit, sent an answering call over the valley. Back came her call and thereafter, for several minutes, call answered call. She would come, had in fact already started, and if she arrived while there was light to shoot by, all the advantages would be on my side, for I had the selecting of the ground on which it would best suit me to meet her. November is the mating season for tigers, and it was evident that for the past forty-eight hours she had been rampaging through the jungles in search of a mate, and that now, on hearing what she thought was a tiger answering her mating call, she would lose no time in joining him.

Four hundred yards down the ridge the path runs for fifty yards across a flat bit of ground. At the far right hand side of this flat ground the path skirts a big rock and then drops steeply, and continues in a series of hairpin bends, down to the next bench. It was at this rock I decided to meet the tigress, and on my way down to it I called several times to let her know I was changing my position, and also to keep in touch with her.

I want you now to have a clear picture of the ground in your mind, to enable you to follow the subsequent events. Imagine then a rectangular piece of ground forty yards wide and eighty yards long, ending in a more or less perpendicular rock face. The path coming down from Thak runs on to this ground at its short or south end, and after continuing down the centre for twenty-five yards bends to the right and leaves the rectangle on its long or east side. At the point where the path leaves the flat ground there is a rock about four feet high. From a little beyond where the path bends to the right, a ridge of rock, three or four feet high, rises and extends to the north side of the rectangle, where the ground falls away in a perpendicular rock face. On the near or path side of this low ridge there is a dense line of bushes approaching to within ten feet of the four-foot-high rock I have mentioned. The rest of the rectangle is grown over with trees, scattered bushes, and short grass.

It was my intention to lie on the path by the side of the rock and shoot the tigress as she approached me, but when I tried this position I found it would not be possible for me to see her until she was within two or three yards, and further, that she could get at me either round the rock or through the scattered bushes on my left without my seeing her at all. Projecting out of the rock, from the side opposite to that from which I expected the tigress to approach, there was a narrow ledge. By sitting sideways I found I could get a little of my bottom on the ledge, and by putting my left hand flat on the top of the rounded rock and stretching out my right leg to its full extent and touching the ground with my toes, retain my position on it.

The goats and men I placed immediately behind, and ten to twelve feet below me.

The stage was now set for the reception of the tigress, who while these preparations were being made had approached to within three hundred yards. Sending out one final call to give her direction, I looked round to see if my men were all right.

The spectacle these men presented would under other circumstances have been ludicrous, but was here tragic. Sitting in a tight little circle with their knees drawn up and their heads together, with the goats burrowing in under them, they had that look of intense expectancy on their screwed-up features that one sees on the faces of spectators waiting to hear a big gun go off. From the time we had first heard the tigress from the ridge, neither the men nor the goats had made a sound, beyond one suppressed cough. They were probably by now frozen with fear—as well they might be—and even if they were, I take my hat off to those four men who had the courage to do what I, had I been in their shoes, would not have dreamt of doing. For seven days they had been hearing the most exaggerated and blood-curdling tales of this fearsome beast that had kept them awake the past two nights, and now, while darkness was coming on, and sitting unarmed in a position where they could see nothing, they were listening to the man-eater drawing nearer and nearer; greater courage, and greater faith, it is not possible to conceive.

The fact that I could not hold my rifle, a D.B. 450/400, with my left hand (which I was using to retain my precarious seat on the ledge) was causing me some uneasiness, for apart from the fear of the rifle's slipping on the rounded top of the rock—I had folded my handkerchief and placed the rifle on it to try to prevent this—I did not know what would be the effect of the recoil of a high-velocity rifle fired in this position. The rifle was pointing along the path, in which there was a hump, and it was my intention to fire into the tigress's face immediately it appeared over this hump, which was twenty feet from the rock.

The tigress, however, did not keep to the contour of the hill, which would have brought her out on the path a little beyond the hump, but crossed a deep ravine and came straight towards where she had heard my last call, at an angle which I can best describe as one o'clock. This manoeuvre put the low ridge of rock, over which I could not see, between us. She had located the direction of my last call with great accuracy, but had misjudged the distance, and not finding her prospective mate at the spot she had expected him to be, she was now working herself up into a perfect fury, and you will have some idea of what the fury of a tigress in her condition can be when I tell you that not many miles from my home a tigress on one occasion closed a public road for a whole week, attacking everything that attempted to go along it, including a string of camels, until she was finally joined by a mate.

I know of no sound more liable to fret one's nerves than the calling of an unseen tiger at close range. What effect this appalling sound was having on my men I was frightened to think, and if they had gone screaming down the hill I should not have been at all surprised, for even though I had the heel of a good rifle to my shoulder and the stock against my cheek I felt like screaming myself.

But even more frightening than this continuous calling was the fading out of the light. Another few seconds, ten or fifteen at the most, and it would be too dark to see my sights, and we should then be at the mercy of a man-eater, plus a tigress wanting a mate. Something would have to be done, and done in a hurry, if we were not to be massacred, and the only thing I could think of was to call.

The tigress was now so close that I could hear the intake of her breath each time before she called, and as she again filled her lungs, I did the same with mine, and we called simultaneously. The effect was startlingly instantaneous. Without a second's hesitation she came tramping with quick steps through the dead leaves, over the low ridge and into the bushes a little to my right front, and just as I was expecting her to walk right on top of me she stopped, and the next moment the full blast of her deep-throated call struck me in the face and would have carried the hat off my head had I been wearing one. A second's pause, then again quick steps; a glimpse of her as she passed between two bushes, and then she stepped right out into the open, and, looking into my face, stopped dead.

By great and unexpected good luck the half-dozen steps the tigress took to her right front carried her almost to the exact spot at which my rifle was pointing. Had she continued in the direction in which she was coming before her last call, my story—if written —would have had a different ending, for it would have been as impossible to slew the rifle on the rounded top of the rock as it would have been to lift and fire it with one hand.

Owing to the nearness of the tigress, and the fading light, all that I could see of her was her head. My first bullet caught her under the right eye and the second, fired more by accident than with intent, took her in the throat and she came to rest with her nose against the rock. The recoil from the right barrel loosened my hold on the rock and knocked me off the ledge, and the recoil from the left barrel, fired while I was in the air, brought the rifle up in violent contact with my jaw and sent me heels over head right on top of the men and goats. Once again I take my hat off to those four men, for, not knowing but what the tigress was going to land on them next, they caught me as I fell and saved me from injury and my rifle from being broken.

When I had freed myself from the tangle of human and goat legs I took the .275 rifle from the man who was holding it, rammed a clip of cartridges into the magazine and sent a stream of five bullets singing over the valley and across the Sarda into Nepal. Two shots, to the thousands of men in the valley and in the surrounding villages who were anxiously listening for the sound of my rifle, might mean anything, but two shots followed by five more, spaced at regular intervals of five seconds, could only be interpreted as conveying one message, and that was, that the man-eater was dead.

I had not spoken to my men from the time we had first heard the tigress from the ridge. On my telling them now that she was dead and that there was no longer any reason for us to be afraid, they did not appear to be able to take in what I was saying, so I told them to go up and have a look while I found and lit a cigarette. Very cautiously they climbed up to the rock, but went no farther for, as I have told you, the tigress was touching the other side of it. Late in camp that night, while sitting round a campfire and relating their experiences to relays of eager listeners, their narrative invariably ended up with, 'and then the tiger whose roaring had turned our livers into water hit the sahib on the head and knocked him down on top of us and if you don't believe us, go and look at his face'. A mirror is superfluous in camp, and even if I had had one it could not have made the swelling on my jaw, which put me on milk diet for several days, look as large and as painful as it felt.

By the time a sapling had been felled and the tigress lashed to it, lights were beginning to show in the Ladhya valley and in all the surrounding camps and villages. The four men were very anxious to have the honour of carrying the tigress to camp, but the task was beyond them; so I left them and set off for help.

In my three visits to Chuka during the past eight months I had been along this path many times by day and always with a loaded rifle in my hands, and now I was stumbling down in the dark, unarmed, my only anxiety being to avoid a fall. If the greatest happiness one can experience is the sudden cessation of great pain, then the second greatest happiness is undoubtedly the sudden cessation of great fear. One short hour previously it would have taken wild elephants to have dragged from their homes and camps the men who now, singing and shouting, were converging from every direction, singly and in groups, on the path leading to Thak. Some of the men of this rapidly growing crowd went up the path to help carry in the tigress, while others accompanied me on my way to camp, and would have carried me had I permitted them. Progress was slow, for frequent halts had to be made to allow each group of new arrivals to express their gratitude in their own particular way. This gave the party carrying the tigress time to catch us up, and we entered the village together. I will not attempt to describe the welcome my men and I received, or the scenes I witnessed at Chuka that night, for having lived the greater part of my life in the jungles I have not the ability to paint word-pictures.

A hayrick was dismantled and the tigress laid on it, and an enormous bonfire made from driftwood close at hand to light up the scene and for warmth, for the night was dark and cold with a north wind blowing. Round about midnight my servant, assisted by the Headman of Thak and Kunwar Singh, near whose house I was camped, persuaded the crowd to return to their respective villages and labour camps, telling them they would have ample opportunity of feasting their eyes on the tigress the following day. Before leaving himself, the Headman of Thak told me he would send word in the morning to the people of Thak to return to their village. This he did, and two days later the entire population returned to their homes, and have lived in peace ever since.

After my midnight dinner I sent for Kunwar Singh and told him that in order to reach home on the promised date I should have to start in a few hours, and that he would have to explain to the people in the morning why I had gone. This he promised to do, and I then started to skin the tigress. Skinning a tiger with a pocket-knife is a long job, but it gives one an opportunity of examining the

animal that one would otherwise not get, and in the case of
man-eaters enables one to ascertain, more or less accurately, the reason for the animal's having become a man-eater.

The tigress was a comparatively young animal and in the perfect
condition one would expect her to be at the beginning of the mating season. Her dark winter coat was without a blemish, and in spite
of her having so persistently refused the meals I had provided for her
she was encased in fat. She had two old gunshot wounds, neither
of which showed on her skin. The one in her left shoulder, caused
by several pellets of homemade buckshot, had become septic, and
when healing the skin, over quite a large surface, had adhered permanently to the flesh. To what extent this wound had incapacitated
her it would have been difficult to say, but it had evidently taken
a very long time to heal, and could quite reasonably have been
the cause of her having become a man-eater. The second wound,
which was in her right shoulder, had also been caused by a charge
of buckshot, but had healed without becoming septic. These two
wounds received over kills in the days before she had become a
man-eater were quite sufficient reason for her not having returned
to the human and other kills I had sat over.

After having skinned the tigress I bathed and dressed, and though
my face was swollen and painful and I had twenty miles of rough

going before me, I left Chuka walking on air, while the thousands of men in and around the valley were peacefully sleeping.

I have come to the end of the jungle stories I set out to tell you, and I have also come near the end of my man-eater hunting career.

I have had a long spell and count myself fortunate in having walked out on my own feet and not been carried out on a cradle in the manner and condition of the man of Thak.

There have been occasions when life has hung by a thread and others when a light purse and disease resulting from exposure and strain have made the going difficult, but for all these occasions I am amply rewarded if my hunting has resulted in saving one human life.

GLOSSARY

anna, 16th part of a rupee.
babbler, long-legged thrush.
basonta, bushes.
Bhutia, man from across the border.
charpoy, Indian bedstead.
chital, spotted deer.
chowkidar, watchman.
chukor, hill partridge.
cooee, signal call used in the bush.
dak, relay of men for post or
    transport.
Dak Bungalow, an inn for travellers on
    a dak route.
drag, the trail, line of scent.
durbar, public audience or levee.
ghat, landing-place, passage down to
    a river.
ghooral, mountain goat.
godown, a warehouse or store for
    goods.
gur, crude sugar.
jaggery, a coarse brown sugar made
    from palm sap.
kakar, barking deer.
karphal, a tree producing sweet berries.

khud (side), ravine, precipice.
langur, a long-tail monkey.
machan, a platform in a tree, used
    for observation.
mahseer, large Indian freshwater fish.
mugger, broad-nosed crocodile.
nullah, a stream, river-bed,
    watercourse.
paddy field, rice field.
Patwari, village registrar or
    accountant.
pea-fowl, pea-cock, pea-hen.
pipal-tree, the sacred fig of India.
pug, footprint.
pugrees, turban.
ringals, stunted bamboos, hill
    bamboos.
'Ram nam sat hai', 'The name of Rama
    is true'.
rowkah, dry watercourse.
sadhu, a Hindu ascetic or holy man.
sahib, 'Sir'; also, an Englishman or
    European.
sal, a valuable timber tree.
sambur, deer.

sari, a long garment of cloth or silk worn by Indian women.

'Satya bol gat hai', 'In truth lies salvation'.

scree, heap of stones, or rocky debris.

semul-tree, silk cotton-tree, *Bombax malabaricum.*

serow, Asiatic antelope.

shaitan, devil, evil spirit.

shikar, shikari, hunting, hunter's guide.

Tahsildar, chief revenue officer.

terai, a belt of marshy land between the foot-hills of the Himalayas and the plains.

zamindar, landowner paying the government a fixed revenue.

PUBLISHER'S NOTE

JIM CORBETT

Jim Corbett was born in 1875 in Naini Tal, an Indian hill station in the Himalayas. He grew up in a large family—he had twelve brothers and sisters—but his father died when he was 4. Their homestead was surrounded by jungle, and Jim spent his boyhood studying wildlife, collecting bird's eggs and learning to hunt. Although he and his younger brother were saved by their old collie from an attack by a Himalayan bear when he was only 4, he had little fear of the "jungle folk" and, later in his life, preferred to observe and photograph the animals of Northern India than to harm them. When he was 54 he started filming tigers, calling them to him and standing as close as ten feet away, while whistling some soft jungle bird song to cover the whir of the camera.

He seldom killed an animal except from necessity, though he became well known as the "Tiger Man" for his jungle campaigns against man-eating tigers and leopards. In his concern for the protection of the wildlife of India and Africa, where he spent half the year, he was a conservationist ahead of his time. India's first national park was named in his honor.

Jim Corbett wrote six books: *Man-eaters of Kumaon, The Man-eating Leopard of Rudraprayag, My India, Jungle Lore, The Temple Tiger* and *Tree Tops*. *Man-eaters of Kumaon* became a best-seller, was widely translated throughout the world and was made into a motion picture.

He died in Africa at 80 years old.

GEOFFREY C. WARD

Geoffrey Ward, with his wife, Diane Raines Ward, wrote *Tiger Wallahs: Encounters with the Men who Tried to Save the Greatest of the Great Cats*. He is an American historian, biographer and writer of television documentaries who spent part of his boyhood in India and writes about her still-astonishing wildlife as often as he can. His books include *A First Class Temperament: The Emergence of Franklin Roosevelt*, for which he won the National Book Critics Award and the Francis Parkman Award, and *The Civil War*, the companion volume to the celebrated PBS television series. He lives in New York City.

RAYMOND SHEPPARD

Raymond Sheppard was born in England in 1913. He studied at the London School of Printing and Graphic Arts, and drew at the London Zoo and the Natural History Museum. He became a free-lance artist at 21, specializing in drawing animals and birds, and he became an admired illustrator of natural history books. During

World War II he was attached to the RAF Photographic Section. He died in 1958.

VICTOR & MARIA LAZZARO

Victor and Maria Lazzaro are artists living in Redding, Connecticut. They attended Cooper Union, where they first met, and have been collaborating ever since.

ABOUT THE ADVENTURE LIBRARY

The Adventure Library is a book club offering its members handsomely designed and printed hardcover editions of the great books of high adventure: the enduring classics of exploration, discovery, and survival. These editions, which are not available in bookstores, include new introductions, annotations, maps, illustrations, and other material.

Adventure Library volumes are printed on acid-free paper and their fine-quality bindings are Smythe-sewn for permanence.

For further information write to:
> The Adventure Library
> 79 Nash Road
> North Salem, New York 10560